HIDE A
DAGGER
BEHIND A
SMILE

USE THE 36
ANCIENT CHINESE
STRATEGIES TO SEIZE
THE COMPETITIVE EDGE

KAIHAN KRIPPENDORFF

avon, massachusetts

Published by
Adams Media, an F+W Publications Company
57 Littlefield Street, Avon, MA 02322. U.S.A.
www.adamsmedia.com

ISBN-10: 1-59869-380-8
ISBN-13: 978-1-59869-380-5

Printed in the United States of America.

J I H G F E D C B A

Library of Congress Cataloging-in-Publication Data
Krippendorff, Kaihan.
    Hide a dagger behind a smile / Kaihan Krippendorff.
        p.   cm.
    Based on concepts from the ancient Chinese text, The
Secret art of war : the 36 stratagems.
    Includes bibliographical references and index.
    ISBN-13: 978-1-59869-380-5 (pbk.)
    ISBN-10: 1-59869-380-8 (pbk.)
    1. Competition—Management—Case studies. 2. San shi
liu ji. 3. Strategy—Case studies. 4. Problem solving—Case
studies. 5. Industrial management—Case studies. I. Title.
HD41.K69 2007
658.4'012—dc22   2007039126

This publication is designed to provide accurate and authoritative information
with regard to the subject matter covered. It is sold with the understanding
that the publisher is not engaged in rendering legal, accounting, or other
professional advice. If legal advice or other expert assistance is required, the
services of a competent professional person should be sought.
    —From a *Declaration of Principles* jointly adopted by a Committee of the
American Bar Association and a Committee of Publishers and Associations

Many of the designations used by manufacturers and sellers to distinguish
their product are claimed as trademarks. Where those designations appear in
this book and Adams Media was aware of a trademark claim, the designations
have been printed with initial capital letters.

This book is available at quantity discounts for bulk purchases.
For information, please call 1-800-289-0963.

CONTENTS

PART I
YIN YANG POLARITY
1

PART II
WU WEI: GO WITH THE FLOW
59

PART III
WU CHANG: CONTINUOUS CHANGE
107

PART IV
SHANG BING WU BING: INDIRECT ACTION
163

ACKNOWLEDGMENTS

The book is like a snapshot of a conversation I have been holding with many like-minded people over the past ten years. I unfortunately only have space here to thank a portion of this community. Above all I thank my wife, Pilar Ramos, and my son, Lucas Somar Krippendorff, for being the purpose of me completing this book. Dr. Kathryn Harrigan, my professor at Columbia Business School, first encouraged me with the idea that I could write a book. Others who provided academic support include Dr. Ming-Jer Chen, Dr. Costas Markides (London Business School), Dr. Sumantra Ghoshal (now deceased, London Business School), Dr. Steve Heine (Florida International University), Dr. Alan Carsud (Florida International University). I thank my father, Dr. Klaus Krippendorff (University of Pennsylvania), for expanding my thinking over countless engaging conversations.

My colleagues at The Strategy Learning Center, especially AnaMaria Rivera, contributed ideas and support the research. This work is far more powerful thanks to the case ideas and insights shared by Doug Muir, Ruedi Müller, Verne Harnish, Zaki Mustafa, Stephannie Wasserstein, Ned Bowman, Tereza Sommerfeld, Enrique Riquelme, Evan Shelan, and Maritza Morales. My former colleagues at McKinsey & Company continue to serve as mentors and friends, including David Wenner, Jacques Antebi, Juan-Jose Gonzalez, Brad Hoover, Tim Lukes, and Joanna Popper.

In my attempt to capture the subtleties of the Thirty-Six Stratagems as accurately as I can, I depended heavily on a small network of generous friends. Qin Chen spent countless hours with me explaining and critiquing my interpretation of each stratagem. I first asked Christina Zhu about the stratagems in 1999. She has continued to answer my questions energetically. Teresa Chu, Harry Wang, and Alex Tsui helped keep my interpretation of the Chinese philosophy behind each stratagem on target.

I also thank my mother, Sultana Alam, for inspiring me and my agent, Laurie Harper, for guiding me.

Kaihan Krippendorff
Miami, Florida
February 2007

PREFACE

In March 1220 AD, the defenders of Bukhara made a fatal mistake. This ancient Muslim city in what is now Uzbekistan was about to fall prey to one of history's most daring military maneuvers. Genghis Khan had appeared as if from thin air.

When he first set his sights on Bukhara, he appeared to pursue a conventional approach, sending his army to attack cities standing between his homeland, Mongolia, and his target. But while the defenders of Bukhara monitored their adversary's progress, Genghis Khan secretly prepared a detachment for a march most thought impossible. He drove his men farther than any army had ever covered—across 2,000 miles of mountains, deserts, and plains—and appeared unexpectedly at Bukhara's doorstep. Surprised, Bukhara swiftly joined a long list of cities outwitted by Genghis Khan.

How did Genghis Khan conceive of an option none expected?

History's greatest military strategists—Alexander the Great, Napoleon Bonaparte, Sun Tzu—won with creativity rather than strength. They shared an unnatural ability to see and choose strategic options others ignored.

I believe we all have the capacity for unlocking such strategic creativity. We can, with the right tools, approximate with a method that others exercise naturally.

This book offers a toolkit, fashioned by an ancient Chinese text called *The Thirty-Six Stratagems*, that is surprisingly effective at triggering creative thought. The text's thirty-six metaphors are more than colorful phrases. They comprise a comprehensive vocabulary of competition. The stratagems use words not commonly applied to business—such as *ladders* and *mountains* rather than *scale* and *competencies*—but their function is the same as your current business vocabulary: to help you understand and influence competitive environments.

Since 2003 I have seen the stratagems reveal unexpected plans for achieving goals in a wide variety of contexts, including negotiations, business growth, international expansion, mergers/acquisitions, and politics. I hope this book will further expand the growing number of modern-day strategists who are using the Thirty-Six Stratagems to design innovative solutions.

INTRODUCTION

An Ancient Toolkit

In 2003 I ran a workshop for fifteen executives of a multinational company. For three years the company's revenues in a key international market had been in decline. After numerous traditional initiatives (pricing changes, marketing campaigns, etc.) proved ineffective, the group had run out of ideas. They saw no compelling solution to their problem.

We looked at the challenge through new perspectives, using six metaphors found in the ancient Chinese strategy text *The Thirty-Six Stratagems* as "lenses." In four hours the team generated more than 100 new strategies for reversing their downward market-share trend.

Once stuck with no solution in mind, the group now saw abundant possibilities. Experiencing this rapid "un-sticking," and the subsequent growth of the company's business, convinced me that the Thirty-Six Stratagems are more than a collection of colorful phrases. They are effective tools for conceiving of strategic options. They are the fundamental patterns of competition and can help you become a more creative and effective strategic thinker.

The Patterns of Competition

A Chinese proverb proposes that "there are just thirty-six strategies under the sun." With just three primary colors, Pablo Picasso painted vibrant masterpieces. Amadeus Mozart composed his works within a scale of just eight primary notes. Dissect William Shakespeare's prose and you will eventually arrive at just twenty-six letters.

Perhaps, then, this proverb is pointing to a truth. Peeling back the blended gradations of competition will eventually reveal a limited set of building blocks, the fundamental patterns of competition. I believe this is true because it fits what we observe in other domains (art, music, prose) and because I have tested for these patterns. Since 1995, when I first came across a translation of *The Thirty-Six Stratagems*, I began collecting competitive business cases and classifying them according to the text, asking, "What stratagem explains this move?" or "What stratagem would have led to this strategy?" I collected about 300 cases overall. All fit one or more of the stratagems.

I then put the Thirty-Six Stratagems through a more rigorous assessment. I identified what I believe to be the 100 most competitive companies of the decade and classified their successes according to the Thirty-Six Stratagems. (See Appendix C for more detail on this research.)

I believe most studies of corporate competitiveness flock too eagerly to admired companies such as General Electric or Southwest Airlines. While such companies offer valuable lessons, they are not in the top group of competitive companies. Instead, I took an impartial approach to identifying competitive companies. I assembled financial data on 9,000 publicly traded companies worldwide, of which 3,000 had at least a decade's worth of financial history available. For each of these 3,000 companies, I calculated a "competitiveness" score equally composed of three metrics:

1. **Revenue growth:** average revenue growth of each company over a ten-year period ending in 2005.
2. **Profit margin:** average earnings before the interest, taxes, depreciation, and amortization (EBITDA) margin over the same period.
3. **Value creation:** average total return to the shareholders over the same period.

The 100 companies with the highest competitiveness score are the most competitive of the past decade. They are the fastest growing, most profitable, and most value-creating publicly traded companies in the world.

The Most Competitive Companies of the Decade*

1. Abertis Infraestructuras S.A.
2. Adobe Systems Inc.
3. Advanced Info Service Plc
4. Advanced Semicon Engineering
5. AES Corporation
6. Altera Corporation
7. Altran Technologies S.A.
8. American Eagle Outfitters, Inc.
9. Amgen Inc.
10. Amorepacific Corporation
11. Antofagasta PLC
12. Apollo Group Inc.
13. Applied Materials Inc.
14. ASSA ABLOY
15. Astra International Terbuka
16. ATI Technologies Inc.
17. Autostrade S.p.A.
18. Barr Pharmaceuticals Inc.
19. Biogen Idec Inc.
20. BKW Energie AG
21. Brookfield Properties Corporation
22. Capita Group Plc
23. China International Marine Containers
24. China Southern Glass Holding
25. Compañia Sudamericana De Vapores
26. Cinram International Inc.
27. Cisco Systems Inc.
28. CJ Corporation
29. Clear Channel Communications
30. Compuware Corporation

*Publicly traded companies that have produced the highest revenue growth, EBITDA margins, and total return to shareholders over a ten-year period.

I then analyzed the history of each of these 100 most competitive companies to assess whether their success—as explained by the companies themselves and by industry experts—can be linked to one or more of the Thirty-Six Stratagems. I discovered that every case can be explained by these strategems. Therefore, the stratagems are the patterns of competition, a comprehensive vocabulary for understanding and managing competitive dynamics. Learning them can help you approximate the skill of expert strategists.

The Mind of the Expert Strategist

Since the 1940s scientists have been studying how experts are able to conceive of and choose better solutions than novices. They have written volumes on expert chess players, surgeons, baseball players, card players, wrestlers, software programmers, writers, dancers, mathematicians, and historians. Notably unrepresented in this research are people skilled at solving political, military, or corporate problems.

This research, however, offers insights into how expert strategists outthink their competition and highlights the critical role the Thirty-Six Stratagems can play in your search to become a more effective strategist. This leads to five key points:

1. All strategic games (e.g., chess, go, etc.) are composed of distinct phases such as the "opening," "middle game," and "end game." Although logic is useful for solving problems during the "end game," it is ineffective during earlier phases because a player faces too many options to logically analyze each branch down to its end point.

2. All options cannot be analyzed during the early phases of a game because the human mind lacks the processing power and working short-term memory to do so. To use logic in the middle of a chess game, for example, would require processing millions of moves per second and retaining millions of possible outcomes. Humans process about four moves per second and can retain only up to nine things in working memory, so humans do not use logic in complex games.

3. To overcome these limitations, experts use "patterns" or "chunks" rather than logic. Just as a child learning to read evolves from seeing letters (e.g., *c*, *a*, and *r*) into seeing words (e.g., *car*), expert strategists develop a high-order vocabulary. While a novice is playing with pawns and knights, the expert is playing with moves or patterns (e.g., "the Lasker–Bauer combination") and is therefore able to retain far more pieces in his or her short-term working memory.

4. To consistently beat the competition requires building a larger vocabulary of patterns. Master chess players, for example, recognize twice as many patterns as experts. Grand master chess players recognize about three times as many as masters.

5. *The Thirty-Six Stratagems* offers a comprehensive vocabulary of patterns for understanding, predicting, and influencing competition. The stratagems explain the rise of each of the 100 most competitive companies of the decade and every competitive strategy case against which they have been tested. By learning these stratagems, you can stock your reservoir of patterns and become a more creative and effective strategist.

History of the Thirty-Six Stratagems

More than 2,500 years ago, military and political minds in China began to debate how to make a science of strategy by distilling their collective knowledge into a few universal principles. The process took more than a thousand years, and it produced a catalog of thirty-six strategies for gaining, expanding, and retaining power: *The Thirty-Six Stratagems*. Less famous in the West than many of its sister texts, including Sun Tzu's *The Art of War*, Lao Tzu's *Tao Te Ching*, and the most ancient of Chinese classical texts, the *I Ching*, *The Thirty-Six Stratagems* is perhaps more directly applicable to strategy development than these others.

The text compiles the lessons of more than twenty generations. (By comparison, most strategic texts capture the lessons of little more than a lifetime.) It compresses this information, even more completely than other texts, into thirty-six patterns captured in just 138 Chinese characters.

To appreciate the amount of experience recorded in *The Thirty-Six Stratagems*, consider what the cultures outside China experienced over the course of the stratagems' formation:

- Athens rose to culturally dominate Greece and was then defeated by Macedonia's Alexander the Great.
- The Roman Empire was founded and expanded into Greece, Persia, the Middle East, and North Africa, eventually conquering the Greek city-states.
- The Persian Empire rose to power and, 500 years later, fell to Rome.
- Prince Siddhartha Gautama was born in India, took the name Buddha, and founded Buddhism.
- Christianity was born, and 600 years later, Islam followed.

During this time, China generated some its greatest thinkers including Lao Tzu, Sun Tzu, and Confucius and experienced the transition of eleven dynasties. It built the Great Wall and the Silk Road.

The true age of *The Thirty-Six Stratagems* is difficult to pinpoint because it has no single author. Rather hundreds of politicians, military leaders, and citizens contributed to its development by passing the stories down through generations, distilling and refining them with each telling until their bare essences remained. The storytelling that led to *The Thirty-Six Stratagems* began sometime before 500 BC and was completed sometime between AD 500, when the text is first mentioned in historical records, and about AD 1600, when an unknown "author" compiled the stratagems into a handwritten book titled *The Secret Art of War: The Thirty-Six Stratagems*.

The text of *The Thirty-Six Stratagems* belongs to the same body of military work as Sun Tzu's *The Art of War* and is closely linked to Lao Tzu's *Tao Te Ching*. All three texts teach readers how to navigate and gain advantage in dynamic environments; they were the products of a turbulent era in China's history known as the Warring States period. This period began when a loosely unified China splintered into separate states that battled each other for power. Seven states quickly dominated the others, and for the next 200 years, they engaged in a dynamic sequence of battles, shifting alliances, and political gaming.

Interestingly, business today is shifting into a similarly fluid, dynamic, competitive environment. Falling communication costs, blurring industry boundaries, and the proliferation of decentralized threats make the lessons synthesized in *The Thirty-Six Stratagems* critical to success.

Structure

This book is designed to be used more than read straight through, but it is structured to allow both. The Thirty-Six Stratagems are grouped into sections that mark four major differences between Taoist and traditional Western perspectives. These four perspectives serve as hidden "laws" derived from cultural conditioning that restricts thinking and limits options. The stories you heard as a child, the books you read, your successes, and your failures influence how you perceive and act as an adult. Such conditioning can help you avoid making a bad decision. Ask any venture capitalist if she would rather invest in an entrepreneur who has experienced failure or one who has not and she will choose the former because someone who has failed is unlikely to fall into the same trap again. The problem, however, is that experience is rarely applied objectively or consciously. Rather, experiences are converted into a bundle of knee-jerk responses (fire = pain, so retract; height = danger, so avoid). These "laws" of response, woven together with thousands of other rules, create conditioning. They serve as protection from obvious threats but often rely on the same restricted set of response patterns. These hidden laws limit reactions and sometimes force poor decision-making, particularly in response to unusual situations.

>   **First Law: Ying Yang: Polarity.** Westerners believe they can pursue good and banish bad, but this assumption runs counter to the Taoist understanding, which doesn't judge anything. There is no "good" or "bad"; they are simply two sides of the same coin.

Second Law: Wu Wei: Go with the grain. Westerners equate yielding with weakness and overcoming adversity with strength. Taoists take the opposite stance: They value "going with the grain," which often leads to the opposite answer to the same question.

Third Law: Wu Chang: Continuous change. Westerners believe the past determines the present and that change connects static moments. Assuming instead that the present determines the present, and that change is continuous, as the Taoist perspective suggests, leads to the selection of different courses of action.

Fourth Law: Shang Bing Wu Bing: Indirect action. Westerners prefer to meet an adversary head-on; the Eastern preference for indirect action often seems impractical, deceitful, or indicative of weakness. Embracing indirect action puts powerful new tactics into Western hands.

The book concludes with three appendixes to help you incorporate the stratagems into solving everyday challenges.

1. The Thirty-Six Stratagems as Problem-Solving Tools. I have seen the stratagems used to generate creative solutions to immediate strategic problems such as preparing for an important negotiation, planning for a sales call, or launching a product in a new market. Appendix A offers a guide for using the stratagems to rapidly solve such challenges.

2. Rapid-Cycle Strategy Innovation. Highly competitive companies are able to rapidly cycle through the strategy development process—from identifying that change is required to generating options to choosing and executing them. This section walks the reader through a process my colleagues and I have found helps companies become more versatile and dynamic organizations.

3. Research. This section provides greater details on the research that went into the book, including how I identified what I deem to be the most competitive companies of the decade.

Ethics

When first introduced to the stratagems, people often question the ethics of using them. The stratagems are aggressive and often suggest tactics that, at first glance, may fall outside your comfort boundaries. There are three reasons, however, to come to terms with and override this reaction. First, the stratagems are at work today determining the success and failure of corporations and other organizations. They are time-tested and proven effective in war, politics, and business. To defend yourself against them, you must be able to recognize them. Second, unethical ideas often trigger exciting ethical ones. Organizations that do not give people the room to discuss the outlandish kill off high-potential ideas too soon. It is perfectly acceptable to conceive of something unethical; it is the choice that you make, not the idea that you have, that is important. I have sat through innumerable brainstorming sessions in which someone meekly shares an unethical idea. Someone else, using this idea as inspiration, shapes it into an exciting ethical path. Some people are naturally gifted with the ability to conceive of unorthodox ideas. Others are good at shaping them into something usable. If you block out the conception and discussion of unethical options, you kill the creative dynamic, the playing with ideas, that leads to truly innovative thinking. Third, a stratagem is a trigger that can produce 500 ethical ideas and 500 unethical ones. To throw the stratagems away to avoid the unethical suggestions means losing the ethical ideas as well. This is akin to throwing the baby out with the bath water.

PART I

YIN YANG POLARITY

"Heaven is yin and yang, cold and hot, the order of the seasons.
"Going with it, going against it—this is military victory"
—Sun Tzu, The Art of War

The first assumption from which to attempt to break free is that there can be good without bad. This assumption is basic to Western thought. In fact, it is hard to imagine another view because ambitions are founded on the pursuit of good without evil.

Western upbringing teaches the pursuit of good without bad, health without sickness, happiness without sadness, strength without weakness. Companies want profit without loss, growth without decline, and strength without competition. Yet this ambition runs counter to the Eastern way, in particular the principle of polarity, which says that bad necessarily accompanies good (not judgments but two sides of the same coin) and that decline follows growth. Companies that embrace polarity create options and goals that other companies do not have. These companies are perplexing with their ability to outmaneuver competitors, to lock in consumers, and to control their environment. According to Yin Yang, we work with the natural laws that bind good and bad to achieve the equilibrium we prefer.

1

Instead of trying to dominate markets by consistently beating competition, organizations should seek harmony with their opponents. From the Western perspective, this may seem impractical or weak; but in practice, it is neither. Polarity helped emperors navigate some of China's most turbulent and violent eras: the Spring and Autumn period (770–476 BC), when the centralized feudal system that had maintained relative calm disintegrated; and the Warring States period (475–221 BC), when forty-four feudal states battled each other for land, conquering each other until only seven kingdoms, all of roughly equal strength, remained. Constant, fluid contention in the forms of war and political gaming typified these periods. Out of this environment, philosopher Lao Tzu (c. 551–479 BC) created the *Tao Te Ching*, which, like Niccolò Machiavelli's *The Prince*, was meant to guide leaders to greatness.

In Chapter 2, Lao Tzu wrote:

> *Being and non-being create each other.*
> *Difficult and easy support each other.*
> *Long and short define each other.*
> *High and low depend on each other.*
> *Before and after follow each other.*
> *There the Master [one who understands the Tao]*
> *acts without doing anything*
> *and teaches without saying anything.*
> *Things arise and she lets them come;*
> *things disappear and she lets them go.*
> *She has but doesn't possess,*
> *acts but doesn't expect.*
>
> —*Lao Tzu,* Tao Te Ching, *Chapter Two*

The polarity principle does not imply complacent acceptance. On the contrary, it is an alternative way to achieve ambitions. Lao Tzu argues that in working with, rather than against, the laws of nature—by accepting that everything is connected with its opposite—goals can be achieved more quickly and with less energy, and results will be more permanent.

The polarity principle has two key implications for business:

1. It is usually better to seek balance with, rather than try to destroy, the competition.
2. The environment (e.g., competitors, consumers, markets) can be better controlled by embracing the complex and interdependent nature of the situation.

Do not always try to eliminate the competition. Indeed, companies often depend on their competition for ideas, to energize their workers, and to protect them against other competitors. The most competitive companies—whether slow (e.g., Cablevision), old (e.g., Coca-Cola), or fast (e.g., Virgin)—dance with their competitors to gain advantage. Indeed fourty-four of the 100 most competitive companies of the decade have in some way embraced their competition to gain an advantage (i.e., their rise over the past decade can be explained in part by the use of one of the stratagems in this section).

When asked about the entry of Microsoft into the gaming business, Kazuo Hirai, president and chief operating officer of Sony Computer Entertainment America, said, "Am I worried? I was asked the same question six years ago about Nintendo and Sega. I think they have a lot to contribute to ensure the growth of the interactive entertainment sector. And if they bring a healthy dose of competition, it bodes well for the industry."[2] This is the attitude of a company that embraces polarity.

Embracing the complexity of one's environment reveals new strategic possibilities. The tendency is to cut problems into separate, more easily digested pieces in order to apply logic and derive a solution. But this strategy masks the interesting relationships among all the players. Creative and competitive companies constantly play with relationships to squeeze out an advantage and profits.

The stratagems in this section will help you apply the polarity principle to your immediate situations. You will see that, while based on a philosophy fundamentally different from those of the

West, polarity is regularly at work, helping the most competitive companies build advantage over their peers, consumers, and allies.

> *"Know how to use your enemies. Grasp things not by the blade, which will harm you, but by the hilt, which will defend you. The same applies to emulation. The wise person finds enemies more useful than the fool does friends."*
>
> —*Baltasar Gracian,* The Art of Worldly Wisdom[3]

TO CATCH SOMETHING, FIRST LET IT GO

"Press the enemy force too hard and they will strike back fiercely. Let them go and their morale will sink. Follow them closely, but do not push them too hard.

Tire them, and sap their moral. Then you will be able to capture them without shedding blood. In short, a careful delay in attack will help bring victory."

—*From* The Thirty-Six Stratagems

It is often better to let an opponent escape. Trying to beat a surrounded opponent is costly in time, money, energy, or lives, because the opponent, having less to lose, will fight more fiercely. A victory so won also is less permanent. A defeated opponent will look for revenge, but one who submits voluntarily can become useful.

Key Elements

You capture your enemy.

Though you are able, you do not kill your enemy.

This stratagem points out two truths:

1. Dominating your opponent often requires more energy than it is worth.

2. Force can win hands but rarely hearts.

"A prince ought to inspire fear in such a way that, if he does not win love, he avoids hatred; because he can endure very well being feared whilst he is not hated . . ."

—*Niccolò Machiavelli,* The Prince[4]

The Demise of "God's Machine"

In the mid-1990s, two Silicon Graphics engineers, Mike Ramsay and Jim Barton, believed the television industry was on a path to transformation. Digital storage technological advances had been driving down hard-drive prices for years, and Ramsay and Barton believed large hard drives, with the capacity to store hours of video, would soon become affordable. This would spread the ability to store and manage digital video beyond the domain of television and movie professionals, into the hands of common TV viewers.

In the summer of 1997, Ramsay and Barton founded TiVo Inc. with the aim of challenging the incumbent television industry with user-friendly digital video recorders.

The company seemed to have done everything right. It identified an emerging market before anyone else, designed a superior product consumers loved, launched first, established a brand, and secured critical patents. But history proves that a careful follower often outwits a visionary innovator. Cable providers eventually took TiVo's innovation for themselves with the stratagem *To catch something, first let it go.*

TiVo's machine was revolutionary. It empowered television viewers as no competing product could. With the press of one button, a viewer could record every episode of her favorite program. She could later watch the show on her own schedule, no longer at the discretion of TV network programmers. She could pause to answer the phone and fast-forward through the slow parts. She could watch an entire baseball game in forty minutes by fast-forwarding between pitches and, by skipping commercials, get through a half-hour program in just twenty-two minutes. She could even create her own television line-up, watching recorded programs in any order she desired.

> *"When the position is such that neither side will gain by making the first move, it is called temporizing ground.*
>
> *"In a position of this sort, even though the enemy should offer us an attractive bait, it will be advisable not to stir forth, but rather to retreat, thus enticing the enemy in his turn; then, when part of his army has come out, we may deliver our attack with advantage."*
>
> —Sun Tzu, The Art of War[5]

TiVo consumers became the "raving fans" of marketers' dreams. Many claimed TiVo had changed their lives and tired their friends with endless sermons on the topic.

The industry granted equally fervent praise. *BusinessWeek* profiled TiVo's product in 1999 with an article titled "Here's TV's Next 'Next Big Thing.'"[6] Michael Powell, then chair of the Federal Communications Commission, called TiVo "God's machine."[7]

Industry leaders appeared equally impressed. TiVo's early investors included Cox Communications, AOL TimeWarner, the Walt Disney Company, and Sony. When the company first issued stock to the public in September 1999, asking $16 per share, investors immediately drove the stock price up 87 percent. TiVo seemed uniquely positioned to revolutionize television.

But cable companies watched from the wings with an alternative plot in mind. They were letting TiVo walk into a trap.

Cable companies saw that while viewers who tried TiVo's digital video recorder (DVR) loved it (97 percent said they were "very satisfied" and would recommend TiVo to a friend), TiVo had a hard time convincing new users to try a DVR. The general public could not quickly grasp what a DVR was or why they should want one. The success of DVRs would come only through an extensive and costly consumer education campaign.

Who should pay for such a campaign? Consumers adopting DVRs would generate new revenue that would benefit many, including TiVo, electronics manufacturers (who produce the boxes), cable providers (from higher monthly fees), networks (from viewers spending more time watching television), and television producers (for the same reason). But while TiVo—a publicly traded company with thousands of investors and just one product—needed to launch the campaign immediately, other media players could be patient. Cable companies faced little urgency because they calculated they could easily leverage their relationships with millions of television viewers to later erase any lead TiVo might gain.

Between 2000 and 2003, TiVo invested $270 million to build awareness and adoption. Cable companies watched.

The cable firms decided to be passive. They avoided participating in the DVR revolution, repeatedly turning down opportunities that would have allowed them to launch DVRs at little to no cost. TiVo could push DVRs into millions of households by integrating its technology into a cable company's cable box. It signed a deal with DirecTV to do this and enjoyed spectacular results (the DirecTV deal eventually created 70 percent of TiVo's users). Then TiVo approached most major cable companies with the identical offer, but each cable company—even TiVo's early investors, Cox Communications and AOL TimeWarner—refused.

Through TiVo's efforts, DVRs eventually broke into public consciousness. Viewers began asking for them. They often called cable providers to learn more. When calls came in earnest, cable companies were ready to seize the opportunity TiVo had ushered in. They offered DVRs integrated into cable boxes manufactured by Motorola, Scientific-Atlanta, and other third-party consumer electronics companies.

While TiVo charged $200 for its box, a DVR from a cable provider costs a fraction of that amount. Cable providers are happy to lose money on the hardware because they make up these losses in the increased monthly fees they earn from DVR customers who must upgrade to digital cable service.

Cable companies let TiVo go and then easily eroded TiVo's early lead. TiVo's stock price, once $30 per share, has stagnated at about $6 per share for the past several years. It commands less than a third of the DVR market and is expected to continue losing share.

Cable companies allowed an innovative competitor to enter their domain, watched patiently as TiVo launched a revolution, and, at the moment of ripeness, used their superior position to take over.

The 100-Year Game of Cat and Mouse

Coca-Cola versus Pepsi, the U.S.'s classic corporate rivalry, exemplifies the stratagem *To catch something, first let it go.* The companies first locked antlers at the turn of the twentieth century, and their drama continues to be studied by MBA students in business schools today. But this rivalry is strange because it is one neither company wants to win completely.

In 1886 a pharmacist in Georgia created Coca-Cola's formula, and a few years later Coca-Cola was introduced as a branded beverage to the public. Seven years later, in 1893, a pharmacist from North Carolina invented the Pepsi formula. Soon after, in a move that would define the hundred-year dance between these rivals, Pepsi implemented Coca-Cola's franchise-based business model. By 1910 Coca-Cola had 370 franchises to Pepsi's 270.

The pattern of competition has remained consistent for a century: Coca-Cola innovates, Pepsi copies; Pepsi innovates, Coca-Cola copies. While each company strives to differentiate itself with a new business model, new channel, or new product, it tries as well to be the same, tracking its adversary's efforts so that it can quickly follow.

- In 1980 Coca-Cola switched from using sugar in its cola to lower-priced high-fructose corn syrup. Pepsi followed suit three years later.
- In 1984 Pepsi switched from saccharine to aspartame to sweeten its diet product. Coca-Cola switched to aspartame six months later.
- In 1984 Pepsi introduced a two-liter bottle. Coca-Cola introduced its own two-liter bottle four months later.

- In 1985 Seven-Up ran a successful advertising campaign extol-
  ling the virtues of being caffeine-free. That same year Coca-
  Cola and Pepsi launched caffeine-free versions of their own
  products.

Pepsi and Coca-Cola are enemies that spur each other to be
better. As Roger Enrico said in 1988 when he was CEO of Pepsi,
"The warfare must be perceived as a continuing battle without
blood. Without Coke, Pepsi would have a tough time being an
original and lively competitor. The more successful they are, the
sharper we have to be. If the Coca-Cola Company didn't exist,
we'd pray for someone to invent them."[8]

Coca-Cola and Pepsi play cat and mouse with each other, following closely but never falling too far behind. When one lurches
forward, the other pounces; but the pounces are never fatal. It is
possible to debate their intentions, but the outcome is clear: These
two companies have spurred each other toward greatness for over
a century without either one "winning."

*"Do not pursue an enemy who simulates flight; do not attack sol-
diers whose temper is keen. Do not swallow bait offered by the
enemy. Do not interfere with an army that is returning home. When
you surround an army, leave an outlet free. Do not press a desperate foe too hard. Such is the art of warfare."*

—Sun Tzu, The Art of War[9]

To Capture a Heart, Let It Go Seven Times

In AD 225, three kingdoms ruled China. One of these, Shu, had
been trying unsuccessfully for years to force a group of tribes in its
southern region into submission. The Shu ruler instructed an advisor, Zhuge Liang, to resolve the problem.

With his superior military power, he could have forced a decisive
victory over the renegade tribes. But he worried that such a victory
would be costly and short-lived. The resentment it would generate
would complicate efforts to rule the region. He decided instead to
win the tribe members' hearts and set out to do so by implement-

ing the stratagem *To catch something, first let it go*. He set his sights on the king of the southern tribes, Meng Huo. In the first battle between Meng Huo's tribal army and the Shu army, it became clear that the tribal army was no match for the well-trained and equipped Shu. The Shu captured all three of Meng Huo's generals. But rather than close in on victory, Zhuge Liang fed Meng Huo's generals well and released them. The generals, who expected to be executed, were naturally grateful.

In response, Meng Huo launched an attack himself, and through some deft maneuvering and trickery by the Shu army, was taken prisoner. But Zhuge Liang again acted strangely. Rather than imprisoning or executing Meng Huo, he simply asked his captive to pledge allegiance to the Shu kingdom. Meng Huo refused but promised that if he were captured a second time he would admit inferiority and submit to Shu rule. Zhuge Liang had Meng Huo untied, treated him to wine and good food, and released him. When Shu officers asked Zhuge Liang why he did not execute the enemy king to end the siege definitively, Zhuge Liang explained that he was trying to win the hearts of the southern tribes, not merely defeat their armies.

Meng Huo planned a second attack. His general, who earlier had been captured and released by Zhuge Liang, failed and almost lost his life as punishment. These two events—being released by the enemy and then nearly being killed by his own ruler—shifted the general's allegiance. He captured Meng Huo and presented him to Zhuge Liang. For a second time, Meng Huo was a prisoner of the Shu. For a second time, Zhuge Liang asked Meng Huo to submit. For a second time, he declined. And for a second time, Zhuge Liang had Meng Huo untied, fed, and released. Meng Huo returned home, hunted down his general, and had him executed.

Meng Huo then planned a third assault. This time, he had his brother and a large entourage dressed as civilians bring gifts to Zhuge Liang. Once inside Zhuge Liang's camp, this band prepared to take the Shu forces by surprise and capture Zhuge Liang. But Zhuge Liang saw the trap coming. When the attack came, his men were prepared. They captured Meng Huo, who led the attack, but again he refused to submit, and again Zhuge Liang released him. This continued four more times.

In one instance, Meng Huo and his men fell into a trap laid by the Shu army. In another instance, a king loyal to Meng Huo turned on him, capturing and delivering him to Zhuge Liang. In yet another, Meng Huo and an entourage pretended to surrender but when searched were revealed to be carrying daggers and swords with which they planned to kill Zhuge Liang. Each time Meng Huo was asked to submit, he refused and was released.

After the sixth capture, few supporters remained. Meng Huo mounted a seventh attack on a Shu outfit. The outfit played a game of cat and mouse for two weeks, setting up camp, pretending to retreat, and setting up camp again. In the last move of this pursuit, Meng Huo's army found itself trapped in a valley. Most of the army died. Meng Huo found himself captured for the seventh time. By now he had little support and the morale of his troops was flagging, so Meng Huo submitted to Zhuge Liang and to Shu rule of his tribes.

Zhuge Liang rewarded him with a kingdom, land, and dominion over the southern tribes. When asked why he returned Meng Huo to power rather than put a Shu ruler in his place, Zhuge Liang explained that the people of the southern tribes would be more loyal to Meng Huo than to a Chinese ruler and that by playing cat and mouse he had won Meng Huo's heart. The victory, therefore, was more stable.

"Nothing in the world is more soft and yielding than water. Yet for dissolving the hard and inflexible, nothing can surpass it. The soft overcomes the hard, the gentle overcomes the rigid. Everyone knows this is true, but few can put it into practice."

—*Lao Tzu*, Tao Te Ching[10]

Summary

Most businesses focus on destroying their competition, assuming they are better off without it. They confuse the means (defeating the competition) with the goal (e.g., value creation, profit generation, mission fulfillment). This is like eating a cookbook (the means) because you confuse it with the food (the real goal).

To catch something, first let it go shows that optimal success often depends on your competitor's success, or at least its continued existence. This stratagem reveals a model for competition fundamentally different from the traditional Western concept that dominates business thinking today. In place of the usual concept is a model in which competition is codependence, a dance rather than a war. This model will open your thinking and allow you to see new strategic possibilities. It encourages you to ask, "What if we do not actually want to beat our competition—what would we do differently?"

Applying the give-and-take of the polarity principle to value, as the next stratagem describes, can similarly liberate your thinking.

STRATAGEM TWO

EXCHANGE A BRICK FOR A JADE

"Use a bait to lure the enemy and take him in."
—From The Thirty-Six Stratagems

On the surface, *Exchange a brick for a jade* means simply to trade something of little value for something of more value, which may seem to be advice that is as wise and as useless as "Buy low, sell high." But its deeper lesson has formed the core strategy with which companies such as Microsoft, Sony, and Gillette have established long-term control over their markets. Six of the most competitive companies of the decade succeed in part through their adherence to this principle. The keys to its success rest on two human tendencies that Taoism and Buddhism attempt to eliminate:

1. Value is relative. Yet we act as if one value is commonly shared.
2. We confuse what we value with what others value.

Key Elements

You give your adversary something on which you place relatively little value.

In exchange, your adversary gives you something you value much more.

14

Commitment as a Jade

Consumers often give up value because there is no market for it or because they have no way to realize the value. Companies such as Microsoft and Sony have built their businesses to a great extent on spinning this consumer tendency into profit.

When you consider buying a product, you judge its fair price by comparison to alternatives. If you're shopping for a video game console, for example, you might compare the price tag of, say, Sony's PlayStation 3 to that of Microsoft's Xbox 360. If no close substitutes exist, you might try a more distant comparison—comparing the price of the game console to the cost of seeing a movie every week for a year, for example.

Unfortunately, you may exclude an important variable from your calculations: the full value the seller (i.e., Sony or Microsoft) realizes from establishing a relationship with you. This value is almost always higher than the profit the seller generates from the first sale. In other words, jade is often given up for bricks because the consumer does not appreciate the worth of what he or she is trading. The jade he or she gives up is dependence.

Sony is willing to lose $100 to $150 on each PlayStation 3 it sells because with each sale it establishes a codependent relationship with a new consumer. This allows Sony to shift from a one-off relationship to a long-term one within which it can put polarity to work. It can use this relationship to generate attractive, long-term profits—initially from software sales, but eventually from Internet services, movie rentals, and any number of yet-to-be-imagined products.

Of course, modern Western strategists might name this strategy "switching costs," a move that blocks a consumer from buying software for other systems. The ancient Eastern concept of polarity—the accepting of good with bad or short-term loss for long-term gain—is a different explanation for the same strategy. And when the ancient polarity concept is used rather than the modern switching costs concept to explain Sony's strategy, Microsoft's seemingly abrupt decision to enter the video game business in 2000 becomes less puzzling.

Microsoft also relies heavily on *Exchange a brick for a jade.* Indeed, some argue that Microsoft's strategy is dictated as much by this principle as by its core product—software. Microsoft built its business by distributing DOS and Windows so widely that they became standards, thereby establishing millions of codependent relationships with computer makers and consumers. The resulting mass of relationships eventually resembled a monopoly position in the software sector. Microsoft's success comes from expanding and leveraging these relationships, not just from building better-performing software.

Microsoft's rivals sometimes focus their criticism primarily on Microsoft's technical abilities. They fail to understand that Microsoft depends on its relationships as much or more than it depends on its software competencies. Rivals misread the source of Microsoft's power.

While Linux and other open-source programmers publicly scoff at Microsoft's software (when, for example, Microsoft warns them against incorporating Microsoft code into their open-source products), they are blind to the fact that Microsoft's dominance is built on relationships, not purely on technical ability. While one-product software companies must compete solely on technical ability, Microsoft can create more value, even with less technically capable software, through the relationships it affords consumers who use its software.

If Microsoft did not hold a strong position on nearly every computer, the source of its advantage might erode. This is probably why Microsoft responded more urgently to Sony's video game console than to Linux's community of programmers. Microsoft can beat Linux—even when that software is superior—by enabling easier connectivity and communication. But if people were to shift to Sony's hardware, Microsoft's ability to ensure connectivity would fall under threat.

When Sony announced that it planned to add Internet capability to its PlayStation 2 game console in 1999, it threatened Microsoft's core asset: relationships. Microsoft, a software company that had never taken the video game segment seriously nor produced hardware, suddenly decided to do both. The company understood what Michael Ribero, an executive vice president of game publisher Midway Games Inc., saw: "Game consoles can be a kind of Trojan horse in the living room. You start playing games and then eventually use the console for other entertainment or for e-commerce."

In the first half of 2000, Microsoft announced plans to enter the interactive gaming business with its first game console, the Xbox. While Microsoft's new business was radically different from its traditional one, the company's core strategy remained the same: *Exchange a brick for a jade.* Microsoft launched the Xbox prepared to lose about $125 on each console it sold. Its aim was to protect its consumer relationships and gain new ones, through which the company could profit from future sales of games, Internet services, and e-commerce capabilities for the Xbox. Microsoft has since captured 30 percent of the game console market with industry analysts predicting it should command a 40 percent share in coming years.

Value Is Relative

Chuang Tzu, a Taoist philosopher and a contemporary of Lao Tzu, was known for his humorous and colorful stories. One of his favorite themes was that value is relative. In other words, what is considered good or bad, beautiful or ugly, valuable or worthless, does not exist as an absolute. Rather, it depends on one's point of view.

One of his stories centers on an old tree most people found worthless. It was so knotted that it offered not an inch of flat wood, making it useless to carpenters. It was so ugly no painter wanted to paint it or gardener decorate it.

But the characteristics that made it worthless to carpenters, painters, and gardeners were considered quite important by the tree itself. Indeed they saved the tree's life. Because no one saw value in cutting the tree down, it grew unharmed for hundreds of years. Chuang Tzu's lesson is that value depends on perspective. It is not absolute.

You Confuse Your Value with Others'

Another story, by an unknown author, describes an old monk who lived by himself in an ample but modest home. One evening a thief, believing the house empty, broke in. He found very little of value: some pots and some food. As he rustled around looking for something worth taking home, he was startled to find the monk quietly meditating in one of the rooms.

The monk greeted the thief and asked what he wanted. When the thief explained that he was there to rob whatever he could find of value, the monk apologized: "I am sorry you have gone through such trouble and I have nothing of worth to give you. Here, take my clothes. They will surely get you more money than those pots or that food." The thief took the clothes and left the house.

The monk, now naked, returned to his meditation. Looking out his window at the sky, he thought, "I wish I could have given him the moon. It is so beautiful."

One lesson from this story (and there are a few) is that outward measures of a thing's value can hide its true worth. The thief was so entranced by the value of clothes that he could not appreciate the moon. Ironically, the thief had to steal the clothes, but he already "had" the moon in that he could use it to light his way home and enjoy its beauty. But because no market price for the moon existed, he had no basis for valuing it.

Summary

Exchange a brick for a jade is a simple but powerful concept that has delivered dominant positions to many leading companies. Sony dominates interactive games (53 percent of the market share for consoles), Microsoft dominates operating systems, and Gillette dominates razors (profiting from blades rather than razors).

The Game Group, a British electronics retailer, has dominated its peers by building an unprecedented customer loyalty program. Seventy percent of the company's sales are purchased with a Game Group loyalty card. Each time a customer uses a card, the Game Group gives away redeemable points in exchange for loyalty. This has moved the retailer into a codependent relationship with customers, through which it has driven sales growth averaging 40 percent per year for the past eight years (compared to the industry average of 6.5 percent). What American Airlines did to revolutionize airlines in the 1980s, the Game Group is doing for the electronics retailing business.

All companies depend *on* consumers, but those that establish a similar dependency *by* consumers on the company, move these relationships into polarity. This unlocks the potential to generate attractive long-term rents.

Two truths about value:

1. Value is relative (yours is unlikely to match mine).
2. Understanding the difference between what you value and what others value creates opportunities for you to exchange bricks for jades to entice consumers into codependent relationships.

You can also entice competitors into dependency. The next stratagem shows that doing so enables companies to increase their competitiveness and even to turn disadvantage into advantage.

INVITE YOUR ENEMY ONTO THE ROOF, THEN REMOVE THE LADDER

"Expose your weak points deliberately to entice the enemy to penetrate into your line, then surround him by cutting off his exit."

—From The Thirty-Six Stratagems

Stratagem One, *To catch something, first let it go*, warns against surrounding an enemy because a surrounded enemy is willing to fight to the death. This stratagem, *Invite your enemy onto the roof, then remove the ladder*, offers situations in which you should surround your opponent. In removing your opponent's ladder, you prevent an escape; you force your opponent to compete where you hold the advantage.

The "ladder" in this stratagem symbolizes a path of entry and escape. A ladder allows one to ascend the battleground and escape if necessary. Without an escape ladder, your opponent is forced to fight uncomfortably on a roof he does not understand.

Key Elements

You entice your adversary to enter your area of control.

You cut off your adversary's escape routes.

This disadvantages your adversary and motivates your people.

Microsoft Lures Britannica onto Its Roof

In 1988, *Encyclopedia Britannica* was the world's leading English-language encyclopedia. Originally published in Scotland in 1768, it was also one of the oldest encyclopedias. Through 130 years of publishing, updating, and republishing, it built two seemingly insurmountable assets: credibility and deep content. These assets were key success factors in the encyclopedia business. Consumers, who had to invest more than $1,000 for a complete set of volumes, demanded that the content be authoritative and exhaustive. These assets were also defendable. Any new competitor would have to invest in years of losses as it built and rebuilt content, slowly establishing its credibility, to catch up. Britannica's foundation seemed secure.

However, in that same year, 1988, Microsoft set its sights on the encyclopedia business. It hired a visual designer into the company's multimedia group to begin designing the "look" of a hypothetical electronic, multimedia, CD-based encyclopedia.

For five years Microsoft designed, built, and assembled the pieces of what it hoped would offer a superior value proposition to established encyclopedias. It borrowed credibility and content from *Funk & Wagnall's Encyclopedia* and added features that would differentiate its product from Britannica's:

Searchability. Users could search for information in multiple ways. In addition to the traditional alphabetical method, users could search by keyword and by category.

Multimedia. Microsoft's research showed that children learned more when presented with colorful pictures and moving images, so Microsoft included 800 full-color maps (with voice pronunciations, a "zoom" feature, and 100 historical maps), 100 animations, and seven hours of sound (including historic speeches, famous pieces of music, nature sounds, and foreign languages).

More graphics. Microsoft offered 7,000 illustrations and photographs. A twenty-foot historical timeline—from 15 million BC to the present—allowed users to click on and explore historic events.

Cross-links. Thousands of cross-links enabled users to jump easily from one topic to a related one.

More timely. Electronic content is easier to update than print (e.g., adding a paragraph does not require reformatting all subsequent pages, as is the case with actual books), so Microsoft could promise the content would be fresher.

By the time Microsoft completed development of its encyclopedia, which it named *Encarta,* in 1993, Britannica's advantages no longer seemed so secure. To round out its list of advantages, Microsoft leveraged something Britannica could not: cost. It only cost about $1 to produce a CD. So Microsoft could, and did, price *Encarta* far below a *Britannica* set—at about $300, *Encarta* was less than a third Britannica's cost. A reviewer wrote in the *Guardian,* "For less than the cost of a *Britannica* [book set], you can now buy a multimedia personal computer with CD-ROM drive and the leading electronic encyclopedias."[11] *Encarta* quickly became the top-selling educational CD.

Microsoft's aggressive pricing removed Britannica's ladder. Had Microsoft priced *Encarta* in line with a set of *Britannica*, its value proposition might have been sufficiently comparable to allow the two products to coexist. Consumers who wanted in-depth content would buy books, and those who wanted multimedia would buy *Encarta.* But by pricing *Encarta* at $300, Microsoft left little choice for Britannica but to follow suit. Britannica had to cross the river to Microsoft's roof because its roof was eroding. How long would consumers be willing to pay so much more for a product with clear disadvantages?

Britannica responded two years later with its own electronic encyclopedia. But when it did, it stumbled, because it was forced to rush into a business it did not understand, and because it was playing by rules that gave Microsoft the advantage.

Britannica introduced its CD product in 1995, but because the company did not have the skills or time—it took Microsoft five years to develop *Encarta* while Britannica had less than two—the first Britannica CD was little more than *Encyclopedia Britannica* text in electronic form. The company hoped its superior brand name and content depth would compensate for a multimedia deficit.

Consumers might have accepted this proposition had Britannica not committed a fatal pricing error. Perhaps because it did not understand the CD-ROM market or, more likely, because it wanted to prevent cannibalization of its core product, Britannica priced its CD product at $1,000—three times the price of Encarta. Sales were, naturally, unimpressive.

Finally, in 1997, after two years in the market, Britannica accepted its new reality and began playing by the new rules. It slashed its price to match competition at $125 and added Web links and multimedia content to its latest release.

Britannica had better but still spotty success online. It was the first to offer an online service, *www.eb.com*, which allowed users, for a fee, access to Britannica's thirty-two volumes of content. The site switched fee structures a few times, and in 1999 Britannica decided to try an advertising-based model. It created Britannica.com to offer users full access to Britannica's volumes at no cost. The site was so popular that it crashed and was down for three weeks.

Before 1993, *Britannica* was the leading encyclopedia, with impressive sources of strategic advantage and 250 years of experience. Yet in just a few years, a new brand nearly toppled this institution. It did so not by force, nor by direct competition. Rather, it invited Britannica onto its roof, where multimedia skills rather than heritage determined success, and then removed the ladder. Britannica could no longer return to its old world where credibility and deep content alone guaranteed success. Britannica now finds itself battling in a starkly modern setting, fighting with CD-ROM based competitors, free online encyclopedias (e.g., Wikipedia), and search engines (e.g., Google) that are capturing a growing share of the consumer's search for knowledge.

As you can see in this example, by removing your enemy's ladder, you can force him to compete where you hold the advantage. This is risky. Your adversary can become desperate and difficult. But if applied in the right situation, as the following story shows, it can provide a steady foundation for victory.

Removing Your Enemy's Ladder

In 206 BC the Han kingdom unified China. During the subsequent Han dynasty, which lasted more than 400 years, China
experienced a renaissance that included the revival of Confu-
cianism, the invention of paper (a thousand years before paper
appeared in the West), and the writing of the first dictionaries
and general histories of China. This renaissance owes much to
the Han's martial capabilities and adept use of stratagems. The
Han ruled by force, regularly attacking rebel kingdoms to keep
them within the fold.

In one such instance, a famous general, Han Xin, traveled
to quell two revolts. While he was on his way, a third kingdom
attempted to stop him. When Han Xin reached the Wei River,
he found an army of 200,000 soldiers ready to battle him on
the other side. Han Xin appeared to have three choices, none
attractive: He could attack; but his solders, wading through
water toward an enemy on solid ground, would be at a severe
disadvantage and likely lose their lives. He could return home;
but in failing his emperor, he might lose his own life. He could
wait; but his opponent had no reason to attack or to leave. Han
Xin would not reach the revolts in time and still would fail his
emperor.

Han Xin applied the stratagem *Invite your enemy onto the roof,
then remove the ladder.* He ordered his solders to dam the river
upstream with sandbags. As night fell, so did the water level. In
the morning, Han Xin attacked. His solders easily crossed the
shallow river. Their opponent was prepared but no longer held a
clear advantage.

Soon after the two armies engaged, Han Xin ordered his soldiers to retreat. The opposing general sensed that Han Xin was
about to fall and ordered his troops to follow. When half the
opposing army had crossed the dry river, Han Xin ordered his
soldiers, who had been hiding near the dam, to quickly dismantle
the barrier. Pent-up waters crashed down, drowning the half of the
opposing army still in the river's path.

In one move, Han Xin had done the following:

- Cut his opponent's size in half (from 200,000 to 100,000 soldiers)
- Obtained the advantage of terrain (he was now on high ground with freedom of movement, while his opponent was on low ground and restricted by a river)
- Shifted from attacker to defender

Han Xin used *Invite your enemy onto the roof, then remove the ladder* to manipulate his attackers into a precarious position and defeat them with minimal loss of his own soldiers' lives.

Strategically creative corporations use a maneuver similar to Han Xin's to win markets. By luring a competitor out of her market and into yours in such a way that the competitor cannot return, you can quickly change the rules of competition in your favor to topple even a more powerful incumbent. Microsoft's entry into the encyclopedia business illustrates this clearly.

Summary

You have considered dancing with your competitors (*To catch something, first let it go*). Why not also consider embracing them firmly? Invite your competitors to compete directly with you. This can drive your managers to higher levels of performance and can potentially switch the rules of competition to your favor. Who, after all, is better suited to compete on your roof than you?

LURE THE TIGER DOWN FROM THE MOUNTAIN

"Use unfavorable natural conditions to trap the enemy in a difficult position. Use deception to lure him out. In an offensive that involves great risk, lure the enemy to come out against you."

—From The Thirty-Six Stratagems

A permutation of the tactic *Invite your enemy onto the roof, then remove the ladder* is to lure your adversary out of his stronghold and onto neutral territory and leave open his escape. Both tactics advise inducing your adversary to leave his comfort zone, but the second involves no ladder. Rather, by pulling your adversary onto terrain on which you can beat him, you benefit by forcing one of three outcomes:

- If your adversary refuses to leave his stronghold, you can advance unchallenged.
- If your adversary leaves his stronghold, you can beat him, force him to retreat to his stronghold, and thereby ensure he will not attack again.
- If your adversary leaves his stronghold, you can take it and leave him isolated.

The tiger, which is indigenous to the mountains, is difficult to hunt in its natural terrain. By luring it out of the mountain, onto the open field where you each have a better chance of winning, you remove its advantage and put its stronghold at risk. This is the most popular stratagem among the decade's most competitive companies. Eighteen of the 100 most competitive explain their growth at least in part by having the discipline to stay out of their competitor's strongholds.

Key Elements

Your adversary is in a stronghold.

You avoid his stronghold by sticking to your own.

This lures your adversary out or prevents him from attacking you.

You either attack your enemy on open ground or attack the stronghold.

CarMax Lures Its Competition into the "Retail Game"

When a local entrepreneur asked Austin Ligon, then senior vice president of strategy at the electronics retailer Circuit City, if he might be interested in the used-car business, Ligon was intrigued.

This implausible idea—that an electronics retailer could sell used cars—took richer, more experienced competitors by surprise. Circuit City's used-car business outmaneuvered its rivals to emerge as the United States' only superstore chain for used cars. Pulled by a competitive vacuum, CarMax has tripled revenue over the past five years and continues unchallenged.

In 1993, Ligon first considered the used-car business. While few links between used cars and electronics were evident, Ligon had reasons to believe Circuit City could become a viable player. Three factors led him to this conclusion.

First, the competition was disinterested and fragmented. New-car dealers, who collectively owned 65 percent of the market, viewed used cars as a secondary business. It provided some extra income when new-car sales were down and it allowed them to lure new customers by offering to credit them for trade-ins. Thousands of small used-car dealerships fought over the remaining 35 percent. None held more than 1 percent of the market.

Second, demand was stable. Unlike new-car sales, which spiked and fell erratically with changes in exchange rates and other economic factors, used-car sales remained fairly constant year after year.

Most important, however, Ligon and other executives at Circuit City believed they could transform the experience of buying a used car. When they interviewed used-car buyers and asked them what they enjoyed about the process, they got blank stares. Used-car buyers could list countless reasons they disliked the experience, but rarely could they provide a balancing virtue.

The "used-car salesman" lived up to his stereotype. This reminded Circuit City of its roots. Years ago, the stereo salesperson enjoyed as poor a reputation. Circuit City helped transform this image by bringing respectability to stereo sales. The company's executives felt they could do the same with used cars. Ligon convinced Circuit City's CEO and its board to invest $50 million to launch CarMax.

CarMax could choose either of two general approaches. It could do what most would expect and become a used-car dealer. This approach would entail hiring reputable used-car dealers and dealership managers, learning best practices, and launching a head-on attack on used-car dealers. Or CarMax could ignore best practices and approach used-car selling as a retailer. Circuit City forwent the obvious and chose the unorthodox approach. It decided to become a "retailer" of used cars rather than a conventional dealer. This decision involved a series of subsequent choices, which ultimately made it almost impossible for incumbent used-car dealers to compete with the newcomer.

A retailer will naturally approach the challenge of selling used cars differently than a car dealer. Retailers provide shopping experiences. Dealers manage salespeople. Retailers optimize operations and inventory. Dealers negotiate higher prices.

Drawing on Circuit City's heritage, CarMax made a set of decisions only a retailer would consider:

1. The company offered to appraise and buy any car, even if the seller was not planning to buy its replacement from CarMax. Car dealers had long ago adopted the practice of linking their purchase of a used car with the sale of a new one, even using "guaranteed trade-in values" to attract new car buyers.

2. Circuit City invested $65 million into a technology platform for tracking key indicators. The system recorded customer visits, finance penetration, used-car purchases across demographics and markets, sales data from wholesale auctions, and the number of sales consultant–customer engagements. With this system, CarMax built a proprietary algorithm for calculating the probability of an incoming car being sold. When an owner brought in a used car, a CarMax staff member entered the car's year, color, make, mileage, any body damage, even noting if the car had an odd smell, into the system, which estimated at what price CarMax needed to buy the car to be reasonably sure it would sell quickly (ideally within one month).

3. The company paid salespeople a flat dollar commission so they had no motivation to push a one-year-old Mercedes onto a buyer seeking a four-year-old Ford. While this compensation structure was obvious to retailers, car dealers saw it as revolutionary.

4. While dealerships forced buyers to finance with their sister finance arm (e.g., a VW dealership only offers financing from VW's finance division), CarMax offered quotes from competing firms. After a customer chose a car, the respective CarMax sales associate would walk her to a terminal where she could enter personal data to receive quotes from CarMax's financing division and at least one competing provider.

5. CarMax hired retailers to run its operations, not car people. Indeed, none of CarMax's top management had experience selling cars.

Circuit City entered the used-car business, but it refused to become a used-car dealer. It held to its roots. "We are not a dealer. We are a retailer," CarMax's chief executive officer Ligon explained.

CarMax planned to grow slowly, but as soon as it opened six stores, the competition took notice. "After our sixth store opened, our competitors came after us. We had underestimated how aggressively they would come, especially AutoNation," said Ligon.[12]

AutoNation, a car-dealer superstore chain founded by the management team behind Blockbuster, was attempting to consolidate independent car dealerships as they had done years earlier with video stores. After noticing CarMax's early success, AutoNation decided to attack.

AutoNation faced the same choice CarMax had faced at its inception: *retailer or dealer?* While Circuit City stuck to what it knew best, AutoNation chose to venture out of its comfort zone. Rather than building a business that leveraged its experience in car dealerships, it chose to copy CarMax's retail model. It entered the same markets CarMax had and adopted CarMax's "no hassles" sales scheme.

Copying CarMax's flat dollar sales commission was easy. Duplicating other elements of CarMax's model was another ballgame. It demanded abilities AutoNation lacked. The company could not, for example, replicate CarMax's technology platform. It would not abandon its long-time practice of preferring to buy used cars from customers who bought new cars at the same time.

AutoNation was well funded. It hired top executives from GE and McDonald's. But, in sharp contrast to CarMax, most of AutoNation's managers came from car dealerships, so its culture, practices, and beliefs were rooted in car dealing.

AutoNation's strategy was inspired by its Blockbuster history: *Build scale.* It bought every used-car superstore chain it could find, consolidating CarMax's entire competitive set under one roof. But the scale advantages never materialized. AutoNation lost about $1 billion over three years, and in 1999, it abandoned the used-car business and converted its used-car superstores into new-car dealerships. From used to new, from "no hassle" to negotiation, from retailer to dealer, AutoNation retreated back into its stronghold and took all of CarMax's head-to-head competition with it.

In the absence of competitive resistance, CarMax's growth tripled in three years, and the company continues to grow.

A Tiger Loses Her Mountain

Toward the end of the Han dynasty (221 BC–AD 220), China's warlords had consolidated power so only a few independent states remained. South of the Yangtze River two rivals emerged: Sun Ce and Liu Xun. They eyed each other carefully. Whichever one survived would rule all of southern China.

Liu Xun's capital was difficult to attack. It was well fortified, surrounded by mountains, and reachable by only a few narrow routes, each of which he could easily defend. Sun Ce had little hope of taking Liu Xun directly so he and his advisors devised a plan to lure Liu Xun down from his mountain.

In AD 199, Sun Ce sent an emissary to Liu Xun. The emissary carried precious gifts and a letter. In the letter, Sun Ce praised Liu Xun for his military might and acknowledged his own inferiority. Liu Xun was pleased by the words.

In the letter, Sun Ce went on to complain about another state, Shangliao, that regularly attacked his territory. Shangliao, he explained, although small, was too large for Sun Ce to handle alone. He proposed that Liu Xun attack Shangliao with Sun Ce providing reinforcements. This, he argued, would offer three benefits: Victory would be assured because Liu Xun's powerful forces reinforced with Sun Ce's smaller army would overpower their enemy. The victory would deliver Liu Xun great wealth, because Shangliao was rich. And in the process, Liu Xun would expand his territory, becoming even more powerful.

Liu Xun was intrigued by the proposal. He consulted his advisors, one of whom argued against the plan. This advisor did not trust Sun Ce. He pointed out that defeating Shangliao would be difficult and nearly impossible if Sun Ce failed to provide reinforcements. He warned that if Liu Xun left his stronghold with his army, the stronghold would be vulnerable—and Sun Ce might attack it.

But Liu Xun, hungry for wealth and power, ignored this advice. He ordered his generals to prepare for battle.

Liu Xun's forces marched to Shangliao and surrounded the city. Tired from travel, they were unprepared for the vigorous defense the city's army had prepared. Complicating their situation further, Sun Ce's reinforcements never appeared. Arrows rained from the city, cutting down Liu Xun's forces. Their siege failed.

Meanwhile, Sun Ce learned of Liu Xun's expedition and ordered his troops into action—not to support Liu Xun but to attack his stronghold. Liu Xun had left behind only a small secondary force, which Sun Ce easily overpowered.

Liu Xun returned with his soldiers, defeated, tired, and now demoralized at finding their home conquered. They could not take back their city. After some effort, they surrendered to Sun Ce. The tiger was unable to return to her mountain.

Summary

Just as a tiger presents minimal threat on the open field, your competition can exert no advantage if you force them into a game in which they hold no advantage. Steve Jobs, for example, bought the movie animation company Pixar for $10 million, then sold it to Disney for $7.4 billion. By refusing to make movies by Hollywood's rules—hiring digital animation experts instead of actors, keeping its teams collaborating for years instead of assembling and releasing them for each movie as Hollywood does—Pixar played a game it could win. Disney attempted to compete with Pixar, could not match its digital animation capabilities, and gave up trying.

Your competitor is skilled at playing her game in her market. Competing with her head-on probably carries unnecessary cost and risk. Even the odds, possibly even reverse them, by refusing to play your adversary's game.

BEFRIEND THE DISTANT ENEMY
TO ATTACK ONE NEARBY

"It is more advantageous to conquer nearby enemies, because of geographical reasons, than those far away. So ally yourself temporarily with your distant enemies in spite of political differences."

—*From* The Thirty-Six Stratagems

It is comfortable to draw clear lines between supporters and competitors, yet doing so is becoming more difficult. This stratagem shows that by selecting the right supporters and targeting the right competitors, you can play one off the other and become more powerful.

When companies defined themselves by industry, identifying competitors was straightforward: If a company played in your industry it was a competitor; otherwise, it was not. Now lines are blurring. Companies increasingly define their businesses along dimensions that cross industries. Few thought Microsoft would threaten Sony's PlayStation, for example, or that Virgin, a record company, would threaten British Airways. While companies in unrelated industries are finding themselves unexpected rivals, other companies in the same industry increasingly find themselves allies. Identifying the right competitors and the right allies is becoming more complicated and a more important determinant of success.

The Thirty-Six Stratagems was born in a similarly fluid environment. This fifth stratagem offers some advice for navigating the web of alliances: Ally with competitors that are more "distant" from you and attack competitors that are "nearer" to you.

Key Elements

You ally with a distant enemy.
You attack a nearby enemy.

Honda Befriends a Bicycle Company

Looking from the sidewalk of any major Western city into the street, you would assume that the largest motorcycle manufacturer in the world must be Honda, Suzuki, or Kawasaki. You would be wrong. The world's largest motorcycle manufacturer is not BMW, Ducati, or Harley-Davidson either. Almost no one in the United States or Europe has heard of the world's largest manufacturer of two-wheel vehicles, even though it produces more than 3 million bikes a year, including the world's most popular motorcycle, the Splendor. The largest two-wheel motor vehicle manufacturer in the world is India's Hero Honda. It owes its success to an unlikely paring of two distant enemies: a motor company and a bicycle distributor.

Honda had been waiting for years to sell motorcycles in India. Its motorcycle business is extremely profitable. It produces just 15 percent of the company's revenue yet generates 50 percent of the firm's operating profit. India, with nearly one billion people, in which 70 percent of motor vehicles are two-wheelers, promised an extraordinary opportunity to expand this profitable business. However, Indian government protection did not allow foreign firms in the market.

In the early 1980s, the rules changed. India's domestic firms, who were enjoying a near-monopoly, could not meet demand. The leading motor scooter producer, Bajaj, was struggling under demand many times its annual output. Its customers put up with a six-month waiting list for new scooters. The Indian government responded by allowing foreign companies to enter India through minority joint ventures with local Indian companies. Honda finally had its chance.

To begin selling in India, Honda had to choose a business partner. It had many well-suited partners to choose from because several domestic motor-scooter companies had established themselves under India's protective laws. The logical choice would be a company with experience building motors, assembling motorcycles or scooters, and a network established to sell them. Honda could easily plug its brand and motor design expertise into such a partner.

One of the Indian companies that courted Honda was a family-owned bicycle firm. Founded by two brothers in the 1950s, Hero had built a network of independent bicycle dealers and had established one of India's leading bicycle brands.

While Hero did not hit the top of Honda's potential partner list initially, Honda was intrigued by two factors. First, Hero had already begun adopting "just in time" (JIT) inventory practices. Pioneered by Honda and other Japanese manufacturers, this practice of minimizing inventory by ensuring parts are delivered only at the time needed was beginning to revolutionize the designs of manufacturing floors throughout the developed world. Honda executives were surprised to see an Indian bicycle company embracing such an innovative practice so early. This signaled that Hero and Honda shared a culture of operating discipline.

Second, through forty years of selling bicycles, Hero had blanketed India with a large network of independent bicycle dealers. It had organized hundreds of suppliers who delivered just in time. By partnering with Hero, Honda could potentially convert bicycle dealers into motorcycle dealers and could source materials through Hero's vast supplier network.

While Honda's competition partnered primarily with Indian motor companies to create TVS Suzuki, Bajaj Kawasaki, and other joint ventures, Honda aligned with a bicycle company to create Hero Honda.

Hero Honda launched several innovations over the years that established its dominance. It was the first to introduce a four-stroke engine in India. This technology, for which Honda is famous, dramatically increases fuel efficiency and reduces maintenance costs, making Hero's motorcycles attractive options for price-sensitive Indian riders.

While its competition preferred to run their own dealerships, Hero Honda used Hero's experience managing independent dealers to establish a powerful network of 5,000 outlets. Hero Honda sales agents traverse the country to visit dealers and every day sent postcards to headquarters with information on stock position, turnover, new purchases, projected demand as well as recent competitor action in the region.

On the back end, Hero Honda coordinates over 300 suppliers who supply parts and materials just in time. Where it makes sense, the company has backward integration: It rolls its own steel, produces its own casting, and owns its own auto components companies.

The innovative strategies needed to build a bicycle business proved an ideal complement to Honda's motor design and manufacturing capabilities. Had the company partnered with a "nearby" enemy, it might have remained in a crowded pack of good motorcycle companies including Suzuki and Yamaha. Instead, by partnering with a distant enemy, Honda became outstanding. It helped create the largest motorcycle company in the world.

Unifying China by Befriending Distant Enemies

During the Warring States period, China consisted of seven kingdoms, each pursuing dominance over the known world. Their contentious balance lasted for 250 years until Qin, one of the largest states, upset it. Qin ultimately enveloped the other kingdoms and unified China by acting on the principle *Befriend the distant enemy to attack one nearby*.

An advisor of the Qin emperor encouraged him to attack a state that, while quite distant, was weak and therefore easy prey. The emperor found this advice sound and was ready to act when another advisor warned he should do the opposite. The advisor argued that Qin should not attack the smaller state because other large states, threatened by Qin's expansion, would come to the target state's defense. Indeed, the states near to Qin had already entered an alliance to defend themselves. The advisor also noted that attacking and ruling a distant state would require more resources and introduce more logistical problems than would attacking and ruling a neighbor.

Instead, the advisor suggested seeking alliances with distant states to attack neighboring ones.

This strategy had two key benefits: Qin would be the primary benefactor of these alliances because each nearby state, once taken, would naturally fall under Qin control. And such alliances would put outlying states off their guard by calming their fears of being future Qin targets (which, of course, they were). This would make conquering neighboring states easier, because outlying states would not come to their defense. It also would allow Qin to take the outlying states by surprise later.

The king followed this advice. He befriended distant states and attacked the ones nearby. This disrupted the natural alliance Qin might have otherwise encountered and paved the way for the Qin kingdom to take over the entire country. For the first time in history, China was unified. Qin was its ruler.

Summary

You can increasingly find allies among competitors, and competitors among seemingly unrelated companies. This creates opportunities. Try looking for—even creating—"distant" enemies with whom to achieve common goals (attacking "nearby" enemies). By avoiding knee-jerk reactions to friend and foe, new opportunities will emerge.

KILL WITH A BORROWED KNIFE

*"Your enemy's situation is clear but your ally's stand is uncertain. At
this time, induce your ally to attack your enemy in order to preserve
your strength. In dialectic terms, another man's loss is your gain."*

—From The Thirty-Six Stratagems

Indirect attacks on your adversary are more likely to catch opponents off-guard. When an attack comes from a third party
rather than from you, its effectiveness multiplies. This stratagem
contemplates having someone else attack your adversary. Even if
your adversary looks in the right direction, he or she is likely to
look to the wrong person and so still fails to see your approach.

The most obvious application of this stratagem to business is to
have one competitor attack another or to use one supplier to negotiate a better price with another. Companies often do this. But
useful "borrowed knives" can be found across your industries' value
chain. Here you will see how one company successfully wielded a
"borrowed knife" up its value chain, among suppliers to establish a
bargaining position and lock in new profits.

Key Elements

You induce a third party to attack your enemy.
You take no direct action.

Influence Your Adversary with a Third Party by Borrowing a Foe

Your adversaries' adversaries are likely to be your friends. In one famous case, Coca-Cola showed this to be true. Coca-Cola attacked its adversary by manipulating a competitor.

In the mid-1980s, Coca-Cola and Pepsi had been using the NutraSweet brand of the chemical aspartame to sweeten their diet products. They used the same brand of sweetener because the supplier, Monsanto, held a patent on aspartame production. However, this patent would soon expire—in 1987 in Europe and in 1992 in the United States.

Once the patent expired, Coca-Cola and Pepsi could potentially switch suppliers. This clearly would lower costs. But both beverage companies had good reason to stay with Monsanto: Whoever switched suppliers would have to remove the NutraSweet brand from its can. If Pepsi did this and Coca-Cola did not, Pepsi would lose consumers to Coca-Cola. If Coca-Cola did this and Pepsi did not, Coca-Cola would lose consumers to Pepsi. In other words, unless someone upset the balance, neither drink company would switch. And because neither beverage company would switch, no new competitor would have reason to enter the aspartame market. The economics of entering the aspartame market without the possibility of gaining one of the two largest accounts were unattractive. Monsanto's hold appeared firm.

To free itself from this trap, Coca-Cola borrowed a knife: a new aspartame producer. It encouraged the Holland Sweetener Company to develop an aspartame business to compete with Monsanto once Monsanto's patents expired. The Holland Sweetener Company, betting that Coca-Cola would become a customer, built capacity in Europe in 1995, two years before Monsanto's patent was due to expire there. It then developed plans to build capacity in the United States.

For the first time, Monsanto faced a genuine threat. Before the Holland Sweetener Company had existed, any threat by Coca-Cola to switch suppliers was impossible. Now such a threat was merely impractical. Before Monsanto's patents expired, and before the Holland

Sweetener Company could begin selling aspartame, Coca-Cola and Pepsi used their newfound leverage to negotiate long-term, low-price contracts with Monsanto, effectively killing the Holland Sweetener Company's chances of survival. It is unlikely that Coca-Cola or Pepsi ever intended to award the Holland Sweetener Company aspartame contracts. The company was a pawn—a borrowed knife.

Coca-Cola's maneuver illustrates one application of the stratagem *Kill with a borrowed knife*. It borrowed a supplier's competitor to attack a supplier. But the stratagem's applications are diverse. Each agent whose actions influence your success is a potential target for this stratagem. Take consumers as an example: Borrowing one consumer to market to another can create "buzz marketing." Or consider the government: Borrowing regulators (e.g., through lobbying) changes the rules of the game to become more advantageous. The list of potential targets is unlimited.

Borrowing a Customer

Several of the fastest growing, most profitable companies of the decade have set in motion a self-generating cycle of customer-to-customer marketing by setting up structures that enable customers to efficiently market to their peers. The community service for which Timberland is famous, for example, fuels this dynamic among its loyalists. Another example is Tiffany & Company. Walk out of a Tiffany store and the distinctive Tiffany bag transforms you into a walking advertisement. Others in the mall see the bag and get the urge to walk into a Tiffany store as well. This is why Tiffany gives its bags such prominence in commercials and why the bag is the one thing in the store you cannot purchase on its own. Are your customers serving as "borrowed knives"?

Two Peaches

The origin of the term *borrowed knife* is unknown. But a story from the Spring and Autumn period (770–476 BC) helps illustrate its essence.

A duke in the state of Qi owed much of his prosperity to three knights, whose abilities and strengths had delivered many victories over the years. Stories of the knights' exploits had propelled them to hero status. The duke, though grateful for the knights' contributions, was concerned by their growing power.

When the knights showed signs of disobedience, failing to salute a high-ranking government official, for example, the duke decided to take pre-emptive action and have them killed.

For political and practical reasons, however, the duke could not act directly against the knights. What soldiers would have the will and courage to confront the state's most capable warriors? And if the soldiers somehow succeeded, how would the duke manage the popular reaction? The duke needed to borrow a knife, and he chose knives that had never failed him before—the knights themselves.

He wrapped two peaches in a gift box and anonymously sent them to the knights with a note that read, "He who has performed the greatest deeds may take a peach." The knights opened the gift and read the note. Then two knights each grabbed and ate a peach, each believing his deeds to be the greatest.

The third knight looked up from the now-empty fruit basket and stared furiously at his colleagues. He called them liars. He accused them of greed and conceit, of breaking their code. He reprimanded them so severely that they took their lives.

When the remaining knight's rage subsided, he came to terms with the finality of his words. He had killed his two dearest companions over meaningless pride. His sense of guilt eventually drove him to suicide. The duke was free, and his hands were clean.

Summary

Using a third party to attack an adversary may be more efficient than attacking directly, and it may require fewer resources. It may also be more effective by catching the adversary off-guard. Before committing resources to direct action, think about borrowing a knife.

Consider the obvious choices (a competitor, a customer, the government, a supplier, etc.), but do not stop there. Only your imagination limits your options.

BESIEGE WEI TO RESCUE ZHAO

"It is wiser to launch an attack against the enemy force when they are dispersed than to fight them when they are concentrated. He who strikes first fails, and he who strikes late prevails."

—From The Thirty-Six Stratagems

B*esiege Wei to rescue Zhao*—the tactic of coordinating your attack with that of an ally to force your adversary to battle on two fronts—can turn the tables of fortune. It is one of the most popular strategies among the world's most competitive companies (14 of the 100 most competitive companies employ this tactic). It can help a weak army steal victory from the jaws of an entrenched defender. It can arm a small, young company with an advantage even in the face of a long-established leader. It can build global brands where none existed.

Key Elements

You are in direct conflict with an adversary.

An ally or another division of yours attacks your adversary.

Your adversary disengages from its conflict with you to defend itself.

Your adversary must now fight on two fronts. This multiplies your chances of success.

Starbucks's Perpetual Siege

Until recently, the local coffee shop was a meeting place for coffee drinkers in the United States. Like the corner grocery store or tavern, the local coffee shop was a product of its neighborhood. Its brand extended no farther than its home area. It drew customers from within its neighborhood's borders and so did not compete with nearby coffee shops.

Today this landscape has shifted. The coffee shop is no longer a local phenomenon. Starbucks has trespassed on the local shops' neighborhoods, creating a chain that spreads across the United States, into Europe, and even Asia. The company has injected new growth in the market, growing U.S. coffee shop revenues by 20 percent a year between 1997 and 2001. It has captured a disproportionate share of this expansion, growing its own revenues by 27 percent a year over the same period. Starbucks transformed the once sleepy, local-centric market into a high-growth market of national and international scope. It has done so by applying the principle *Besiege Wei to rescue Zhao.*

To see Starbuck's method at work, imagine three neighborhood coffee shops in three neighborhoods equidistant from one another. These coffee shops do not compete with one another. The coffee, food, and ambiance are equivalent, and the locations do not bring these businesses into competition because they are not in the same neighborhoods. A customer has no reason to travel out of her way to visit another coffee shop, so her neighborhood coffee shop is content.

Now imagine that two of these three shops merge and coordinate their operations. When one buys coffee, for example, it buys for two stores instead of one and so buys at a lower price. When it places an advertisement, it does so for two stores instead of one and thus can expect a larger return on its investment.

If the two coffee shops share the same name, even more advantages present themselves. By approaching customers on two fronts (i.e., customers see the same name twice a day as they pass through neighborhoods on their way to work instead of just once), they can attract new customers to the market. This two-front attack also allows them to capture a larger share of the market: When one coffee shop wins a new customer, that customer becomes loyal to the sister shop as well and will be more willing to walk out of his way, even walk past a competing coffee shop, to visit the sister coffee shop whose name he recognizes. Loyal Starbucks customers, for example, will walk blocks to find a Starbucks. This loyalty cuts into the market share of competing neighborhood coffee shops (though in the case of Starbucks, neighborhood coffee shops often experience sales growth because overall market growth overcompensates for their market share losses).

The local coffee shop that once lived in relative balance with its competitors must now battle on two fronts. Similarly, customers who once were loyal to one coffee shop are now drawn to others on two fronts.

The outcome that results from applying this tactic is powerful. This stratagem gave both Starbucks and Wal-Mart seemingly unstoppable growth. Starbucks uses its stores to market for one another. Wal-Mart achieves economies on the backend: all the stores in a given area coordinate their supply schedules so they can share the same truck fleet, thereby reducing the cost of keeping their stores stocked. No standalone business can match these kinds of efficiencies. In market after market, two or more Starbucks coffee shops teamed up to beat a local competitor; two or more Wal-Marts teamed up to share distribution costs and beat out a local retailer.

> *"Appear at points which the enemy must hasten to defend; march swiftly to places where you are not expected."*
>
> —*Sun Tzu*, The Art of War[13]

Virgin Besieges British Airways

By 1984, numerous start-up airlines had failed in their attempts to challenge British Airways in the UK. British Airways held near-monopolistic power that seemed to make competition futile. So when the Virgin Group launched Virgin Atlantic, most industry experts were incredulous.

Virgin faced numerous disadvantages. It had less money, capacity, political clout, and experience, and it had no control of the reservation system. Its defeat seemed inevitable.

But Virgin could place a piece on the game board that its predecessors never had. By putting its brand into play, Virgin introduced a powerful new ally. Virgin flustered British Airways and set a course for victory.

Because of its size and reputation, British Airways could deal with almost any direct competitor. But Virgin presented an enigma: It had already developed a strong brand in the music industry. Not only would British Airways have to deal with Virgin Atlantic, but it also would have to deal with Virgin Records. Each record Virgin Records sold helped win over passengers for Virgin Atlantic.

Virgin further complicated British Airways' position by expanding into the radio, television, and hotel businesses. British Airways, under attack from disparate directions, was unable to dispose of Virgin Atlantic with the ease it had put other start-up airlines out of business. In just five years, Virgin Atlantic grew to £10 million in profits. And just five years later, it expanded to Asia and Australia. Virgin learned that using one business to protect another rarely drains resources. Usually both businesses benefit.

The stratagem *Besiege Wei to rescue Zhao* strengthens with use, as Richard Branson, the founder of the Virgin Group, observed:

> As well as protecting each other they [the companies] have symbiotic relationships. When Virgin Atlantic starts a flight to South Africa, I find that we can launch Virgin Radio and Virgin Cola there. In the same way, we can use our experience in the airline industry to make buying train tickets easier and cheaper. We can draw on our experience of entertaining people on planes to entertain people on trains. We can use the cinemas to have people sample our Virgin Cola. We can use our vast stock of entertainment at the Virgin Megastores to make trips to Virgin Cinemas more fun.[14]

Virgin's relatively loose conglomeration of companies provides any individual company an enviable stock of internal "allies" from which to borrow support. Just as a neighborhood coffee shop cannot compete with only one neighborhood Starbucks but must also contend with those in other neighborhoods, businesses taking on Virgin cannot compete with just one Virgin company but must simultaneously combat sister firms battling from entirely different industries. Competing against Virgin requires fighting on multiple fronts.

When Two Plus Two Is Greater Than One

In 354 BC, the Chinese state of Wei laid siege to its enemy, the state of Zhao. The weaker Zhao was unable to ward off its aggressor and appealed for help to an ally, the state of Chi, which was led by a strong general named Tian and a wise strategist named Sun Bin.

General Tian assembled his troops and, together with Sun Bin, planned his strategy. They discussed their options. There were many to consider. Chi's army could supplement Zhao's in any number of ways, such as by fighting alongside Zhao's soldiers or by flanking Wei's solders. Each defensive option had its merits, but Sun Bin offered a superior tactic.

Since Wei's troops were at Zhao's doorstep, Wei's city was left exposed. Sun Bin calculated that by ignoring Wei's soldiers—indeed, by avoiding them entirely—Chi could both save Zhao and capture Wei. Although General Tian found Sun Bin's tactic unorthodox, Sun Bin had demonstrated his strategic skill many times before by using such unconventional tactics. General Tian accepted the plan and attacked the state of Wei directly.

Chi's attack on Wei forced Wei's army to abandon its siege of Zhao and to return home in its city's defense. But the journey tired Wei's soldiers. They arrived home unprepared and disorganized; they lacked the normal advantages of defense. As a result, Chi defeated them and saved Zhao in the process.

Like lions, which often attack in pairs to fluster their target, Chi and Zhao trapped Wei in an impossible dilemma. When implemented correctly, one plus one becomes greater than two.

Summary

The stratagem *Besiege Wei to rescue Zhao* advises using an ally or division to attack a competitor on two fronts. Even very different companies (e.g., a music retailer and an airline) may have enough in common to generate an advantage when properly coordinated. At least ten of the most competitive companies of the decade have used this stratagem to expand rapidly overseas. By using a core local business to provide cover for carefully chosen offshoots in new countries, they safely capture share away from international competitors. Using this stratagem can fluster an adversary and clear the way for seemingly unstoppable growth.

THE STRATAGEM OF SOWING DISCORD

"Use the enemy's spies to work for you and you will win without any loss inflicted on your side."

—*From* The Thirty-Six Stratagems

Corporations are built on relationships, from basic (with employees) to complex (e.g., with specialized outsourcers). Some argue that a corporation's core function is simply to aggregate and coordinate relationships. While these relationships are necessary for a company to specialize and grow, they also expose it to risks that others will use the relationships to harm the company.

Key Elements

You induce your adversary's agent to work in your favor.

You use this agent to topple a critical relationship on which your adversary depends.

"The enemy's spies who have come to spy on us must be sought out, tempted with bribes, led away and comfortably housed. Thus they will become converted spies and available for our service."

—*Sun Tzu,* The Art of War[15]

The War for Talent

As companies lean less on factories and machinery for their competitive advantage and more on people, the talent battlefront is becoming more important. Your ability to compete increasingly depends on how well you develop, retain, and recruit employees. Of these three, the last offers a dual opportunity because when you aim your recruitment efforts at your competition, your success not only strengthens your advantage, it weakens your opposition.

In the high-tech sector, competing through recruitment is commonplace. In January 2002, for example, after database software maker Informix Software lost eleven employees to Oracle, it launched a legal defense attempting to secure a temporary restraining order that would prevent Oracle from recruiting more Informix employees. The tactic failed. That same year, another software firm, Borland International, launched a similar effort against Microsoft. The company had lost thirty-four programmers to Microsoft over a thirty-month period. The company was struggling to emerge from financial trouble and the loss of key employees was, in the words of one industry executive, "like we're in the desert, and Microsoft is stealing our water bottle."[16]

In the competition for talent, momentum is more important than size. When Google picked up speed in 2005, programmers began switching their loyalties. In July of that year, the head of Microsoft's Interactive Services division, Kai-Fu Lee, left Microsoft for Google, setting off a well-publicized volley of lawsuits between the companies. Microsoft sued Google, claiming Lee was in violation of a one-year noncompete agreement. It wanted to restrict Lee from setting budgets, salaries, or guiding research for Google in China because Lee had headed Microsoft's China research initiatives. Google countersued.

The two companies eventually negotiated an agreement with undisclosed terms and called off their suits. But Google continues its strategy of luring away Microsoft talent. It established an office in Kirkland, Washington (six miles from Microsoft headquarters) to court discontented Microsoft talent. The strategy seems to be working. Steve Berkowitz, the head of Microsoft's online unit, sees the talent threat as a top priority. "Microsoft is no longer the primary place for technical talent," he said in a *New York Times* interview, "If there is a superstar, Google will be on their minds."[17]

Coca-Cola Sows Discord in Venezuela

In 1996 Coca-Cola outsold Pepsi in almost every market in the world. In Latin America, Venezuela was the one country in which Pepsi enjoyed a lead. Venezuela was a particular source of pride for Pepsi. Pepsi had outsold Coca-Cola in the country for almost fifty years. Its sales were approaching four times that of Coca-Cola's. But in August of that year, Coca-Cola turned this situation around overnight by applying *the stratagem of sowing discord*.

Pepsi's Achilles' heel was Embotelladoros Hit de Venezuela (EHV), the sole Pepsi bottler and distributor in the country. Despite its long history, Pepsi's relationship with EHV was tenuous. Contrary to industry practices, Pepsi held no equity in EHV. Previous requests by EHV for additional investment from Pepsi went nowhere. So Coca-Cola embarked on a campaign to achieve two things:

1. To induce its adversary's agent (EHV) to work in its favor.
2. To use the relationship with EHV to topple Pepsi's dependence on EHV.

Fifteen hundred years earlier, Zhou Yu, a warlord, achieved the first goal through manipulation (by planting a false letter) and the second goal indirectly (by tricking his opponent to destroy his own critical dependence—his generals). Coca-Cola's method was simpler yet equally effective. Coca-Cola planned to turn Pepsi's agent not through trickery but through entering secret talks with EHV aimed at convincing that company to switch its allegiance. In late August 1996, Coca-Cola and EHV reached an agreement under which Coca-Cola would buy 50 percent of EHV and invest additional money into building its Venezuelan business. The talks were so well hidden that Pepsi was taken by surprise upon hearing that a fifty-year relationship had come to an abrupt end—that Pepsi's only bottler, in the only Latin American country in which Pepsi held a lead, had suddenly switched sides.

Pepsi fought to hold on to its 45 percent market share. It said it would "exhaust all legal remedies in Venezuela and in the U.S."[18] It scrambled to find a new partner. But almost overnight, eighteen bottling plants switched over to Coca-Cola, and 4,000 blue Pepsi trucks were painted over with Coca-Cola's red logo. Pepsi's market share dropped to almost zero, and Coca-Cola's 10 percent share shot up to 50 percent.

Sowing Discord in Cao Cao's Camp

During the Three Kingdoms period (220–591 CE), the warlord of Wei kingdom, a famous poet turned general named Cao Cao, was hunting down a rival warlord, Zhou Yu. Cao Cao was a powerful leader and a highly regarded strategist; he commanded an army superior to Zhou Yu's. Cao Cao's advantages were sound, and he should have easily defeated Zhou Yu. But he had one critical dependence, which Zhou Yu toppled using *the stratagem of sowing discord.*

Cao Cao's critical dependence derived from having grown up on the central plains of China. He and his army were unfamiliar with water and incompetent at waging war in it. Although they consistently routed Zhou Yu's army on dry land, their success ended at the rivers and riverbanks of a wetland area in which Zhou Yu had established his last defense.

Cao Cao had Zhou Yu cornered but was incapable of delivering the final blow. To turn this stalemate in his favor, Cao Cao hired two generals experienced in water-based warfare to train and lead his troops. In a short time, Cao Cao's men would learn enough about swimming through rivers and navigating marshes to complete their victory. The generals became Cao Cao's critical dependence. With them, he would succeed. Without them, success was unlikely.

While his men trained, Cao Cao decided simultaneously to pursue a diplomatic solution. One of his advisors happened to be an old friend of Zhou Yu. So Cao Cao ordered this advisor to visit the enemy and try to convince Zhou Yu to surrender.

After trekking to Zhou Yu's camp, the advisor received a warm welcome from his old friend. Zhou Yu ordered a banquet served with large quantities of food, wine, and laughter. He refused to talk of politics, only old times, giving the advisor no opportunity to discuss surrender.

At the end of the night, Zhou Yu invited the advisor to sleep in his tent. The two settled into bed, closed their eyes, and calmed their breathing. But neither fell asleep. After some time the advisor, believing Zhou Yu actually had fallen asleep and hoping to salvage something of his trip, quietly searched for something of value to bring back to Cao Cao.

He found a letter on Zhou Yu's desk with shocking information. The letter appeared to be from the two generals Cao Cao had hired to train his troops in water-based warfare. In the letter, the generals affirmed their allegiance to Zhou Yu and their intentions to capture Cao Cao and sabotage his siege. The letter, of course, was a forgery planted by Zhou Yu to sow discord in Cao Cao's camp.

The next day the advisor reported the news to Cao Cao, who ordered the two generals executed. With them died Cao Cao's only chance of victory.

Summary

Viewing corporations as webs of relationships reveals interesting opportunities. Each relationship on which your adversary depends is a potential point of influence. By identifying your adversary's most critical relationships and, among those, determining the ones you can best influence, you uncover new tools for achieving your goals.

An interesting spin on this tactic is to play with relationships that do not directly influence your adversary but rather influence how she perceives her options. This indirectly influences her actions. The next stratagem, *Trouble the water to catch the fish*, explains this concept.

STRATAGEM NINE

TROUBLE THE WATER
TO CATCH THE FISH

"When the enemy falls into internal chaos, exploit his weakened position and lack of direction and win him over to your side. This is as natural as people going to bed at the end of the day."

—*From* The Thirty-Six Stratagems

It is difficult to catch a fish with your bare hands because it reacts quickly to your approach. But if you stir up the water around the fish so that it becomes clouded with mud, the fish will not see your hand and will be slow to react. You can then catch the fish more easily.

Companies use this principle to catch consumers. They intentionally link seemingly unrelated products or decouple products that normally belong together to change how customers perceive their options and thereby the value of products they are considering.

Key Elements

You create confusion around your adversary.

You blind your adversary and hinder his or her ability to understand your intentions or see your approach.

"When two fish are locked together in battle, you can get both by catching just one."

—Chinese proverb

By linking or decoupling products, a company stirs the water around customers. They remove their products from direct competition with those of similar businesses and thereby charge a higher price, unrestrained by the bar of comparison. To charge more for your apples, for example, bake an apple pie.

"Confusing" the Media Consumer

Stratagem One (*To catch something, first let it go*) showed that cable companies need not lead. They can give a lead to more innovative companies (e.g., TiVo) and then close in if an innovation proves profitable. Cable companies are able to do this consistently because they have assets to stir the water around their customers.

In 2003, investors were writing obituaries for Comcast, the United States' largest cable company. The company was fending off adversaries on two fronts. Satellite TV companies were convincing customers to cut their cables in exchange for hundreds of channels delivered by air. Telephone companies, facing declining revenue from their traditional telephone business, were investing heavily in high-speed Internet access and video. To survive, Comcast would need to underwrite costly upgrades of its cable infrastructure, which investors feared would bring a low return on their investment. Comcast, the common wisdom held, was a dinosaur facing extinction. But what only a few investors saw was that the company possessed immense strategic potential because it was poised to implement the stratagem *Trouble the water to catch the fish*.

In the face of encroaching competition, Comcast bet on a strategy the industry later called the "triple play." It upgraded its infrastructure so that it could bundle its core cable service with high-speed Internet access and telephone service and thereby pull its offerings from direct comparison with satellite TV and telephone companies. This new bundled service complicates consumers' ability to compare offerings because doing so requires disaggregating the total cost into its elements. If your bundled service costs $100, for example, you must estimate how much of this covers your telephone service, how much covers your television, and how much covers your Internet. If an apple pie costs $5, how much are you paying for the apples?

The results have taken investors by surprise. In October 2002, at the nadir of Comcast's struggle, its stock fell to $19 per share. A few investors, including Warren Buffet's Geico insurance company, saw the strategic value of Comcast's position. They began buying Comcast stock, and the market was happy to sell.

Over the subsequent four years, as the company put its strategy in play, consumers turned increasingly to cable for high-speed Internet access. Comcast's high-speed Internet subscriber base nearly doubled; its profitability began growing for the first time in years (operating profit rose to 38 percent by 2006 after stagnating at about 30 percent); and the company's share price more than doubled to $40 per share.

Today Comcast and other cable companies are adding yet more mud to the water by adding wireless telephone service to their bundle (a "quadruple play").[19]

"Confusing" the Software Consumer

As evidence of this stratagem's potential for creating a long-term advantage, consider Microsoft PowerPoint. It is the leading presentation software in the world. It has grown so popular that many consumers forget that PowerPoint followed behind Harvard Graphics. As Microsoft has done many times (e.g., in the encyclopedia business), it grew from a weak position to oust an established leader and dominate a new market. In this case, Microsoft's success rested in a great part on troubling the water around Harvard Graphics consumers.

Microsoft bundled its PowerPoint product with other products to confuse consumers trying to value the product. Microsoft made significant advances on PowerPoint that brought the program's performance in line with that of Harvard Graphics. To cut into the market, Microsoft could have sold its new

PowerPoint version for significantly less than the $290 that Harvard Graphics charged. But if they did this, consumers might perceive PowerPoint to be inferior. Instead, Microsoft kept the standalone price of PowerPoint high ($339) but bundled it with Word and Excel in its Office suite. Consumers believed they were getting a $399 program (PowerPoint) for free when they purchased Office. This pushed PowerPoint into the lead position.

Water around consumers can also be stirred by taking the opposite approach: decoupling products. Financial institutions, for example, have found attractive profits in decoupling financial products. A bank can split the cash flow of a foreign bond into separate pieces: the principal payments, the interest payments, the cash flow related to foreign currency movements, and so on. Although customers know how to value a complete foreign bond, they have much greater difficulty valuing its pieces. The cash flows from the currency fluctuations on the interest of a foreign bond are much more difficult to understand than the bond itself. Because of this confusion, banks can sell the parts for more than the whole.

Cao Cao Troubles the Enemy Camp

Cao Cao, the warlord of Wei who fell for *the stratagem of sowing discord*, faced a difficult decision while laying siege to a rival city. His forces had established a position outside an entrenched enemy. His army was strong but was running low on supplies—so low, in fact, that his soldiers would likely starve before completing their mission. Cao Cao had two choices: He could retreat or risk losing to hunger. The logical choice was to retreat. This would at least allow him to succeed another day.

But Cao Cao decided to apply *Trouble the water to catch the fish* in the hope of winning the battle quickly.

Cao Cao dressed a group of soldiers in enemy uniforms and had them march toward the enemy camp. At the camp gates, his men convinced the guards that they were reinforcements and entered the enemy camp. Soon after, his men set fire to the enemy's tents and supplies.

As confusion ensued, the enemy's army was torn between dousing the fires and battling the invaders. Complicating the situation, they could not distinguish between their own troops and Cao Cao's, who wore the same armor. Blinded by fire and chaos, the enemy did not see Cao Cao's army advancing from beyond the stronghold's walls. Cao Cao took the stronghold.

Summary

By linking things that are normally separate, or separating things that are normally linked, you can "trouble the water" around your adversaries (consumers, partners, competitors, and so forth). This freezes them (making them less likely to understand your intentions or to see you coming) and increases your chances of success.

PART II

WU WEI: GO WITH THE FLOW

W*u Wei*, a term coined by Lao Tzu, most closely means "go with the flow." It advocates yielding to nature rather than opposing it—being a flexible blade of grass instead of a rigid oak tree.

The West equates power with going against nature's flow, overcoming odds, or forcing an outcome. As Winston Churchill said, "Never give in, never, never, never, never, in nothing great or small, large or petty, never give in except to convictions of honor and good sense. Never yield to force; never yield to the apparently overwhelming might of the enemy."[20]

The underlying Western assumption is that the world is rigid and will not change unless it is acted upon. Great change requires greater effort. The underlying Taoist assumption, however, is that the world is constantly changing and that wise exertion can influence this evolving change with minimal effort. The Taoist view is that when we do not feel tired, we have been efficient in impacting the world. As Lao Tzu wrote in the *Tao Te Ching*:

> *Stiff and unbending is the principle of death.*
> *Gentle and yielding is the principle of life.*
> *Thus an Army without flexibility never wins a battle.*
> *A tree that is unbending is easily broken.*
> *The hard and strong will fall.*
> *The soft and weak will overcome.*

A story by Chuang Zhu, Lao Tzu's most famous contemporary, illustrates this principle well. A prince praised his cook for the skill with which he cut meat, because the meat appeared to fall effortlessly off the carcass. The cook explained that when he first began to cut animals he saw them as whole animals. Over many years of practice, however, he learned to see the animal's separate parts. This allowed him to slice easily around the parts rather than struggling to cut through them. Average cooks need to change their knives once a month. Good cooks do so once a year. But because the cook in this story learned how to cut efficiently, he did not have to change his knife in nineteen years.

> "What the ancients called a clever fighter is one who not only wins but excels in winning with ease."
>
> —*Sun Tzu*, The Art of War[21]

Forty-seven of the 100 most competitive companies of the decade used stratagems that followed the principle of Wu Wei.

REMOVE THE FIREWOOD FROM UNDER THE POT

"When confronted with a powerful enemy, do not fight them head on but try to find their weakest spot to initiate their collapse. This is the weak overcoming strong."

—*From* The Thirty-Six Stratagems

Powerful companies do not attach themselves to one source of control. Understanding the complex interdependence of all things, they broaden their view to reveal unorthodox sources of influence. This is seeking the path of least effort and resistance.

Companies like to oversimplify the dynamics of competition. Competition consists of three players: the company, the competitors, and the consumers (the 3-C model). Within this framework, companies focus on key competencies such as being "customer-centric," or "technology driven."

These simplifications help direct employees and educate investors, but they also limit options. Companies without such preferences for simplicity play with greater freedom. They move pieces their competitors never knew were on the game board. While one company decides where to exert power, its opponent, following the stratagem *Remove the firewood from under the pot*, attacks the source of this power. This is one of the most popular tactics among the

decade's most competitive companies. Fifteen of the 100 emerged
as important companies at least in part because they exercised it.

Key Elements

Rather than engage your adversary head-on, attack his or her
source of power.

This weakens your adversary or hinders his ability to attack.

You defeat your weakened adversary.

Attack the Fuel

Throughout history, corporate battles have been waged over the
issue of supply. When Apple launched its first iPod, for example,
it signed an exclusive agreement with Toshiba, which prevented
competitors from following quickly. Toshiba had developed a revolutionary new hard drive that would allow Apple to introduce
an MP3 player that approximated the size of flash-memory-based
players but held ten times the number of songs. By locking up
Toshiba's supply, at least temporarily, Apple made it impossible for
competitors to match the iPod's performance.

To hinder its adversary, Pepsi, Coca-Cola attempted to "lock
up" corn syrup supply by signing large long-term supply contracts
with corn syrup manufacturers. To strengthen its competitiveness
selling consumer media devices in the late 1980s, Sony purchased
Columbia Pictures and CBS to ensure these companies would not
deny content to Sony.

Perhaps the best-known application of this tactic involves Minnetonka, the inventor of Softsoap. The small company realized that if
its new Softsoap products were successful, more powerful consumer
goods companies such as Procter & Gamble and Colgate-Palmolive
would quickly introduce their own liquid-soap products and leverage
their marketing and distribution muscle to overtake Minnetonka. So
the company signed large long-term contracts with the manufacturers
of the pumps that were needed to produce liquid-soap products.

By locking up a large share of the pump supply, Minnetonka
hindered P&G's and Colgate-Palmolive's attempts to follow

with competing products (because these companies could not get enough pumps). This strategy afforded Minnetonka sufficient time to establish a defensible position. While most small companies that go head-to-head with P&G and Colgate-Palmolive fail, Minnetonka survived.

In each of these cases, the attacker targeted its enemy's source of power. This approach allows a more efficient application of power than does the traditional approach of attacking the enemy directly.

Remove the Patents

In 1993, Barr Pharmaceutical was an average generic drug manufacturer, indistinct from hundreds. Years of struggling with the FDA for product approval had pushed back the company's revenues to $58 million in revenue, down from $70 million three years prior. But that year, the company changed its strategy. Once it began focusing on the "fire" rather than on the "pot," the company started growing again. Over the ten years ending 2006, the company grew revenues 560 percent to $1.3 billion while stretching its operating margin to 41 percent from just 6 percent.

The company triggered growth by systematically removing inputs large drug companies depended on to protect themselves against competition: patents. In March 1993, Barr settled a patent challenge with Zeneca Inc. over a breast cancer treatment drug called tamoxifen citrate. Zeneca vigorously defended its right to exclusively market the drug but eventually gave in by giving Barr nonexclusive rights to distribute a generic version of this drug in the United States. With that news, Barr's stock immediately rose 30 percent.[22] The drug grew to produce about 75 percent of the company's sales.

This success in attacking Zeneca's patent led Barr to shift its focus toward patent litigation. In 1993, Barr's CEO stepped aside to allow a former litigator, a partner at the law firm that represented Barr, to take over. The litigator-turned-CEO launched a strategy challenging select patents of large drug companies. The company challenged Glaxo Wellcome's patent of the AIDS drug

AZT. It attacked DuPont Merck's rights to warfarin sodium, an anticoagulation agent.

In just ten years, Barr Pharmaceutical lurched out of a crowded pack to become one of the largest generic drug companies in the world. It did so by systematically removing the patents big drug companies depended on to compete.

Han Starves Rebels

In 154 BC, nine states collaborated to stage a rebellion against the ruling Han empire in China. The Han general calculated that he did not have the power to quell this uprising head-on. So he attacked the rebels' supply lines.

He ordered his primary troops to assemble as if preparing for battle while he led a smaller group of lightly armed troops around the battlefield. This smaller group raced behind the massing rebel forces and took up position on a key route on which the rebels would later depend for supplies.

The Han general then ordered his primary troops to engage the rebel force without launching a genuine attack. The main forces engaged. The rebels were pleased that they were sustaining the "attack" so well; after some time, however, they realized their supply lines had been cut. Their soldiers grew hungry and thirsty, but no food or water came to recharge them. Forced to fight on, the soldiers lost first their passion, then their energy, and finally their will to rebel. In this way, Han ended the rebellion with little cost or effort.

Summary

Attacking your adversary's supply lines requires less effort than directly attacking your enemy. A hungry adversary is easier to take. So cut off your adversary's supply lines, starve him, and then attack.

> *"When the soldiers stand leaning on their spears, they are faint from want of food. If those who are sent to draw water begin by drinking themselves, the army is suffering from thirst."*
>
> —*Sun Tzu*, The Art of War[23]

SHUT THE DOOR TO CAPTURE THE THIEF

"When dealing with a small and weak enemy, surround and destroy him. If you let him retreat, you will be at a disadvantage in pursuing him."

—*From* The Thirty-Six Stratagems

When your adversary is relatively weak, you can seize the moment without attacking directly. Rather it is both effective and efficient to simply contain him. Surrounding your adversary is effective because it prevents him from launching a later counterattack somewhere else. You have, in effect, neutralized him. This tactic is efficient because it often requires less energy than a direct attack and yet provides the same benefit of rendering your adversary unable to cause you harm.

As industries' structures evolve, power shifts from one company to another, from buyers to suppliers, and from customers to companies and back to customers. Strive to build on each favorable shift of power. The principle of Wu Wei implies choosing the time and the methods that minimize effort. This means exerting control over your adversaries when they are weak or divided, moving around them rather than directly at them.

Key Elements

You encounter a moment when your opponent is weak, divided, or dispersed.

You capitalize on this moment by surrounding your enemy, preventing escape, but avoiding direct attack.

Shutting In Your Customers

Your customer is a capricious friend, quick to sample your competitor's offer. You may wonder what she says about you in private or whom she visits when she's out of sight. For much of her life, you cannot see or influence her. But you do enjoy moments of control. If you can recognize and capitalize on these moments, you may seize a profitable advantage over your competition.

As the 1990s began, for example, Barnes & Noble embraced a new concept in book retailing that would transform its industry. Until then a bookstore was for buying books: The customer knew what he or she needed, visited a store, asked for the book, purchased it, and walked away.

Barnes & Noble recognized it was forfeiting a moment of control by too easily letting customers walk out of its doors. By thinking through what else a customer might want to buy while inside a store, it conceived of a web of new businesses to surround its clientele. Barnes & Noble expanded the book-shopping experience to include comfortable couches for browsing, a café offering food and drink, children's play areas, and larger magazine and music sections. The company widened its aisles and scattered reading chairs throughout to encourage clientele to linger. If the amount a customer spends depends on the number of products available for purchase and the amount of time she or he browses in a store, Barnes & Noble multiplied both parts.

Barnes & Noble's new "superstores," at six times the size of traditional bookstores, redefined the experience and economics of the bookstore. In 1989 Barnes & Noble operated 23 superstores; today they run more than 700. Superstores generate 85 percent of the company's sales.[24]

Like most significant innovations, the book superstore concept now seems obvious. It seems a simple enough exercise to explore what else you might sell store visitors. Yet before Barnes & Noble, no major book retailer had answered the inquiry with courage. The inquiry transformed an industry and generated millions in profit and value.

Nearly 10 percent of the decade's most competitive companies I studied have applied this stratagem to secure advantage. The Capita Group, the United Kingdom's leading business-process outsourcing firm, has grown its revenues 2,000 percent in ten years by systematically adding new services it thinks customers will need, from the common (back-office administration and HR outsourcing) to the complex (IT integration and facility design). Retailers Ross Stores and H&M have outgrown their peers over the past ten years in part by answering the question: What else might our customers need once they are in our stores?

Nintendo Shuts the Door to Secure Success

Consider how Nintendo capitalized on its strength early in the video game wars. As a pioneer and early leader, Nintendo commanded the largest user base of any game console manufacturers. This made Nintendo the software developers' favorite platform. Developers could make much more money writing programs for Nintendo than they could anywhere else.

Of course, Nintendo also depended heavily on its game developers. It needed an attractive library of proprietary games to maintain its lead. So the company decided to exert its power over game developers, not by attacking them directly (e.g., by taking them over) but by containing them. Nintendo built a security chip into its console to prevent gamers from using software from other systems. As a result, developers could not reach Nintendo consumers by developing for other platforms. This tactic forced developers to sign exclusivity agreements that prevented them from selling a title to another company for two years after it had been released on Nintendo.

Software developers had two options: They could build software for non-Nintendo consoles with no hope of selling to Nintendo's wide user base, or they could write for Nintendo exclusively. Developers consistently and logically chose option two.

By shutting the door on developers, because developers had no freedom to sell to others when Nintendo was the only game in town, Nintendo was able to set up a barrier to entry that extended its competitive lead for years.

Qin Shuts the Door on Zhao

In 260 BC, the armies of two great states, Qin and Zhao, met in a decisive battle. By seizing on a moment of weakness, Qin shut the door on—and, as a result, soundly defeated—its enemy.

The armies of Qin and Zhao were locked in an even battle when the Zhao army replaced its experienced commander with a less experienced but promising new one. The Qin general saw this switch as an opportunity to apply the stratagem *Shut the door to capture the thief.*

The Qin army attacked the Zhao army and then feigned a retreat to draw the Zhao troops in pursuit. The new Zhao commander pushed his troops in pursuit into Qin territory. But he soon realized his mistake. The Qin army had retreated to the sides rather than straight back and had reassembled behind the Zhao forces. The Zhao general and his 40,000 troops were surrounded. The army tried to retreat, but the Qin had trapped them.

The Qin did not close in for the kill. They held their position for over a month, during which time the Zhao army repeatedly tried to break Qin's grasp. Qin never gave in but never closed in either.

As supplies ran low, the Zhao soldiers grew weak. Without outside communication, they grew desperate. Finally, after forty-six days, the Zhao commander gathered his best troops and made a final attempt to break out. He died in the process.

With the Zhao soldiers leaderless, hungry, and desperate, the Qin marched in and slaughtered the remaining Zhao soldiers, thus ending the long rivalry.

"That the impact of your army may be like a grindstone dashed against an egg—this is effected by the science of weak points and strong."

—*Sun Tzu,* The Art of War[25]

Summary

When handed an opportunity, surround your adversary and prevent his escape. By following that course, Nintendo and the Qin each removed their adversary's threat and Barnes & Noble captivated its customers to transform its industry. Instead of attacking your adversary, if you contain him, you can secure power while preserving your energy.

REPLACE THE BEAMS WITH ROTTEN TIMBERS

"Make the allied forces change their battle formation frequently so that their main strength will be taken away. When they collapse by themselves, go and swallow them up. This is like pulling back the wheels of a chariot to control its direction."

—*From* The Thirty-Six Stratagems

Wu Wei implies attacking where your efforts are most rewarded. By destroying your adversary's support structure, you can bring her down completely and efficiently.

The terms *beam* and *pillar* here have literal military meanings. They relate to battle formations. A typical battle formation in Chinese warfare consisted of two axles: a central axle (called the "heavenly beam"), which extended from the front to the rear of a formation; and a horizontal axle (called the "earthly pillar"), which connected the left and right flanks. The best soldiers fought along one of these axles.

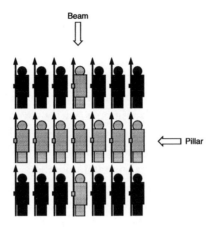

This stratagem advises you to manipulate your opponent's axles so that they lose their integrity. Like rotten timbers, they will crumble. In the ensuing chaos, you can easily secure victory.

Key Elements

Your adversary's advantage is built on key support structures.

You attack these structures.

By breaking these key support structures, your adversary's integrity falters; then you take him.

"When the general is weak and without authority; when his orders are not clear and distinct; when there are no fixed duties assigned to officers and men, and the ranks are formed in a slovenly haphazard manner, the result is utter disorganization."

—*Sun Tzu*, The Art of War[26]

Your competitor's advantage is constructed like a house. On the surface, it appears to be a cohesive whole. But dissection reveals some elements, such as painted sideboards, that are cosmetic; others, such as beams, that provide critical support; and still others, such as the foundation, that are too fundamental to upset. Companies that damage other companies' critical yet vulnerable supports can decrease their adversaries' advantage with minimal effort.

This is like destroying a house by knocking down its supporting beams.

Competitive Beams

Selling beer in Britain is a lucrative proposition. About 80 percent of British adults regularly visit pubs, with an average of three visits per month, and they spend about £20 billion each year.

For decades, a few national British chains exerted protected dominion over pub-goers, maintaining their control by locking up pub locations. When entrepreneurs tried to expand their pub chains beyond a few locations, they would hit a growth ceiling because there were no pubs available for sale.

Like countless aspiring pub owners before him, English-born, New Zealand–raised Timothy Martin hit this ceiling in 1981. Perhaps because of his relative inexperience in pub operations—the twenty-six-year-old had only two years previously opened a small pub and was now looking to expand—Martin saw a strategic option that his predecessors did not, one that disrupted the structural hold major British pub chains had enjoyed over pub locations for decades. His decision laid the foundation for the fastest-growing public company in Britain (and the ninth-fastest growing one in Europe).

Martin was an uninspired law student in London who sought consolation at the end of his day by visiting a pub. Because he couldn't find a pub in his neighborhood, he regularly took a taxi to a certain one across town. This pub was unique for two reasons: It was small (a 500-square-foot former betting shop), and it offered a wide selection of regional beers at a time when most pubs served only a small set of national beers.

Martin enjoyed spending time at the pub far more than he did with his law books. When he learned the pub owner earned £500 per week, he decided to switch careers. He sold his apartment, which had appreciated by £10,000, took out a £70,000 mortgage, and bought the tiny betting–shop–turned–pub.

Martin immersed himself in the pub business. His zeal and the pub's unique location helped build a loyal following. Two years later he needed more room, but when he looked to purchase a new location, he ran into the national chains. He could not find a pub for sale.

Rather than struggle against the national chains, Martin went around them. Inspired by the betting-shop history of his current pub, Martin purchased a car showroom. This would be his new pub.

The strategy worked. Not only did it differentiate Martin's pubs from others by providing unique experiences, it eliminated a competitive "beam" the national British chains relied on to pre-empt competition.

Over the next two decades, Martin expanded by purchasing unusual locations and converting them into unique pub experiences: banks, grocery stores, theaters, auto dealerships. The uniqueness of each location became a trademark of Wetherspoon, Martin's new pub chain. More important, it eroded the structural underpinnings of an advantage his larger competitors had depended on for years.

Today, Martin's pub company generates £850 billion in revenue. Over the past decade, it has grown 35 percent per year, faster than its industry and peers, which post between 1 percent and 10 percent growth. Indeed, his company has grown faster than any other company in the United Kingdom.[27]

Jin Topples Qin

In AD 383, during the Six Dynasties Period in China, two empires of unequal power—Qin and Jin—faced off in a stalemate. The smaller empire saved itself by manipulating its adversary's beams.

The stronger empire, Qin, was attempting to destroy a much weaker one, Jin. The Qin army was encamped just across a river that bordered Jin territory. Despite Qin's relative strength (Jin was smaller and undergoing internal conflict), there were two reasons the Qin general did not want to cross the river to attack the enemy. First, some clever maneuvering by Jin had given him the false impression that the Jin army was less vulnerable than it actually was. Second, the army that crosses the river is always at a disadvantage to the one waiting on the shore. For this second reason, the Jin army also refused to cross the river—hence the stalemate.

To break the stalemate and free his empire from threat, the Jin general devised a plan to disrupt the Qin army's axles, destroy the integrity of its formations, and force it to retreat.

His first step was to send an envoy to the Qin general with a deceptive proposition that he pull back his troops to allow the Jin army to cross the river. The two could then fight on solid ground and settle the conflict.

The Qin general conferred with his advisors and decided on the following plan: He would accept Jin's proposal and order his troops to retreat. But once the Jin army was halfway across the river, he would reverse his orders and attack. The Jin army, caught in the river, would fall quickly.

The Jin general expected, even counted on, Qin's deceit. He ordered a few of his men to dress as Qin soldiers and infiltrate the Qin camps to spread a rumor that their general had discovered the Jin army was actually much stronger that he originally believed them to be and that he feared they would lose the battle if the Jin crossed the river.

The next day the Qin general ordered his troops to retreat as promised. The troops did not know that this retreat was prearranged, and they took it as a sign that the rumors were true—that the Jin army really was much stronger and they were at risk of losing their lives. So instead of retreating in an orderly manner, panic broke out. The Qin soldiers abandoned their formations, dropped their weapons, and ran.

The Qin general lost control in the chaos. He ordered his troops to return to battle, but their formation and command-control structure had fallen apart, and the orders disappeared in the wind. His men kept running. His house crumbled because his beams and pillars had been destroyed. Jin was saved.

Summary

Jin and Wetherspoon each focused their efforts on the support structures on which their adversary most depended. By pulling out these supports, they diminished the integrity of their opponent's resistance until they collapsed.

THE STRATAGEM OF THE BEAUTIFUL WOMAN

"When faced with a formidable enemy, try to subdue their leader. When dealing with an able and resourceful commander, exploit his indulgence of sensual pleasures in order to weaken his fighting spirit. When the commander becomes inept, his soldiers will be demoralized, and their combat power will be greatly weakened. This stratagem takes advantage of the enemy's weakness for the sake of self-protection."

—*From* The Thirty-Six Stratagems

The "beautiful woman" here symbolizes something your adversary needs or desires. By introducing whatever this thing is, you can control your adversary's behavior by distracting him or manipulating him. In this way, your adversary becomes your puppet.

Key Elements

Your adversary has a weakness or need.

You bait your adversary by feeding this weakness or need.

This encourages your adversary to act in a way counter to his benefit.

You take advantage of his misstep.

Beautiful Money

To win adoption of a technology, service, or other innovation typically requires enrolling critical gatekeepers. If you can identify these players and target their unique weaknesses or needs, you can unlock their gates with ease.

Successful corporate innovators often implement this strategy through the placement of carefully designed strategic investments. In the late 1990s, for example, QUALCOMM was fighting heatedly for the world to adopt its wireless technology, Code Division Multiple Access (CDMA). This required that AT&T Wireless and other mobile phone operators agree to build their systems using CDMA. If an operator chose CDMA, then phone makers such as Motorola would begin building CDMA handsets setting off a virtuous cycle of growth. But QUALCOMM's advances went unnoticed because most operators around the world were leaning toward an alternative technology called Time Division Multiple Access (TDMA).

Mobile phone players in United States and other developed countries were fairly entrenched in their technology commitments. Convincing them to switch to CDMA was akin to entering a crowded battlefield. In comparison, the battlefield in developing countries, where mobile communications was a relative novelty, seemed unguarded. QUALCOMM saw a way to influence developing countries to adopt CDMA.

Exponential growth of mobile phone usage in developing countries demanded large infrastructure investments. To remain competitive, phone operators would need capital to build new towers and expand their networks. QUALCOMM channeled its high-flying stock and robust cash flow to begin investing in mobile phone operators in select developing markets.

In 1997 and 1998, the company invested heavily in foreign operators. It purchased a 50 percent interest in Chilesat PCS for $42 million. The following year, it committed $110 million to Pegaso Telecommunications in Mexico and OxPhone Pty, Ltd. in Australia, along with Metrosvyaz Ltd. and Orrengrove Investments Ltd. in Russia. QUALCOMM was not interested in entering the phone-operator business. Indeed it later spun off all of its mobile phone–operator investments (see *Let the plum tree whither in place of the peach*). Rather, the company made these investments to build influence and push phone operators to choose CDMA over other options. By identifying and playing to a critical need, QUALCOMM altered the calculations of mobile phone operators in developing countries, giving them a compelling reason, beyond purely technical considerations, to prefer QUALCOMM's proprietary technology. CDMA became a preferred technology platform in much of the developing world not necessarily because it was a better choice but because QUALCOMM designed an influencing strategy to stack the cards in its favor.

A Woman Topples an Empire

Around 200 BC, a ruthless warlord, Dong Zhou, indirectly controlled the Han Empire through a puppet emperor. He strengthened his power by adopting a powerful warrior, Lu Bu, as his son, thereby ensuring Lu Bu's and the army's loyalty. With this solid power base, Dong Zhou was able to rule with a heavy hand and with little fear of attack. He developed a reputation for regularly beheading those who betrayed, contradicted, or opposed him.

The governor of one of the empire's provinces feared it was only a matter of time before he, too, was condemned, so he devised a plan to remove Dong Zhou from power. He applied *The stratagem of the beautiful woman*.

The governor first found a stunning young woman who was willing to help him execute his plan. He then invited Lu Bu to his house for dinner and had the young woman serve Lu Bu wine. The young woman quickly intrigued Lu Bu. His curiosity grew as he drank, and eventually he asked the governor about the young woman. The governor said she was his niece and offered her to Lu Bu as his wife. Lu Bu eagerly accepted and made arrangements for a wedding. The governor's first stone was in place.

Next, the governor invited Dong Zhou over for dinner. And again, in a similar fashion, the governor conspicuously displayed the young woman so that Dong Zhou became enamored and inquired after her. The governor told the warlord she was his maid and offered her to the warlord as his concubine. The warlord enthusiastically accepted and arranged for his people to pick her up the next day. The governor's second stone was in place.

Through the woman, the governor gained influence over the two most powerful people in the empire. The governor used this influence to play Dong Zhou and Lu Bu against each other. Each thought the other was trying to steal the woman against her will. The woman lied to each to reinforce this belief, asking the warlord to protect her from the warrior and vice versa.

The rivalry between the warlord and his chief warrior heated up. Neither was willing to give in. Lu Bu eventually killed Dong Zhou and so freed the governor and the Han Empire from Dong Zhou's oppressive rule.

Summary

You can use that which your adversary wants or needs to induce him to follow your wishes. Lu Bu dangled a woman on his hook; QUALCOMM dangled investment.

This tactic may seem elementary at first, but this is because its scope is often unnecessarily limited. Companies tend to consider only levers of influence that are consistent with their environment. For example, if they want to influence a supplier, they concentrate on levers that fall within the scope of a buyer-supplier relationship (e.g., payment terms and logistics); if they want to influence a distributor, they consider margins and marketing support.

Companies that think beyond the limits set by context and consider a broad array of options can exert greater power more efficiently. They uncover unorthodox sources of leverage for which their adversaries are unprepared.

BEAT THE GRASS
TO STARTLE THE SNAKE

"Any suspicion about the enemy's circumstances must be investigated. Before any military action, be sure to ascertain the enemy's situation; repeated reconnaissance is an effective way to discover the hidden enemy."

—*From* The Thirty-Six Stratagems

In the context of the Thirty-Six Stratagems, Microsoft's persistent trial-and-error approach to pursuing new business opportunities is best referred to as *Beat the grass to startle the snake*. This tactic suggests that rather than committing to a full attack, make a series of smaller attacks in order to learn your adversary's strengths and likely responses. With this knowledge, you can defeat your adversary more easily.

Key Elements

You are unsure of your enemy's strength or strategy.

You launch a small-scale or indirect attack on your adversary.

Your adversary reveals her strength or strategy by her response to your false attack.

You plan your real attack with this new knowledge.

When you approach a bush in which you fear a poisonous snake hides, you can beat the bush with a stick. If a snake is hiding, it will either strike or run away. Either way, you will know if the bush is safe, and with this information, you can decide where to place your next step.

Miyamoto Musashi, a famous Japanese sword master and author of *The Book of Five Rings*, calls this tactic Moving Shadows:

> In large-scale military science, when you cannot discern the enemy state, you pretend to make a powerful attack to see what they will do. Having seen the opponent's methods, it is easy to seize victory by taking advantage of the different tactics specially adapted to each use.[28]

Moving Shadows is something you do when you cannot discern what an adversary is thinking. This stratagem delivers power by inducing an adversary to react, thereby extracting information about the adversary's strength or intentions. Action is pregnant with information. A story of two master swordsmen illustrates this well.

Two swordsmen, both old and experienced, stood opposite each other prepared to spar in competition. The referee announced that the match had begun, but neither swordsman moved. They stood still for several minutes until the referee called the match a draw. Neither moved because action would reveal information (e.g., how the opponent's weight was distributed, the direction of his momentum) that his opponent could use against him. If you force your opponent to react without committing yourself, you gain an advantage.

Microsoft Persists

Most Westerners perceive the success of high-growth companies to be built on exhaustive analysis followed by the execution of bold strategies. Yet this is rarely the case. Only seven of the 100 most competitive companies of the decade have explicitly adopted this approach. In accordance with Wu Wei, successful companies more often take a series of small incremental steps that preserve energy, minimize risk, and allow them to "feel out" the market.

Microsoft regularly turns to this same pattern of trial and error when it builds a new business. It is not that Microsoft identifies opportunities before its competition; indeed, Microsoft is often a follower. The image of Microsoft using its unprecedented cash reserves to thrust into new businesses is, for the most part, inaccurate. Microsoft follows a patient, deliberate approach that allows it to feel out the competition as it works its way into a leading position over the course of several years.

Consider Microsoft's entry into the Internet and later the server market. When the company introduced its Web portal in the mid-1990s, industry experts believed it had missed its opportunity to be an Internet player because Yahoo! and AOL had already built insurmountable leads. Commentators often mentioned the fact that Bill Gates did not refer to the Internet in the first version of his 1995 book *The Road Ahead*. The publisher rapidly produced a revised version that did, but Microsoft persisted in its Internet strategy, buoyed by strong cash reserves and minimal debt.

In comparison to Yahoo!'s and AOL's breakneck rise to power, MSN's decades-long effort seems like a slow plod. Its execution was plagued with mistakes—and with each mistake, onlookers cheered for the smaller, independent companies. This taught the software giant lessons about the Internet and the new economy. Therein is a key to Microsoft's success. Most observers interpreted Microsoft's failures as faults. But these missteps also offered lessons. With each loss, Microsoft learned about its market and its competitors. Its next attack was informed by this new knowledge. Through a sequence of minor battles, Microsoft learned. With each loss, it grew more familiar with competitive and consumer dynamics to cut further into its competitors' leads. After fifteen years MSN has persisted as one of the Internet's most popular Web sites. It attracts nearly 500 million unique visitors worldwide each month[29] and is the third most-popular search engine after Google and Yahoo!

Its server software business followed a similar pattern. When Microsoft first entered the segment in 1998, industry experts discounted, even poked fun at, the company's prospects. Microsoft's product, SQL Server, was far weaker than Oracle's and IBM's offerings. But Microsoft persisted. Every few years, it launched an improved version that responded to competitive and customer reactions. It slowly built a legitimate position. Today it captures the third highest share of server revenue.

H&M Plods . . . Quickly

Over the past decade, H&M has emerged as one of the fastest growing and most profitable retailers in the world. It owes its recent success to a great extent to its application of *Beat the grass to startle the snake*.

The company was founded in Sweden in 1947. It grew from a local success story into a European one, expanding into the UK and continental Europe. Then it set its sites on the United States. As of 2007, H&M operated more than 1,300 stores in twenty-four countries.

Its philosophy is inconsistent with that of other global retailers such as the The Gap because H&M takes small steps instead of big ones and adapts to local tastes instead of standardizing for scale.

When H&M enters a new market it tests out a merchandise mix, keeping inventory levels and costs low. The new store carefully tracks local customer buying habits, whether they buy more children's clothes or men's or women's or a family mix. The company replenishes stores faster than its peers so it can adjust each store's merchandise mix almost immediately. When a store finally gets its mix right, it maximizes growth.

This trial-and-error strategy has fueled growth and profit margins at nearly twice the industry average over the past decade. In 1995, H&M sold $1.7 billion. In 2005, it sold $11 billion.

> *"Float a trial balloon to see how well something is accepted and received, especially when you doubt its popularity or success."*
>
> —*Baltasar Gracian,* The Art of Worldly Wisdom[30]

Beat an Assistant to Startle a Magistrate

Although this stratagem is much older, its modern name originates from a story during the Tang dynasty (618–907 CE). The story centers on a provincial magistrate who regularly accepted bribes. His citizens, who were fed up with the corruption, issued a formal complaint. But rather than directly implicate the magistrate, they issued charges against one of his assistant magistrates. Perhaps the citizens feared the response that a direct attack on the magistrate might evoke. Perhaps they were not sure whether the magistrate was actually involved. Either way, their tactic had the desired effect: They startled and exposed the snake. The magistrate felt the threat and ended his corrupt practices. In a moment of anxiety, the magistrate wrote: "You merely beat the grass but by doing so startle the snake within."

Summary

By staging a small uncommitted attack, you can learn how your adversaries and markets will react to a real attack. Even companies that can afford a full attack may find the fastest leap to dominance is to take short steps. Subsequent attacks then become better informed and, thus, more effective.

LOOT A BURNING HOUSE

"When the enemy falls into severe crisis, exploit his adversity and attack by direct confrontation. This is the strong defeating the weak."

—From The Thirty-Six Stratagems

Businesses that consistently seize on others' misfortunes build power. They act like water, exerting pressure on all surfaces, so that the moment an opening appears, they are already advancing. A key element of this approach is to see opportunity where others see trouble. Birds fear floods. But the bird that can become a fish will thrive where other birds perish. Such flexibility is in accordance with Wu Wei. Thor Industries' aggressive, fluid opportunity chasing is an example of the stratagem *Loot a burning house.*

Key Elements

Trouble strikes.

Your adversary freezes or retreats.

*"You capitalize on your adversary's inaction or retreat to build power
"When the [enemy] is in chaos, take him."*

—*Sun Tzu*, The Art of War[31]

Looting Burning Buses

Wade F. B. Thompson and Peter B. Orthwein knew next to nothing about the recreational vehicle (RV) business when they bought HI-LO Trailer, a small RV manufacturer, in 1977. But their willingness to buy when others wanted to sell, combined with their complementary financial and marketing skills, proved sufficient to compete. Today their company, Thor Industries, (named for the first two letters of each partner's name, *Th* and *Or*) is the United States' leading producer of RVs. It commands a nearly 30 percent market share, having grown revenues by 450 percent over the past ten years to $2.6 billion.[32] The courage to move in when others are rushing for the exits can generate attractive returns.

Thompson and Orthwein first got a taste of the ancient stratagem *Loot a burning house* in 1980 when, with just three years of industry experience, the two bid for an American RV icon, Airstream.

Throughout the 1940s and 1950s, Airstream became a symbol of American culture. Its distinctive bullet-shaped silver trailers could be seen hitched to autos throughout the United States. Known for its design and durability, the Airstream trailer served as a way for American families to explore their country at a time when family journeys across the States became symbolic of post–World War II mores. Even today, when you imagine the classic RV, you are probably unconsciously visualizing the Airstream.

By 1980, however, Airstream was on the verge of failure. The company had been sold in 1967 to Beatrice Foods, which wanted to diversify beyond its core food businesses. While Airstream had become an important contributor to Beatrice Foods' profits, the 1970s oil crisis kept would-be RV travelers at home and pushed Airstream's profits into negative territory. In 1979, Airstream reported a loss of $12 million on sales of $22 million.

In 1980, Beatrice CEO James Dutt determined that Beatrice should sell all non-core companies, as well as any company that couldn't produce at least a 20 percent return on net assets for Beatrice. Airstream, Dutt determined, had to go.

The market for buses and RVs at the time was poor. Few wanted to bet on Airstream's future. But two entrepreneurs who had entered the RV business just three years prior decided to ignore consensus and bid for Airstream. The two formed a new company, Thor Industries, in August 29, 1980, to buy the Airstream business from Beatrice. They paid $22 million for a company that, at the time, was losing $12 million per year.

The investment paid off. The two implemented a set of operating and marketing initiatives that simultaneously built up Airstream's top line while it restrained its costs. Within their first year of ownership, the entrepreneurial team increased revenue to $26 million and profit to $1 million (a $13 million turnaround in profit).

Thompson and Orthwein continued their strategy of *Looting a burning house* throughout their careers:

- In September 1988, Thor acquired El Dorado, a troubled Kansas-based company that produced buses. Under Thor, El Dorado more than quadrupled revenue to become the largest small bus manufacturer in the United States.
- In 1982, Thompson and Orthwein purchased Commodore Corporation's RV business. Again, under Thor, Commodore's business soared.
- In 1991, Thor purchased Dutchman, which became Thor's largest "towable" RV company (i.e., an RV to be towed behind users' main vehicles).

Moving in when others are exiting, and buying when common wisdom drives the competition to sell can lead you to attractive competitive advantages. Thor went public in 1984, and that same year *Forbes* magazine ranked Thor sixth out of 200 best small companies in the United States. In 1987, *Money* magazine named Airstream travel trailers one of the ninety-nine "best-made products" in America. Over the past ten years, Thor's revenues have grown over 450 percent, while its profit margin has nearly doubled to 10 percent.[33]

Yue Crouches for Fifteen Years

In the fifth century BC, the states of Yue and Wu were at war. In a decisive battle in 498, the Wu army took the king of Yue prisoner and forced him into slavery. For the next three years, he groomed horses for the king of Wu. He worked without protest. Indeed, he behaved so respectfully and obediently that he won the Wu king's trust. Eventually the Yue king gained his freedom and returned to his home.

Although the king of Yue yearned for revenge, he waited. In the years that followed his release, he continued to act respectfully toward Wu and purposely stayed close to Wu's king. He regularly sent gifts of gold and money to strengthen the foundation of trust between the two nations.

During this time, the Yue king rebuilt his army. This task took several years. Once it was complete, more than five years later, he had the strength to attack Wu and exact his revenge.

But he did not. He sent gifts, maintained his friendly countenance, and waited.

Ten years after the Yue king's release, a drought hit Wu, and the Yue king sensed his moment approaching. When the king of Wu foolishly executed his most capable advisor, the Yue king prepared to strike. And in 482, when the king of Wu led his most capable troops out of the capital to meet with rulers from surrounding states, the Yue king finally seized the moment and unleashed his revenge. He attacked and took the Wu capital.

The king of Yue sat poised for fifteen years, waiting patiently for a sign of fire. When Wu's house started to burn, he advanced. His timing gave him a clean victory and a satisfying revenge.

So in war, the way is to avoid what is strong and to strike what is weak.

> "Water shapes its course according to the nature of the ground over which it flows; the soldier works out his victory in relation to the foe whom he is facing.
>
> "Therefore, just as water retains no constant shape, so in warfare there are no constant conditions."
>
> —*Sun Tzu,* The Art of War[34]

Summary

This stratagem advises capitalizing on trouble. Trouble creates opportunities. If you are willing to jump into the fire while others are running away, you may take easily what you would otherwise have at only heavy price. Ten percent of the decade's most competitive companies used this tactic in some form to seize an advantage.

SOMETIMES RUNNING AWAY IS THE BEST STRATEGY

"To avoid combat with a powerful enemy, the whole army should retreat and wait for the right time to advance again. This is not inconsistent with normal military principles."

—*From* The Thirty-Six Stratagems

There are three options when facing an adversary you cannot defeat: surrender, make peace, or retreat. If you surrender or make peace, you limit future options. These are at least partial defeats. But if you retreat, you preserve your strength and maintain the possibility of exerting your power either at a later time or in a different place. Nearly 10 percent of the decade's most competitive companies began their rise with some kind of retreat. Chinese military history is filled with stories of armies that came back from retreat, often after decades, to claim ultimate victory.

Key Elements

You face a powerful adversary.

You retreat.

You exert your preserved power somewhere else or at some other time.

Jobs Trims the Apple Tree

As 1997 came to a close, Apple Computer announced that it would lose money again; this represented its sixth straight quarter of losses. The company's board had ousted Steve Jobs a decade earlier, and the procession of CEOs who followed him had eroded the company's "cool." Once a highly desired brand, Apple was becoming like any other computer company and risked bankruptcy as a result.

Apple's fall and subsequent rise illustrates the principle behind *Sometimes running away is the best strategy*. It seems logical that new products and markets will add to growth. But by resisting this logic—by "running away" from good businesses and attractive markets—companies can often grow more quickly.

The Apple board first chose a marketing guru, John Scully, the former president of PepsiCo, to replace Jobs. Scully began to move Apple away from its marketing roots while investing in new technology research projects including the development of the Apple Newton, the world's first hand-held personal digital assistant (PDA). New product development projects flowered under Scully, but few bore fruit.

Scully repositioned Apple more deeply in the realm of high technology and focused on pursuing the same corporate clients that Microsoft, Oracle, and Sun Microsystems fought over. For example, he took an expensive risk in translating Apple's operating system into a platform robust enough for corporate use. However, Apple's strengths were inappropriate for competing with the computing giants that were targeting corporate accounts. Apple was outstanding at building aesthetic products that appealed emotionally to consumers. Corporations bought computers through layers of procedures that prevented emotional purchases from slipping through. They did not care about, or at least were not willing to pay for, more aesthetic machines.

The CEOs who replaced Scully, Michael Spindler and then Gil Amelio, sustained Apple's expansion into head-to-head competition. This began to have an impact on Apple's core consumer business, because, as Apple's attention broadened, it began to make mistakes. It recalled a new line of laptops in 1995 after two models caught fire. It ran into a component shortage that left consumers around the world waiting for $1 billion worth of computers.

Ironically, the more products and markets Apple took on, the less it sold. Between 1995 and 1997, the company's share of desktops halved from 8 percent to about 4 percent while its share of laptops fell from 7.6 percent to 3 percent.

After the company announced losses of $708 million in the first three months of 1997, its board decided to look for a new chief executive (the company's third in four years). During the search, Steve Jobs took the role of interim CEO.

Jobs had been working with the company for about six months as an "informal advisor" and so had a good grasp of the direction in which Apple needed to head. During his first months as interim CEO, Jobs held group meetings with hundreds of managers. He asked uncomfortable questions such as, "If you had to cut half your products, what would you do?" He was looking for projects to cut and told Apple managers he would keep only projects that were both strategic and profitable. Anyone who wanted to keep funding for any unprofitable strategic project would have to lobby for it.

Jobs's goal was to cut 70 percent of Apple's R&D efforts. "We've reviewed the road map of new products and axed more that 70 percent of them, keeping the 30 percent that were gems."[35] He cancelled some of Apple's best-known efforts including the Newton, Apple's revolutionary PDA. Some say he did so because the idea was not his own; rather, it was cultivated by John Scully. In the end, Jobs cut more than the 70 percent he promised, reducing the number of R&D projects from 350 to 10.

By pulling out of contests Apple could not win, Jobs could now refocus on areas in which the company could dominate. He prioritized a few exciting new products (e.g., the iPod) and began making the Apple brand "cool" again with investments in new marketing and branding initiatives.

In January 1998, Jobs was concluding a ninety-minute speech attended by 4,000 Apple fans. He began walking off the stage, but then, as if suddenly remembering, he stopped, turned to the crowd, and said, "I almost forgot. We're profitable." This was Apple's first profit in six quarters. The trend continued. Revenue began to march steadily upward from $6 billion in 1998 to $14 billion in 2005. By "running away," Apple unleashed growth.

Surrendering to Return

In 1403, during the Ming dynasty, the Ming emperor was considering suicide. His stronghold had been surrounded by an enemy force and was about to fall. But one of his eunuchs stopped him. The eunuch explained that he had instructions from the emperor's grandfather to direct any emperor who faced an apparently hopeless situation to open a particular chest.

The emperor agreed. He looked in the chest his grandfather had prepared and found a monk's robe, a razor, a diploma, and some silver. His grandfather's message was clear. He escaped through a hidden passage to a monastery, put on the robe, and shaved his head. Disguised as monk, the emperor fled the city as it burned down.

After the siege, the people assumed the emperor had died in the fire. But he had retreated to a remote monastery in the mountains where he lived in obscurity. For the next forty years, the emperor practiced the rituals and discipline of a monk.

A rumor began that the old emperor was actually still alive. To address this rumor, the new emperor launched an official inquiry. The inquiry concluded that the rumor was true. The reigning emperor found the old emperor and invited him back into the city, where he was treated with honor. The old emperor lived out the rest of his life in comfort and died a palace guest. He owed this comfortable ending to having run away.

Summary

The most clever and powerful are willing to retreat. They do not equate retreat with failure. This is as true for corporations as it is for nations. Though driven to surmount odds, powerful companies recognize when to yield and choose the battles that most reward effort. This requires transcending an attraction to big challenges (a tendency strengthened by past successes). It requires recognizing retreat as an offensive option, one that has benefited armies and politicians for millennia.

SEIZE THE OPPORTUNITY TO LEAD THE SHEEP AWAY

"Exploit any minor lapses on the enemy side, and seize every advantage to your side. Any negligence of the enemy must be turned into a benefit for you."

—*From* The Thirty-Six Stratagems

The name of this stratagem originates from a Chinese folktale about a destitute traveler who, while walking along a country road, comes across a flock of sheep. He fantasizes about having one of the sheep to eat or sell. As he makes his way through the flock, however, he notices a shepherd is guarding the sheep.

He sets his hopes aside and continues walking. Just before he leaves the flock, he looks toward the shepherd and notices two things have changed. First, the shepherd has walked up a hill. Second, the shepherd is now staring in the opposite direction.

Some quick mental calculations reveal an opportunity. If he took a sheep, the shepherd would not see him because his back is turned. If the shepherd did turn around, he would not be able to descend the hill in time to prevent the theft. And if the shepherd did run down the hill, he would choose not to chase the peasant because doing so would leave the remainder of his flock unguarded.

Recognizing the shepherd can do nothing to prevent him from stealing a sheep, the peasant casually picks one up and walks away.

Taking advantage of our opponents' inaction is in harmony with seeking the path of least effort. Similar to the stratagem *Loot a burning house*, which advises seizing each opportunity that trouble may offer, the stratagem *Seize the opportunity to lead the sheep away* demonstrates that companies can expand their power by punishing their competitors for each mistake they make.

Key Elements

Your adversary fails to act (e.g., because he is distracted).

You take advantage of this moment to advance.

By the time your adversary realizes his mistake, you have already taken the advantage.

"The good fighters of old, first put themselves beyond the possibility of defeat, and then waited for an opportunity of defeating the enemy. . . . To secure ourselves against defeat lies in our own hands, but the opportunity of defeating the enemy is provided by the enemy himself."

—Sun Tzu, The Art of War[36]

Apple Catches Sony in the Jaws of Conflicting Agendas

After Steve Jobs took back control of Apple, he set his sights on a new adversary: Sony. For two decades, Sony had dominated the world of portable music. With its Walkman line, Sony remained the leading producer of traditional portable music devices (i.e., cassette, CD, and radio players) and digital MP3 players. But in the early 2000s, Sony's long-held advantage disappeared when Apple's iPod became the world's leader just three years after its introduction.

Ironically, Sony fell victim to the same stratagem to which it owed its initial success. Fifty years prior, Sony had overtaken both RCA and GE in the radio market by seizing an opportunity that the incumbents had refused to embrace. In 2005, Sony found its role reversed as Apple took over the digital music market.

At first, the MP3 player market was relatively small. Even as recently as 2002, only 5 million portable devices had been sold since their introduction in 1998, according to the Consumer Electronics Association.[37] Two barriers were restraining growth of the digital music player market: the lack of available of music for download and the unmanageable size of players.

Music was difficult to find at that time because major record labels, fearing piracy, resisted making their music available in digital form. Instead, they invested heavily in a two-pronged attack on the growth of digital music. On one front, they launched legal campaigns against those encouraging its spread. They sued file-sharing sites and lobbied for stricter regulations. Simultaneously, they began preparing for the rising world of digital music by developing software and systems, digital rights management technology, that would protect their music ownership. Until this technology could be put in place, the music labels aimed to keep their music on CDs. They avoided making any of their property available for download.

The second limitation on the business was the size of the early MP3 players. Consumers essentially had two choices. Devices based on flash memory were physically small but came with limited memory; they could hold no more than ten songs. The other option was to buy a hard-drive based player, which could hold considerably more music but was heavy and bulky.

Facing these severe limitations, MP3 players failed to gain momentum.

The bonds began loosening in 2000, however, when illegal music-sharing sites were reaching unprecedented audiences. Napster, for example, claimed to reach 50 million users. The success of such sites forced record labels to begin rethinking their legal strategy. At industry strategy meetings, the conversation began to shift from stopping digital music distribution to seeking ways to profit from it. The industry realized that the future was in adapting to and serving the millions of consumers looking for a legitimate digital music option.

Additionally, hard-drive technology was improving. Hard drives were getting smaller and less expensive. In early 2000, Toshiba developed a hard drive capable of storing 1,000 songs that weighed less than 6 ounces.

These two developments, the explosion of digital music sharing and the shrinking of hard drives, created an opportunity for someone to finally introduce an MP3 player that would prove competitive with existing portable music devices, one with access to music (from record labels) and the ability to store many songs in a small package. Sony should have seized this emerging opportunity. In addition to owning the leading portable music brand (the Walkman), Sony had spent years developing its digital-rights technology and even owned a record label (Columbia).

Despite its strength, Sony chose to think instead of act. The company studied the idea of putting a hard drive in an MP3 player but, as Sony Senior Vice President Keiji Kimura explained, "We have many things to resolve."[38] These issues had little to do with the market or technology. Sony wrestled with internal barriers. The company's consumer electronics group wanted to free users to transfer music while its entertainment businesses wanted the opposite.

While Sony was considering how to untangle its conflicting agendas, Apple acted. In October 2001, the computer company launched the first iPod, a 6-ounce 5-GB device that could only be used on a Mac. In July 2002, Apple launched a version compatible with Windows PCs and subsequent versions offered ever-increasing capabilities. Hard drives grew to 30 GB, then 60 GB, capable of storing 15,000 songs and displaying color images. Apple followed with the Micro, the Nano, and even the Video iPod.

As Sony watched and struggled to unlock its conflicting agendas, Apple took over. By 2005, Apple was earning nearly $5 billion from its iPods, while its stock price had grown from $7 to $80 per share in three years. The iPod captured 75 percent of the portable digital music market share[39] and its iTunes music store captured 82 percent of its market.[40]

Sony Moves In as Others Pause

Ironically, Sony built its leadership in consumer electronics with precisely the move it fell to fifty years later.

In just seven years, Sony transformed itself from being a manufacturer of rice cookers for the Japanese market to the world leader in the production of consumer radios. It achieved this by seizing on a unique moment when its competitors could not or would not take advantage of a particular opportunity.

When Bell Laboratories invented the transistor in 1947, the two leading electrical and electronics leaders, RCA and GE, agreed with most industry observers that the transistor would one day replace the vacuum tube. But neither RCA nor GE wanted to adopt transistors quickly. Both companies were heavily invested in products designed for vacuum tubes and felt little competitive pressure. So they hesitated. They made plans to study and further develop transistor technology with the goal of replacing vacuum tubes sometime in the next twenty years.

Akio Morita, the CEO of Sony, recognized RCA's and GE's mistake and took advantage of the opening they provided. In the early 1950s, he bought a license to use the transistor from Bell Labs for just $25,000. He then challenged his engineers to design a transistor radio faster than the industry believed it could be done. In just two years, far fewer than the twenty RCA and GE had anticipated, Sony introduced a portable transistor radio. For one-third of the cost of a traditional radio, Sony offered consumers a product that was a fraction of a traditional radio's size and weight. Sony went on to dominate the world's consumer radio markets.

This tactic is what Peter Drucker calls "entrepreneurial judo." Small attackers can topple large incumbents because the incumbents are too heavily invested in the old way of doing things to embrace a new way.

Sony is not alone in benefiting from this tactic. Home Depot, for example, stole market share from unsuspecting home contractors by convincing consumers to "do it yourself." Contractors could not respond in part because they refused to see Home Depot as a competitor. Coca-Cola's now-famous strategy of attacking water consumers targeted competitors who never had cola on their competitive radar screens. Water companies never saw Coca-Cola as a threat.

Microsoft's seemingly well-calculated strategies tend to depend heavily on this stratagem, as Microsoft's chair Bill Gates admits: "*Most* of our success comes when we end up with a competitor who doesn't do things correctly—that's lucky. You're not supposed to work on a strategy that depends on other people's mistakes, but they've certainly made a lot."[41]

Redefining Clean

Method Home seems poised to corner its competition. Founded in 2001 by Eric Ryan and Adam Lowry, friends from Stanford University, Method is taking a new perspective on cleaning products. The company wants consumers to pull their detergent from under their sinks and put it on display. The two friends—one a chemist, the other an advertiser—developed a line of eco-friendly products contained in high-design packaging.

When they convinced Target Stores to carry their teardrop hand-soap, their company's revenues began ramping exponentially. By 2006 they tracked over 3,000 percent revenue growth and secured the seventh spot on the *Inc.* 500 list of the fastest-growing private companies.[42]

Why have consumer product incumbents Procter & Gamble or Colgate-Palmolive not responded? In part, with revenue of around $20 million in 2006, Method is perhaps too small to draw notice. But viewing Method's attack objectively reveals *Seize the opportunity to lead the sheep away* to be at work.

Traditional consumer product companies are organized by brand. The Mr. Clean brand manager, for example, holds full responsibility for the brand and operates it as an independent company. This brand-centric structure has worked well for over a century.

Method's approach is different. The company is building a lifestyle brand that stretches across multiple products. The Method brand is independent of function. It stands for design and being eco-friendly. The Mr. Clean brand—indeed, each major cleaning supply brand—stands for what it does.

To copy Method's approach, Procter & Gamble, owner of the Mr. Clean brand, would have to give someone oversight over Mr. Clean, Dawn (dishwashing liquid), and Febreze (fresheners). The cost of such a radical reorganization will outweigh the risk Method poses for many years. Until Method reaches a scale sufficient to challenge Procter & Gamble's core business, P&G will be better off letting Method grow. Not unlike RCA let Sony or Sony let Apple's iPod grow.

Seizing the Opportunity to Take an "Ally"

In 770 BC, the state of Song was under siege by an alliance of opposing states. The state of Chen led this alliance. In defense, Song implemented the stratagem of *Besiege Wei to rescue Zhao*. It attacked Chen's capital, forcing Chen's aggressors to call off their siege and leave to defend their homes. Through cunning application of this stratagem, Song freed itself from the threat.

On its return home, the Song army passed through a small state called Tai. Tai had refused to support Song's defense, so Song decided to take the Tai capital in revenge. The Song army surrounded Tai's stronghold and prepared for what promised to be almost certain victory over the weaker Tai state. As it turned out, however, neither state would be victorious.

Tai, facing certain defeat, sent an appeal to Chen for help. When a few days later the Chen army was seen approaching, the Song army called off its siege and hurried home. The Tai army rejoiced. The presence of Chen's powerful army had saved them. The Tai king opened his city gates to welcome the Chen duke and his army.

The Chen duke faced an unexpected opportunity. He stood with his army in front of the open city gates of a strategically important state (Tai was in proximity to Song). Knowing that an attack on Tai would provoke little or no resistance, he marched his soldiers into the welcoming walls of the Tai capital, kidnapped the Tai king, and took over the city.

Just as the traveler in the Chinese folktale took advantage of an inattentive shepherd, Sony took advantage of an inactive RCA,

Apple took advantage of a conflicted Sony, and Chen took advantage of an adversary that it knew could not defend itself. This is the essence of the stratagem. When your adversary is unlikely to react, seize the moment.

Summary

At some time, your adversary will fail to act, either for structural reasons (e.g., Sony's inability to seize the iPod opportunity) or distraction (e.g., since the United States has locked its attention on the Middle East, many experts warn, China is expanding its influence in Asia). By identifying such moments and doing what your adversary will not, you can overcome far stronger competitors with minimal effort.

FEIGN MADNESS BUT KEEP YOUR BALANCE

"At times, it is better to pretend to be foolish and do nothing than to brag about yourself and act recklessly. Be composed and plot secretly, like thunder clouds hiding themselves during winter only to bolt out when the time is right."

—*From* The Thirty-Six Stratagems

Concentrated force generates an opposing force. A key to achieving your objectives with minimal effort is to avoid triggering this opposing force. This stratagem points out that if your opponent views you as crazy, she will no longer feel threatened by your presence and so will drop her resistance. Jones Soda, for example, adopts practices too outrageous to draw competitive retort. Virgin cultivates an image of irrational irreverence that facilitates its entry into new markets.

Key Elements

Your adversary is powerful and/or you are weak.

You appear mad or incapable in order to avoid being perceived as a threat.

When your adversary puts down her guard, you take her.

"Never let them know what you're thinking."

—The Godfather, *Mario Puzo*

How Do You Respond to Turkey and Gravy Soda?

Getting into the soft drink business seems a crazy idea. A swarm of small competitors battle each other in the shadow of two entrenched giants for a market that is stagnating. Any reasonable industry analyst would steer you away from launching a new soda business. But Peter van Stolk was never educated in business and did not know how to analyze an industry. Nor is he a reasonable man.

Ironically, these two traits—making uneducated decisions and acting without reason—actually provided him with an effective competitive shield. By appearing "crazy," he convinced his competitors to ignore him while he established his power base.

Van Stolk made a seemingly illogical decision. Previously, he had founded and grown a $6 million corporation in Western Canada that distributed beverages, including Just Pik't Juices, Arizona Iced Tea, and Thomas Kemper sodas. In 2000, he suddenly decided to sell this successful distribution business and form a company that would produce and market its own brand of soda.[43] By doing so, he was trading a stable enterprise for the quixotic challenge of taking on Coca-Cola and PepsiCo.

Van Stolk's new soda company immediately faced resistance. Distributors showed little interest in carrying his products as many were under pressure from large beverage companies to shun small manufacturers. Even the few distributors who did decide to carry van Stolk's soda had little reason to be proactive in selling the products.

To circumvent this resistance, van Stolk conducted a series of seemingly "crazy" strategic decisions that disengaged his company from the competition. Instead of fighting for shelf space, for example, van Stolk created his own "shelves," coolers emblazoned with his company's brand. Instead of fighting for traditional retailers, he targeted locations that did not normally sell sodas: surfing, skating, and snowboarding shops; tattoo and piercing parlors; unique clothing retailers; and music stores.

To complement these unorthodox distribution choices, Jones Soda made equally "crazy" product decisions. The company dared to produce flavors that few competitors, and surely not conservative Coca-Cola, would dare copy. It started to offer sodas called Blue Bubble Gum, Green Apple, Bada Bing! (cherry and loganberry juices), and D'Peach Mode. For Halloween, it rolls out its Candy Corn–flavored soda, and over Thanksgiving it offers Turkey and Gravy–flavored soda!

Jones Soda wraps these unorthodox drinks in equally unusual packaging. Fans began sending Jones Soda photographs of their babies and pets, asking that they consider using the images for labels. This gave the company another "crazy" idea. It would print consumer-submitted photographs on all of its soda labels. This started a trend, and today customers vie to get their photos on the label. For example, someone can submit a picture of her cat on jonessoda.com, and it will be included in a consumer-judged photo contest. If selected, she may find her cat's image on Jones Soda labels at her local store and around the country.

If you want to avoid the contest and ensure your picture makes it onto a bottle, you can even order customized soda on myjones. com. If you want a case of Turkey and Gravy soda with your family photo on it to serve over Thanksgiving, you can get it for $50. The company protected this "customization" service and now holds the patent on customizing branded merchandising over a computer network. This process has created an intense sense of brand loyalty. As van Stolk explains, "People get fired up about Jones because it's theirs. It's not my soda. When you buy a bottle of Jones Soda there is a person's name on the bottle who took the photo."[44]

Van Stolk empowers his "crazy" distribution and product decisions with equally unusual marketing ones. On one April Fool's Day, for example, Jones Soda issued a false press release announcing they were being acquired by John Deere, the tractor company. The release claimed John Deere wanted a weed-flavored soda. This antic stirred up Jones Soda drinkers and drew a lot of attention. Some were amused, others confused, but most at least heard about it.

Van Stolk's latest idea is create a Board of Directors composed exclusively of children. His chair would be a teenager. While van Stolk admits some regard the idea as "crazy," he thinks allowing seventy-year-old chairpersons to make marketing decisions, as most large companies do, is much crazier.

Jones Soda's unorthodox strategies indeed attract consumers, but more important, they help deflect the competition. Faced with Jones Soda's unusual tactics, most competitors discount the company as a threat too odd and indirect to warrant a response. Yet, countless companies have grown strong under the protective barrier of a "crazy" reputation. Think how Richard Branson and Rupert Murdoch continually build competitive companies under the guise of madness.

The Jones Soda story is short and the company's longevity yet to be proven, but its growth is impressive. Now a publicly traded company, it is growing at 30 percent per year while its stock price has soared 250 percent over the past two years.[45]

If the company continues to use its "crazy" reputation to deflect any serious competitive response, it should continue to grow. As van Stolk points out, "There's so much room to grow—Coke and Pepsi are so big—we've got a long way to go before anyone notices."[46]

Virgin's Crazy Telephone Call to Boeing

In 1984, when the Virgin Group announced plans to enter the airline business, most people wrote off the idea. Many airlines had tried to compete with British Airways, but none had had the financing to persevere against the powerful national airline.

Most companies would fight such pessimism with arguments grounded in rational analysis and strategic logic. However, Richard Branson, the head of Virgin, appeared to do exactly the opposite. He cultivated a seemingly amateurish story about how he came up with his idea to compete in the airline business: An acquaintance happened to give him a proposal for a new airline. Branson called

People's Express (British Airway's competition) over the weekend and was encouraged to find they never answered the phone. This pointed to an opportunity. On Monday, he cold-called Boeing to inquire about leasing a used plane. With that he "had done all the market research [he] felt [he] needed and had made up [his] mind."[47]

Virgin further bolstered an offbeat image with a series of outlandish publicity events. For example, for Virgin Atlantic's maiden transatlantic flight, Branson dressed up as a pirate and filled the plane with champagne and music stars.

These tactics benefited Virgin in more ways than one. They helped build awareness and endearment among the flying public. But the tactics also helped keep British Airways off-guard. It was unclear, for example, how seriously the national airline should take Virgin. Would Virgin's "crazy" image, which contrasted starkly with British Airway's buttoned-up reputation, make Virgin more or less threatening than other start-ups? British Airways ultimately took Virgin's threat seriously and fought back, using all the strength it had. It is difficult to know for sure, but many believe that Virgin's unorthodox approach created a gap or softening in British Airway's response, within which Virgin built momentum. As the *Economist* stated in an article outlining the folly of Virgin's entry into the rail business, "To be fair, back in 1984 Mr Branson's entry into the airline business also seemed both a crazy gamble and a threat to his brand."[48]

Madness Creates Opportunity

In AD 249, General Cao Shuang, who had invested ten years securing near-complete control over his state, lost his power in just four days when he turned his back on a seemingly weak adversary.

Cao Shuang and his adversary, Sima Yi, were officials of the Wei Empire. When the emperor died and enthroned his young son to replace him, both Cao Shuang and Sima Yi were charged with looking after the young prince until he reached sufficient age to rule.

Although they initially enjoyed equal power, Cao Shuang ultimately took power from Sima Yi by demanding complete control
over the military. Marginalized, Sima Yi feared that Cao Shuang
would soon kill him. So he acted crazy. When one of Cao Shuang's
henchmen came to visit Sima Yi, he acted sick and senile. He
spilled soup on his collar to appear weak. He pretended to misun-
derstand their conversation, to appear senile.

Cao Shuang concluded that Sima Yi posed no threat. He let
Sima Yi live and eventually slip from his mind. No longer under
heavy scrutiny, Sima Yi waited patiently for an opening. His
opportunity came when Cao Shuang left the capital with the young
emperor to visit the imperial tombs. Sima Yi quickly gathered his
sons and followers and staged a coup. Four days later, Sima Yi took
control of Wei and had Cao Shuang executed.

By feigning madness, you can bide your time in relative ano-
nymity and wait for the right moment to act.

> *"Make use of folly. Even the wisest person sometimes puts this piece
> into play, and there are occasions when the greatest knowledge lies
> in appearing to have none."*
>
> —*Baltasar Gracian,* The Art of Worldly Wisdom[49]

Summary

To pre-empt opposition, avoid appearing to be a threat. When you
appear crazy instead of calculating, your adversary will discount
your efforts and give you room to succeed.

PART III

WU CHANG:
CONTINUOUS CHANGE

Your mental model for what "change" should be and how it affects you has a powerful impact on your actions. It invisibly guides your thinking, telling you what type of "change" your action will cause, whether or not and even when you can take such action. While your mental model may help you decide which actions to take, it also limits your options and freedom by telling you which action you should not take. Many people find it difficult to see their mental models at work because they have been around nearly their entire lives and are so familiar. They have been so submerged in their mental model of change that they can no longer see them—just as a fish can no longer see the ocean. This is not to say that a familiar model for change is inaccurate or wrong. But by clinging to it consistently, the person grows rigid and predictable.

By dissecting your mental models for change and adopting alternative ones, you can become more competitive. Companies that regularly outmaneuver their adversaries have a reputation for thinking "outside the box," acting in ways that are inconsistent with the dictates of past predictable models. By adopting alternative concepts of change, you too can become an outside-the-box thinker, a more competitive adversary, and more skilled at capturing power. Your first step to freeing yourself from your old model for change—and to becoming a more creative strategist—is to dissect your familiar model, which rests on two key assumptions:

1. That the past determines the present (or cause and effect drive change)
2. That change connects static moments

The Western View

The West's first key assumption about change is that the past determines the present. Change is rooted in cause and effect: A cause in the past effects a change in the present. A Westerner envisions the universe as a game of pool where a linear chain of interactions—one ball knocks against another, propelling it into yet another—explains why any particular ball rests where it does. In other words, he can work backward to understand how a particular ball came to rest where it is and forward to predict what balls he must set in motion to cause a desired result (e.g., eight ball in the side pocket).

Change Connects Static Moments

The second key assumption is that change connects static moments. This means that a Westerner divides his life into two distinct states: rest and motion, static and kinetic, or no change and change. *Change* is what happens *between* states of rest. In fact, *Webster's New Universal Unabridged Dictionary* defines *change* as "the passing from one place, state, form, or phase to another."

A Westerner doesn't question this definition, because it seems to work for him and it helps him manage his life. The underlying belief is that it is easier to play games when the balls are at rest than in motion. In the West, life is like a game of pool, ruled by linear sequences of cause and effect, composed of distinct states of change and static moments. This model is not wrong or more limiting than other models. It's only limiting if it is the only model you choose. You would be better off looking at your problems through different lenses.

The Eastern View

The Eastern view, primarily the Taoist perspective of change, offers an intriguing alternative. Instead of viewing life as composed of static and fluid moments, a Taoist views all moments as change, where the balls never come to rest. This means that instead of looking to the past to understand the present, a Taoist just looks to the present.

A Taoist takes an entirely different approach to understanding the present, believing that she should look at the present—at what is occurring—rather than at the past. This does not mean that a Taoist does not learn from the past; rather, the lessons from the past do not hold predictive value. They may help her recognize patterns (when A happens, B also happens) that in turn help her understand the present and future (A is happening, so B must also be happening). These patterns are evident in all aspects of life, from the flow of a stream around a rock, to the migration of animals through the mountains, to the rise of a new religion around a rigid government. A Westerner might be tempted to explain such a pattern through causal relationships. A Taoist, on the other hand, places little value on this exercise. Explaining patterns through causal relationships does not necessarily reflect the way the universe works, nor does it improve attempts to influence or predict the environment. Instead, learn to recognize life's patterns and look for them in the current moment.

The Eastern point of view is linked to an interesting understanding of the mechanics of change. Westerners view time as a linear sequence of static moments separated by change; the Taoist understanding, however, is cyclical and continuous. Time is a wave in continuous motion (*Wu Chang* translates roughly as "Nothing is constant"). Points on this wave are always either rising or falling. When the traditional Western view says you are at the top of this wave, the Taoist view says you are already falling. When the Western view says you are at the bottom, the Taoist view says you are rising. The following Chinese folk story illustrates this view well:

The horse of a poor farmer ran away. His neighbors visited to offer their condolences, but the farmer said, "Do not feel bad, this may be good fortune." After several weeks, the horse returned to the farmer with another horse of excellent breeding. The farmer's neighbors again visited, this time to congratulate him. But the farmer said, "How do you know this will not lead to disaster?" The farmer bred the horses and became rich. His son liked to ride the horses but one day fell from a horse and broke his leg. When the neighbors came to console him, the father again said, "Do not feel bad, this may be good fortune." A year later barbarians raided the farmer's town and conscripted all young men who could fight. Ninety percent of the young conscripts died in the war, but the farmer's son was left alone because of his bad leg. He lived on.[50]

Most people cling to static moments. Victories and failures mark the completion of discrete periods of change, the end of one moment and the beginning of another. But for those who embrace change as continuous—unbound by wins, losses, new years, and birthdays—a new definition of "winning" emerges and new options appear. A "game" becomes an endless stream of conflicts rather than a closed-ended event. Winning comes to mean defeating an opponent as often as possible over this endless stream of conflict, not just once.

In the Taoist view, no loss is permanent, nor is any win. So exchanging a loss today for future wins becomes more palatable. Indeed, losing is simply an entry to future wins. This is the reason companies that out-think their competitors often appear to take losing positions only to re-emerge as the winner later on. As this chapter shows, many highly successful companies including QUALCOMM, Whole Foods, and Wal-Mart make decisions that initially lead to loss but that position them for future victory. These companies play the next game while their competitors and the pundits focus on the current game. Fifty of the 100 most competitive companies of the decade can trace their rise at least in part to one of the stratagems in this section.

The Taoist view encourages corporations to take longer perspectives. Predicting the future in a linear world driven by causality is difficult, since accuracy drops off quickly with each cause-and-effect calculation. On the other hand, making long-term predictions in a cyclical world where patterns repeat and moments return is reasonable. Nothing changes permanently, so while some of the details may be wrong, the overruling pattern can be predicted quite well.

This was clearly the case with Matsushita. In the early 1930s, Konosuke Matsushita, the founder of the Japanese electrical giant Panasonic, developed ten consecutive twenty-five-year plans that comprised a 250-year corporate strategy. For Western companies using a linear causal model to predict the future, such an exercise would be inaccurate to the point of uselessness. For them, a ten-year planning period is already aggressive.

Understanding Change

	Western	Taoist
Present events are determined by	Past events	Other present events
Time is	Linear	Cyclical
Change occurs	Between events	Continuously
A reasonable planning time frame is	Up to 10 years	Up to 100+ years
Objective	Win this war	Win as many wars as possible

In summary, adapting a Taoist perspective, whereby change is continuous and unending, may feel unnatural. However, the process can enable you to outwit your competition—not because this perspective is absolutely right but because it is different and creative. Companies that adopt this perspective are more comfortable peering into the future. They often give the impression of making losing decisions in the short term that turn out to be winning decisions over the long term. As a result, these companies are able to think one step ahead of their competition. They are already preparing for the next game that will begin when their competition finally catches up to them.

WATCH THE FIRE ON THE OTHER SHORE

"When a serious conflict breaks out within the enemy alliance, wait quietly for the chaos to build. Because once its internal conflict intensifies, the alliance will bring destruction upon itself. As for you, observe closely and make preparations for any advantage that may come from it."

—*From* The Thirty-Six Stratagems

A linear view of change creates pressure to take action. This Western view warns that if you pass up the opportunity to act, your ship will sail. A cyclical view, however, argues that the wind will shift, the rudder will turn, and the ship will return even if this means that the ship circumnavigates the globe before doing so.

Companies that are driven to expand their power and yet are willing to be patient will be more competitive in the long run. The Thirty-Six Stratagems calls this tactic of inaction *Watch the fire on the other shore.*

Key Elements

Your adversary is engaged in internal conflict or in conflict with other allies.

Your attack might unify your adversary (and her allies).

You refrain from acting.

> Allowed to continue, the internal conflict damages your adversary.
> After your adversary is adequately weakened, you attack.

Inaction can be more powerful than action. If aggression drives you to act when you should not, you lose not only power—you also lose opportunity.

The Cost of Action

Stories of companies that acted when they should have held back litter business history. By not considering the reaction an attack might invite, you risk unsettling a salutary balance between you and your competition.

In the mid-1990s the Swiss national postal service (the Swiss Post) found itself in a trying competitive situation. Overall demand had been shrinking as the Swiss turned increasingly to electronic instead of traditional mail. Swiss Post's monopoly on this shrinking market was also slipping to international carriers including DHL and FedEx. Many of the historical legislative advantages the institution enjoyed were being challenged. Swiss Post had grown up under protection. With an office covering every Swiss town, sorting facilities, and a fleet of trucks and planes, the Swiss Post had built unparalleled scale. Now liberalization and globalization were eating into its monopoly. Revenues declined, but the costs of maintaining its real estate and equipment held firm. Swiss Post's size was transforming from an advantage to a liability.

To survive, the postal service needed to change. In 2002 the board reconstituted itself. Several long-serving members and executives left so that a new line of leadership could take over. This new leadership began testing the demand for new businesses including electronic mail and special post boxes serving remote areas.

Swiss Post, adopting the practices of for-profit firms, was following demand. But because it failed to contemplate the competition, this reinvented public service took a costly misstep.

Market research and tests encouraged Swiss Post in 1994 to begin selling paper, pens, and other office products in its stores. The decision seems logical: Customers would easily associate the

Swiss Post brand with office supplies, and Swiss Post's locations enjoyed heavy foot traffic. In that year, Swiss Post enjoyed a significant spike in revenue and credited much of this uplift to its new office-supply business.

But Swiss Post was not convincing people to buy more office supplies. It was convincing them to shift their purchases away from office-supply stores, and these stores, to protect profits, had to respond.

Their response was to match Swiss Post's offer. If customers were now able to mail a letter and stock up on supplies at a post office, office-supply retailers would have to allow the same service. These retailers began offering shipping services through private letter carriers (e.g., DHL) in their stores.

By entering the office-supply business, Swiss Post drew a new class of competitor into the battle. It had to contend not only with private carriers providing service to customers in their offices; additionally, it had to fight the neighborhood office-supply store, which was tempting consumers with a convenient postal service.

The Benefits of Inaction

Inaction can be a powerful and aggressive choice. Puma, for example, made a critical strategic decision in the mid-1990s to stop competing with its traditional opposition, Nike and Reebok. Facing a financial crisis, Puma realized it was incapable of succeeding as an athletic shoe company. So it chose to leave this battle to others.

Instead, Puma reconceived itself as a fashion and lifestyle brand. It began producing sneakers that placed aesthetics over performance. It hired well-known designers to create exclusive Puma shoes. It expanded its apparel business and diversified its product offerings, even producing a Puma bicycle.[51]

The results have been astounding. Fashionable Puma has been outpacing its athletic-oriented rivals, averaging 20 percent annual revenue growth over the past ten years, compared to 10 percent for Nike and just 1 percent for Reebok.

Intel is similarly careful about which battles it chooses. It intentionally holds back from many opportunities in order to avoid competing with customers. It will not, for example, introduce products such as mobile phones or PDAs (personal digital assistants) that depend on Intel chips but would compete with existing Intel customers.

Forgoing such tempting opportunities is difficult. A near-term cost-benefit analysis might prove that such a move would create value; for example, a new Intel-manufactured PDA might generate more profits than Intel would give up in lost customers. But the longer-term lens shows that Intel's policy is highly profitable. Intel remains a trusted supplier of choice for most large electronics companies. Intel may "lose" current battles, such as the PDA battle, but the long-term payoff of steady customer relationships is well worth it.

> *"The most yielding parts of the world*
> *Overtake the most rigid parts of the world*
> *The insubstantial can penetrate continually.*
> *Therefore I know that without action there is advantage.*
> *This philosophy without words,*
> *This advantage without action,*
> *It is rare, in the world, to attain them."*
>
> —*Lao Tzu,* Tao Te Ching[52]

Cao Cao Lets a Family Destroy Itself

In AD 200, there was a turning point in the war between Cao Cao and a rival warlord, Yuang Shao. In that year, Cao Cao inflicted a number of victories over Yuang Shao and built momentum that demoralized his opponent. In 202, the shame of constant defeat led Yuang Shao to sickness and then death. He had three sons, all of whom desired to succeed him.

In a break with tradition, the eldest son was passed over, and power was given to the middle son. The youngest son supported this decision. Naturally, the eldest did not. So the Yuang brothers began to fight for control.

Cao Cao saw the brothers' internal conflict as an opportunity, and he attacked. But his threat convinced the Yuang brothers to set aside their quarrels and unite in defense. Cao Cao pulled back from his offensive in order to give the Yuang brothers' conflict more time to gestate. The brothers quickly picked up their differences, which again escalated into battles.

Over the next three years, Cao Cao capitalized on the Yuang brothers' disunity. He picked off four of their provinces and convinced many of their subjects, including their generals, to defect. But he held off launching a full direct assault.

By 205, Cao Cao's soldiers attacked and killed the eldest brother. By this time Cao Cao had taken control of a great portion of the Yuang family's territory. The two remaining brothers were forced to flee their kingdom. They found shelter with a nomadic tribe called the Wuhuan. Cao Cao's application of the stratagem *Watch the fire on the other shore* was successful because he had captured all of the Yuang family's territory at minimal cost.

He might have ended his conquest there, but he felt the remaining Yuang brothers still posed a threat. Strains of Yuang loyalty were still woven throughout the populace. If the brothers returned, Cao Cao might face a revolution.

Two years later, in 207, Cao Cao attacked the Wuhuan tribe that was sheltering the brothers. After a long march, Cao Cao's troops crushed the Wuhuan and killed the clan's leader. The Yuang brothers, however, managed to escape. They sought shelter from the leader of a more distant nomadic tribe, Gongsun Kang.

Cao Cao's advisors urged him to continue his pursuit. But Cao Cao declined. He explained that he would simply request Gongsun Kang to deliver the Yuang brothers' heads. His request was soon answered with the arrival of two boxes. Each contained the head of a Yuang brother.

Cao Cao's advisors eagerly questioned how he knew that Gongsun Kang would grant his request. Cao Cao said, "Gongsun Kang has always been wary of the Yuang tribe. He was afraid [the brothers] might usurp his position. . . . If we had pressed them with violent attacks, they would have joined together in defense. But our retreat prompted them to plot against one another."

The first application of *Watch the fire on the other shore* delivered Cao Cao's victory over the Yuang brothers' territory. The second application made this victory permanent.

Summary

Whether in business or war, inaction is a powerful choice. Set aside your focus on winning today's war to appreciate the value of inaction today, which can deliver victory tomorrow.

LET THE PLUM TREE WITHER IN PLACE OF THE PEACH

"When loss is inevitable, sacrifice the part for the benefit of the whole."
—*From* The Thirty-Six Stratagems

As a matter of convenience and habit, companies often concentrate on one war at a time. Yet their goals are likely to reach beyond one war. The next war may be more important than the current one. By losing today to win tomorrow, a company can seize advantages that others overlook.

Companies that give up the tendency to focus on one war at a time may lose one war to win another. Their actions often appear counterintuitive until the next war begins, at which time their actions prove brilliant. This tactic of self-sacrifice adopted is Stratagem Twenty: *Let the plum tree wither in place of the peach.*

Key Elements

You cannot win across all wars and fronts.

You allow your adversary victory on one war or front.

You thereby strengthen your ability to win another war or on another front.

You defeat your adversary.

Sacrifice as a Path to Power

In 1999, one of the world's leading producers of mobile phones announced it was abandoning the business. In exiting, the company admitted falling victim to stronger competition. But what had at first appeared a withdrawal was actually an attack, allowing the former hardware producer to evolve into a technological force.

Fifteen years earlier, seven mobile technology veterans had met in Dr. Irwin Jacobs' den, aiming to revolutionize their industry through a new company called "QUALity COMMunications" (now QUALCOMM). Although they "had no particular product in mind,"[53] as Dr. Jacobs explained, they wanted to apply World War II radio technology to modern mobile phones.

Digital mobile phone use was expanding, and the industry wanted to set a standard for managing the information flow between phones and networks. The Telecommunications Industry Association (TIA) had endorsed a digital technology called Time Division Multiple Access (TDMA). However, QUALCOMM, believing its Code Division Multiple Access (CDMA) technology to be superior, ignored the emerging consensus and introduced its product. For the next six years, QUALCOMM fought to convince the industry to adopt CDMA technology.

Reversing the momentum behind TDMA and the European alternative GSM, looked improbable. It was a classic Catch-22. Nokia, Motorola, Ericsson, and other mobile phone producers were not interested in building CDMA phones because AT&T Wireless and other service providers were not using the technology. At the same time, service providers resisted adaptation because mobile phone producers were not making CDMA compatible phones. To unlock this dilemma and jumpstart CDMA adoption, QUALCOMM decided to produce its own mobile phones and related infrastructure. Only by offering a completely packaged solution could QUALCOMM convince industry players to take a risk on CDMA.

QUALCOMM's strategy worked. Its hardware and infrastructure business exploded, and the company became a well-known mobile phone consumer brand.

To accelerate its rise, the company began placing significant strategic investments in developing markets. In 1997, it entered Chile, purchasing a 50 percent interest in Chilesat PCS for $42 million. In 1998, it committed $110 million to Pegaso Telecommunications in Mexico and OxPhone Pty. Ltd. in Australia along with Metrosvyaz Limited and Orrengrove Investments Limited in Russia.

By 1998, QUALCOMM was a major player in three distinct mobile communications areas: manufacturing, operating, and technology development. Although this strategy was delivering impressive growth, cracks were beginning to show.

Conflicts of interest emerged to damage QUALCOMM's core business. The company had invested in mobile phone operators to encourage them to adopt CDMA. But the company had not anticipated that this strategy would discourage competing operators—who hesitated to bet on technology owned by their competitors' new investors—from adopting CDMA. Similarly, those manufacturers producing CDMA phones were hesitant to continue imbedding the internal technology because of direct competition from QUALCOMM. As a result, QUALCOMM's hardware and operating businesses were causing its technology businesses to suffer.

Managing these different businesses was also becoming a challenge. In the technology industry, it is common to immediately hire an army of engineers when you get funding (e.g. from a government grant) and then disband them when the project ends. Such rapid labor fluctuations, however, do not work in large-scale manufacturing.

It was becoming increasingly clear that QUALCOMM could not remain competitive. It was struggling to compete with Motorola, Ericsson, and Nokia, who, with over 50 percent of the market, commanded far stronger purchasing power. Though CDMA usage was booming, it paled in comparison to its alternatives (TDMA and GSM).

QUALCOMM's multifront war proved more than the company could handle. Analysts and investors began exerting considerable pressure on QUALCOMM to change course. QUALCOMM reacted quickly, deciding, in 1998, it would immediately begin exiting the hardware business.

On September 24 of that year, QUALCOMM's exit from the hardware business began when the company spun its investments in mobile phone operators off into an independent public company called Leap Wireless International. Six months later, it sold its infrastructure business to Ericsson as part of a legal settlement between the two companies. QUALCOMM transferred 1,200 employees and took in a $240 million charge as part of the deal. Its stock leaped 50 percent in the following week.

QUALCOMM committed to a complete exit from the hardware business in December 1999 when it announced it would sell its entire mobile phone business to Japan's Kyocera. A decade pushing CDMA hardware came to an end. QUALCOMM was no longer a hardware manufacturer.

QUALCOMM's story is not one of failure because, by leaving a game it could not win, it was free to focus its resources on one it could dominate. "We'll do the innovative part and let others do the manufacturing," Dr. Jacobs explained.[54]

The results have been extraordinary. In the four years after QUALCOMM abandoned its hardware business, its patent filings more than doubled (from 700 in 1999 to 1,700 in 2003) and its patents issued nearly tripled (from 325 in 1999 to 1,000 in 2003).[55] While its revenue remained flat, remarkable after shedding so much of its business, its profitability grew 135 percent (from $390 million to $920 million).

By disengaging from the competition, QUALCOMM became distinctive.

The General Sacrifices His Worst Horses

During the Warring States period, the royals and generals regularly entertained themselves by gambling on races among their private stocks of horses. The stakes on these races were high.

One day a well-known military advisor and descendant of Sun Tzu named Sun Bin noticed that General Tian Ji was preoccupied. When Sun Bin inquired, the general explained that his horses, which regularly lost, had cost him significant sums of money. Sun Bin offered to accompany the general to the next match to see if he could devise a strategy whereby the general would win. The general gratefully accepted.

At the race match, Sun Bin learned that the races consisted of three heats. The best horses of the contestants competed in the first heat; their second-best horses, in the second; and their worst horses, in the third. He also noticed that the general's horses were in each instance slightly slower than the competition. This was enough information for Sun Bin to devise a strategy that would ensure victory for General Tian Ji.

After the races, Sun Bin told General Tian Ji that he had a plan. He suggested that the general call another race and be prepared to bet heavily on it. The general had great confidence in Sun Bin, so he planned a high-profile competition. He invited the prince to compete and thousands of peasants and royal subjects to attend. He put much at risk both financially and in terms of his reputation.

In the first heat, Sun Bin advised the general to race his worst horses against the prince's best. The prince easily defeated the general. The crowd cheered; the prince smiled confidently, but Sun Bin remained calm.

In the second heat, Sun Bin advised the general to race his best horses against the prince's second-best horses. The general's best horses, although no match for the prince's best horses, easily defeated the prince's second-best horses. The score was tied one to one.

In the final, deciding race, the general ran his second-best horses against the prince's worst horses and won. By sacrificing his worst horses, General Tian Ji won the tournament and recouped a large share of his losses.

> *"The strategy of guerrilla warfare is manifestly unlike that employed in orthodox operations, as the basic tactic of the former is constant activity and movement. There is in guerrilla warfare no such thing as a decisive battle."*
>
> —Mao Tse-tung, On Guerilla Warfare[56]

Summary

This tactic of sacrifice, of losing today to win tomorrow, has served some of history's most powerful generals and today's most powerful companies. Whether dealing with horse races, wars, or business conflicts, broadening your objectives beyond the current war frees you to seize opportunities that your adversaries cannot see. Tian Ji's willingness to give up a near-term win and QUALCOMM's willingness to give up on hardware profits allowed each to adopt a distinctive strategy and step away from the pack.

THE STRATAGEM OF THE OPEN CITY GATES

"In spite of the inferiority of your force, deliberately make your defensive line defenseless in order to confuse the enemy. In situations when the enemies are many and you are few, this tactic seems all the more intriguing."

—From The Thirty-Six Stratagems

Your competitors study you carefully, trying to assess the threat and anticipate your moves. In response, you go to great lengths to keep information hidden. Indeed, commitment to protecting internal information is so pervasive that an entire industry—competitive intelligence—has flourished around it.

Yet one of the most successful business moves begins with revealing, rather than hiding, information. A carefully staged peek into your strategies, intentions, or capabilities can influence your competitors' actions and deliver an advantage to you.

Key Elements

Your adversary is attacking or preparing to attack.

You reveal your strength or weakness.

Your adversary calls off his attack, because he fears your strength or no longer considers you a threat.

When Strong

A company regarded as a tough competitor can scare away opposition simply by making noise during its approach. Microsoft's worldwide reputation as aggressive, persistent, and usually successful is the weapon the company wields to clear away potential opponents. When Microsoft announces its intention to introduce a new product or enter a new market, would-be competitors recalculate their projections. Investors readjust their risk assessments. Customers rethink their purchases and consider waiting for the Microsoft product. In other words, when Microsoft announces it is entering a new segment, the market makes room. If Microsoft hid its intentions, it would have to spend more to win over customers and investors.

Microsoft implements this tactic intentionally and proactively. It does not depend on the market to link past successes to future success. It makes this linkage explicit.

In revealing Microsoft's "digital home" strategy, which envisions home appliances (e.g., refrigerators, televisions, and systems, such as alarms, and lighting) networked through Microsoft products, Bill Gates said, "The way you get to our vision [of the digital home] is by building individual products that are the best in their own categories. It's like Microsoft Office. We built that with Word being the best, Excel being the best. They all had to be the best before the whole integration thing came together."[57] In other words: Competitors, beware.

Microsoft is not the only company to rely on this stratagem. International Game Technology (IGT) is the largest designer and producer of slot machines and video-gaming machines in the world. The company sells two out of every three slot or video machines bought in the world.

In the mid-1980s, IGT was not the dominant player. It was one of six leading producers in its market. To separate itself from the competition, IGT made a strategic decision to invest more heavily than its peers in research and development. Over the subsequent twenty years, these R&D investments began paying off in two ways. First, IGT's technological advances created new betting experiences, which captured new business. For example, the company linked one of its new computerized slot machines to a proprietary network that allowed gamblers in different states to play for the same progressive jackpot. This multistate slot machine was a breakthrough that began separating IGT machines from the pack.

But IGT's commitment to outspend its peers on R&D had a secondary, possibly more powerful, effect. By revealing, even boasting, about the level of its R&D spending, IGT deflated competitive resistance. The company signaled competitors to give up competing with IGT using R&D spending and, possibly, convinced investors to prefer IGT stock because the company was technologically aggressive.

From the mid-1990s, IGT launched a stream of new gaming technologies and expanded into new geographic markets. Over the past decade it has averaged 13 percent annual revenue growth (twice the industry average) and produced a 30 percent profit margin (also twice the industry average).

IGT's success offers the lesson that by committing to a bold strategy and openly sharing it, you may convince the competition to step aside.

Using Weakness to Communicate Strength

During the Three Kingdoms period (220–265 CE), while the kingdoms of Shu and Wei were at war, the prime minister of Shu found himself in an apparently helpless predicament. Taking a break from fighting, he retired to his base city. He sent most of his troops off to battle and ordered half of the remaining troops to leave the city to help move supplies in another town. This left him with just 2,500 troops.

The news of an approaching Wei army, 150,000 soldiers strong, came too late for the prime minister to call back his men. He would have to work with what he had.

His two obvious choices were to flee or to fight, each of which meant death for him and his subjects. The Wei army outnumbered his by sixty to one. If he fought, he would lose. If he fled, the Wei would hunt him down and kill him. The situation's helplessness made his subjects faint, but the prime minister remained calm. He had a stratagem in mind.

As great clouds of dust signaled the approach of the Wei army, the prime minister ordered his soldiers to occupy their posts as usual, threatening to behead anyone who attempted escape. He then opened the city gates and placed twenty soldiers at each gate.

Dressed as civilians, the soldiers pretended to sweep the streets. Finally, the prime minister ascended an observation post, carrying incense and a zither. He lit the incense and calmly played the zither.

Wei scouts were shocked at the strange signs of calm in Shu's city. When they reported that the city gates were open, civilians were sweeping the streets, and guards were at their usual posts, the Wei general was incredulous. He mounted a horse to inspect the scene himself. He too found the same signs of calm. Then, when he heard the prime minister playing serene songs on a zither without a hint of fear in his voice despite the presence of 150,000 troops at his doorstep, the general concluded that the prime minister had set a trap. He explained to his advisors that the prime minister was known for being conservative and careful, and he would not take such a bold position without a powerful stratagem in hand. Wei turned his troops around and left.

Thus Shu's prime minister saved his life and his city. He forced 150,000 enemy troops to retreat with only 2,500 soldiers, open city gates, and a zither.

"Things pass for what they seem, not for what they are. Only rarely do people look into them, and many are satisfied with appearances."

—Baltasar Gracian, The Art of Worldly Wisdom[58]

Summary

Like Microsoft and International Gaming Technologies, Shu simply allowed his adversary a peek behind his city walls. By carefully revealing your strength, strategy, or (in the case of Shu) your level of concern, you can shape your adversary's assessment of his situation. This determines his actions and in turn influences your chances of success.

AWAIT THE EXHAUSTED ENEMY AT YOUR EASE

"To weaken the enemy, it is not necessary to attack him directly. Tire him by carrying out an active defense, and in so doing his strength will be reduced, and your side will gain the upper hand."

—*From* The Thirty-Six Stratagems

Competition is expected to be contained within defined boundaries. For the most part, these boundaries hold: Television networks battle for consumers within the boundaries of the living room, and cereal manufacturers battle within the walls of grocery stores.

Occasionally, however, these battles break out of their borders. Such "new game" events shift power, humbling long-dominant incumbents and crowning young challengers. Indeed, this is one of the tactics most often cited among the decade's most competitive companies. Fifteen of the 100 most competitive companies on my list assign their emergence at least in part to having moved ahead of such "new game" shifts.

Surviving such shifts is difficult because competitiveness on today's battlefield will not guarantee competitiveness tomorrow. Predicting these shifts is also difficult because they happen so rarely.

Clever companies and armies have toppled more powerful adversaries by predicting the battleground to which their conflict would shift, setting up a position there, and waiting for their adversary to approach.

Key Elements

You predict that the battleground will shift.

You set up a defendable position on the new battleground.

You wait for your adversary.

When your adversary arrives, you use your superior position to defeat him.

Because confrontation is viewed as temporary or close-ended, it is expected to remain within defined boundaries. In fact, the first step in assessing a competitive situation is to define the market, which is to define the boundaries within which you plan to battle your competitors.

Often these boundaries have not changed measurably in decades. Indeed, battles rarely break through their boundaries within their "lifetime." But pretending such shifts will not happen rules out any chance of success or advantage. Seeing the game as unbounded overcomes this dilemma.

Battleground shifts become inevitable if a conflict's lifetime is extended—if business is viewed as an endless war, a never-ending stream of battles. "New games" become continuations of old games. They transform the everyday obstacles to something that can be planned for and turned into an advantage. Indeed, long-term success depends on predicting and capitalizing on the unexpected.

As the following cases will show, adaptable companies turn battleground shifts into advantages, overcoming even their largest competitors by identifying new battlegrounds, setting up a defensive position, and waiting for their competition.

> *"One who takes position first at the battleground and awaits the*
> *enemy is at ease. One who takes position later at the battleground*
> *and hastens to do battle is at labor. Thus one skilled at battle sum-*
> *mons others and is not summoned by them."*
>
> —*Sun Tzu*, The Art of War[59]

The Seaman Who Predicted the Ground Would Shift

How does the son of a working-class welder emerge as one of the world's richest billionaires? He sees something others do not; he sees that the battleground is about to shift.

John Fredriksen began his career with an unremarkable first job as a trainee in an Oslo ship-brokering company. He continued to work in the shipping business, becoming one of many obscure private tanker owners. In the 1990s, however, he saw that the world of tankers was about to experience a shift.

Private tanker owners such as Fredriksen had been hurting because of overbuilding in the 1970s. Oil companies exploited the resulting oversupply by pitting ship owners against each other (see the stratagem *Kill with a borrowed knife*) to drive down rates to levels that barely covered costs.

But Fredriksen predicted that many of the tankers built in the 1970s would soon wear out. Tanker supply was about to shrink and this shrinking would shift power away from oil companies toward tanker owners. As he said, "The world has to get crude somewhere, and OPEC is the place. We saw that."[60]

He also saw that oil companies were starting to look for environmentally safe shipping options. These two shifts revealed a new future in which oil companies would be bidding for the few tanker owners that owned newer, environmentally safe tankers.

In accordance with Sun Tzu's ancient principle that one should seize the battleground first, and when common industry wisdom was to avoid the tanker business, Fredriksen began buying tankers. In 1996 he took over a Swedish shipping company called Frontline for $55 million. Over the next three years he continued acquiring tankers, focusing particularly on buying the more expensive but environmentally friendly double-hull tankers.

Fredriksen made another strategic decision that positioned him well for a battleground shift. Instead of entangling his company in long-term contracts, he focused on the "spot market"—the market for shipping oil on short notice. The spot market had two advantages: It offered higher margins, and it gave Fredriksen the flexibility to raise prices with the market.

In 1999 Fredriksen's prediction came true. The battleground shifted when an aging tanker spilled 70,000 barrels of fuel oil off the coast of Brittany. Headlines warning of a major ecological threat drew public attention to the risks single-hull tankers posed to the environment, which in turn sent big oil companies into a frenzy. To avoid such environmental, economic, and public relations disasters, they began looking for double-hull ships to ship their product. They increasingly found themselves negotiating with Fredriksen.

Frontline now commands nearly 25 percent of the world's supertanker spot market. This means that if a company wants to ship oil quickly, there is a one in four chance they will ship it with Frontline. With such bargaining leverage, Fredriksen turned the tables on oil companies. At one time, big oil companies could negotiate tanker owners down to break-even pricing. Now that they need Frontline, they are willing to pay.

In the ten years ending in 2005, Frontline has decisively beaten its competition. It has grown revenue at 55 percent per year versus 15 percent for its peers. It commands 50 percent cash profit margins while its peers produce just 20 percent. And it has produced more shareholder value, delivering on average 60 percent total return to shareholders (TRS) annually versus 30 percent for its peers.

Frontline, the company Fredriksen bought for $55 million is today (in 2006) worth $2.5 billion, making the son of a middle-class welder the richest man in Norway.

Wal-Mart Awaits Its Exhausted Competition

While Wal-Mart's rise to become the world's largest retailer owes its success to multiple factors, it was launched from the platform of *Await the exhausted enemy at your ease.* In 1945, the company that was to become Wal-Mart consisted of one variety store in Newport, Arkansas. In just over thirty years, it became the largest retailer in the world, with more than 3,000 stores in all fifty states and with operations in Argentina, Brazil, Canada, China, Germany, South Korea, Mexico, and the United Kingdom. Wal-Mart owes much of its success to a simple tactic: identifying the next battleground, setting up a stronghold there, and waiting for the competition.

When Wal-Mart began its national expansion in the early 1970s, large retailers such as Sears, JC Penney, and Kmart positioned stores only in large city and town centers. Wal-Mart took the opposite approach: It focused on smaller towns, in part to avoid direct competition and in part because it believed the battleground would shift. As Wal-Mart's founder Sam Walton explained:

> [Our strategy] was simply to put good-sized discount stores into little one-horse towns, which everyone else was ignoring. In those days Kmart wasn't going into towns below 50,000 and even Gibson wouldn't go to towns much smaller than 10,000 or 12,000. We knew our formula was working even in towns smaller than 5,000 people, and there were plenty of those towns out there for us to expand into. When people want to simplify the Wal-Mart story that is usually how they sum up the secret of our success: "Oh, they went into small towns when nobody else would."[61]

Companies that avoid direct competition simply to reduce the cost of battle risk holding a big piece of an insignificant pie. But Wal-Mart was doing more than avoiding direct competition—it was betting that the battleground would move toward small towns and suburbs.

For various reasons that are still the subject of dispute, consumers migrated to suburban neighborhoods and increasingly preferred suburban to city-center retail stores. Leading retailers faced with declining sales in their key locations followed customers into these smaller markets. When they got there, however, they encountered an unexpectedly strong competitor.

Wal-Mart had been waiting for them, fortified with a strong brand and an efficient distribution system. The advantages Sears wielded in serving large urban centers did not carry into Wal-Mart's backyard. Sears fell from leader to follower and still trails.

> *"When two great forces oppose each other, the victory will go to the one that knows how to yield."*[62]
>
> —Lao Tzu, *Tao Te Ching*

Luring an Adversary with Campfires

In 342 BC, three states engaged in war: Wei, Qi, and Han. Wei attacked Han. While Wei was besieging Han, Han asked the state of Qi for help. Qi prepared its army and began marching to the capital of Wei to implement the stratagem *Besiege Wei to rescue Zhao*, just as Chi had done to Wei twelve years earlier. The goal was to force Wei to return to defend the capital and call off its attack on Han.

Remembering the painful consequences of falling for the stratagem, the Wei army, under the leadership of General Pang Juan, pulled back its troops. They rushed home to defend their capital against Qi's attack.

But Sun Bin, the leader of the Qi army, had a new stratagem in mind. He knew that Pang Juan underestimated the Qi army. So rather than attack the Qi capital, he feigned a retreat. He used a creative ploy to lure Pang Juan out of the capital. During the first night of his retreat, he had his army light 100,000 campfires. During the second night, his soldiers lit 50,000, and on the third night, only 30,000.

Pang Juan read this as a sign that the Qi army was dwindling. Tasting an easy victory, he gathered a collection of lightly armed troops and marched them rapidly, at twice the normal speed, toward the retreating Qi army. Sun Bin calculated that at dawn Pang Juan would reach a town called Maling. He set up an ambush there and waited.

The Wei troops arrived on schedule but exhausted from their strenuous march. Sun Bin's army, which was rested, fortified, and

three times the size Pang Juan expected, easily defeated the Wei
troops. Pang Juan committed suicide on the battlefield. Sun Bin
had identified the next battleground, fortified his troops there, and
forced his adversary to become exhausted getting there.

Summary

Insight gave Qi the same advantage that enabled Frontline and
Wal-Mart to topple their dominant adversaries. It allowed each
to turn shifts into advantages by identifying new battlegrounds,
setting up a defensive position there, and waiting. If you take a
short-term view, attaining such insights seems difficult because
battleground shifts seem rare occurrences. But taking a long-term
view makes such insight attainable. What appears a "new game"
on a ten-year scale may be but a blip on a 100-year scale.

EXCHANGE THE ROLE OF GUEST FOR THAT OF HOST

"Whenever there is a chance, enter into the decision-making body of your ally and extend your influence skillfully step-by-step. Eventually, put it under your control."

—From The Thirty-Six Stratagems

If your goals extend beyond the immediate battle, it becomes acceptable to open with a seemingly weak move. A deceptively weak move can serve as a foot in the door that creates an opportunity to infiltrate the adversary and take control. The acceptance of your inferior position acts as your Trojan horse.

This tactic has delivered well-known corporate power reversals. Both Microsoft and Intel, for example, were born from taking a subordinate position to IBM and then building power. The B-2 bomber program, at the mercy of legislators, had to fight for funding at each budget cycle. By shifting production to almost every state, thereby generating jobs in the constituencies of almost every senator, the program changed from the dependent to the depended-upon, almost guaranteeing continued funding.[63]

This pattern—building on a position of weakness to capture control—is Stratagem Twenty-Three, *Exchange the role of guest for that of host.*

Key Elements

Your adversary accepts you as unthreatening.

You incrementally build power over your adversary.

You take control.

Becoming Your Client's Host

Doug Muir faced a decision after September 11, 2001, that would have scared many other pilots. With American travelers staying on the ground, airlines needed to cut costs. Muir, a well-paid senior pilot with a major U.S. airline, was one of the first to receive an offer of furlough as a precursor to unemployment. To Muir, furlough represented a runway to a new career. "I was getting paid to not fly," he recalls thinking.

After a few experiments in various businesses, Muir saw an opportunity to do something new in the mundane business of collecting debts. After some research, he decided to create a subrogation company, one of the many firms that specialize in helping insurance companies collect unpaid obligations. (When two people have a car accident, they exchange insurance information. If the driver at fault does not have adequate insurance or, as is too often the case, has no insurance at all, he or she must make reparations. Often, however, the uninsured driver refuses to pay. The insurance company of the other driver will make several attempts to collect the unpaid amount but if these fail, it will hire subrogation companies to collect. Subrogation companies usually keep 20 percent to 40 percent of what they collect.)

As Muir started his collections business, he realized the industry had stagnated and become inefficient. His insurance company clients sent him boxes of legal documents, which he and his staff dredged through and entered into databases so that they could begin their collection routine. He hired staff to manually enter the data he needed; the process was labor intensive and costly.

Muir wanted his clients to send their documents in digital form. This would save considerable time, but more important, it set in motion a strategic shift that eventually provided him with considerable leverage over his clients.

Muir developed software that automated much of his work and added to it an interface that enabled clients to log on and directly enter required data. Clients liked it because this saved them packaging and shipping time. Muir liked it because it made his collection system almost entirely self-operating. Once clients entered their data, his system could automatically perform three key steps in the collection process: make a phone call, send a letter, and cancel a driver's license.

Everybody won with this solution. But Doug Muir won disproportionately because his software built client dependence.

To see how this worked, consider the typical evolution of a new client. First, a client agreed to test Muir's subrogation service. Company officials sent him their hard-copy information as they did with other subrogation companies. Then Muir suggested they try his digital entry interface. Clients loved it. Sending the information digitally required less time. They were able to shrink their packaging and shipping department because they needed fewer people to photocopy and pack boxes. Clients could move packaging and shipping people into higher-value roles.

Clients gradually moved more of their subrogation business to Muir, each time reducing their shipping departments. As these departments shrank, the clients' dependence on Muir grew. Eventually, the clients became captives. They had reorganized their operations around a digital solution that only Muir's company offered. They could leave Muir only if they made a significant reinvestment in rebuilding the shipping department.

Muir was transformed from guest to host. His captive customers gave him a competitive barrier. After three years growing his business, Doug Muir sold his company to a hedge fund for eleven times his initial investment.

From Buyer to Boss

Wal-Mart offers consumers superior value. It can sell products at lower prices than its competition without forfeiting quality. This unique ability has fueled Wal-Mart's incessant growth and seemingly insurmountable competitiveness. The retailer has been able to do what its competitors cannot primarily because it is able to cut costs out of the supply chain and thereby reduce the costs of the goods it sells. It squeezes the margins of all players in its supply chain from raw material suppliers to manufacturers. To push down manufacturers' margins, Wal-Mart adopts the tactic *Exchanging the role of guest for that of host.*

An Asian apparel manufacturer shared his experience of working with Wal-Mart. He described a process Wal-Mart has repeated with other manufacturers throughout the region. The process overcomes the initial resistance that manufacturers often have to working with Wal-Mart, which, they think, allows manufacturers to earn only extremely low margins.

First, Wal-Mart places a relatively small order that the manufacturer eagerly accepts, because such a small order does not make the manufacturer dependent on Wal-Mart. Wal-Mart then requests additional capacity, which the manufacturer almost always grants. The manufacturer would rather give any extra capacity it has to Wal-Mart instead of investing the time in winning a new customer. The manufacturer's rationale: "with a buyer waiting, why would you waste time hunting down another buyer?" So Wal-Mart's share of the manufacturer's sales has grown from an insignificant 10 percent to a slightly more significant 15 percent.

This development in isolation does not at first noticeably shift the balance of power between Wal-Mart and its manufacturer. But Wal-Mart repeats this process a few times, incrementally growing its share of the manufacturer's production. During this "infiltration" period, Wal-Mart demands good but not overly aggressive prices from the manufacturer. The manufacturer finds it difficult to turn away Wal-Mart's easy business.

After some time, Wal-Mart comes to represent a significant share of the manufacturer's capacity. Wal-Mart then begins demanding deeper discounts. The manufacturer must now choose between cutting margins and losing a large customer, perhaps its largest at this point. The manufacturer naturally acquiesces and cuts margins.

Interestingly, by cutting margins, the manufacturer increases its dependence on Wal-Mart. With lower margins, maintaining high utilization levels (i.e., keeping their machines working) becomes more critical to profitability. So when capacity becomes available, the manufacturer is motivated to sell it quickly; Wal-Mart, with its vast retail network, is the customer most likely to buy extra capacity quickly.

Wal-Mart's process turns an initially weak position into one of dominance. By opening with a seemingly innocuous position then building dependence incrementally, the company effectively reduces manufacturer resistance. This tactic is central to Wal-Mart's overall success. Manufacturer dependence allows Wal-Mart to demand low margins and therefore sell at prices lower than its competitors.

From Guest to Governor

Xiang Liang descended from a long line of generals. However, when his home state, Chu, fell to the powerful Qin dynasty, his family lost power. Even before this happened however, as a youth Xiang Liang had murdered a man and fled from his home with his nephew, Xiang Yu. They took up asylum in the state of Wu. Thus a man destined to lead armies became a lowly administrator, an exile, and an unwilling citizen of the oppressive Qin dynasty. He was, naturally, hungry for change.

Xiang Liang developed a reputation as a strong administrator and leader. The governor of Wu, who had granted Xiang Liang and his nephew asylum, grew to trust them. Over the years, Xiang Liang patiently climbed Wu's organizational ladder. He became a valued advisor to the governor.

In 209 BC, when states and kingdoms throughout the Qin dynasty ignited in revolt, the governor of Wu turned to Xiang Liang. He wanted his state to join the revolt and asked Xiang Liang and his nephew to lead an army.

Xiang Liang saw this as an opportunity to complete his ascent of Wu's governing hierarchy and take control. He asked to confer with his nephew before accepting the challenge. But the plan he and his nephew devised was not what the governor expected.

After Xiang Liang and his nephew jointly accepted the governor's challenge, the three men met to discuss how Wu should join the revolution. In the middle of this meeting, Xiang Liang gave his nephew a secret cue. Without warning or hesitation, his nephew drew his sword and beheaded the governor. Xiang Liang then took the state seals and declared himself governor. To quell the opposition, Xiang Yu swiftly killed any objecting onlookers.

The uncle-nephew team continued their ascent to power. They joined the revolution and won many battles, including the battle for their home state, Chu. Xiang Liang became a contender for the reconquered Chu throne but for political reasons could not secure it. He died in battle soon afterward. Xiang Yu became a contender for rule of the entire dynasty but suffered a similar fate, dying in battle before the dynasty's next ruler was named.

The asylum seekers exchanged their roles from guests to governors. They almost continued their rise to become kings and emperors. Their success lay in timing. By accepting seemingly powerless positions as lowly administrators, they entered the doors of power. By taking small steps, none of which warranted suspicion, they infiltrated their adversary. Once they had built sufficient trust and dependence, they took control.

> "Make people depend on you. . . . You will get more from dependence than from courtesy. He who has already drunk turns his back on the well, and the orange already squeezed turns from gold into mud."[64]
>
> —Baltasar Gracian, The Art of Worldly Wisdom

Summary

Taking power incrementally blurs the line between passive and aggressive and so prevents adversaries from raising their defenses. Because your adversaries are thinking about today's battle while you are planning for tomorrow, they are comforted by their current success and so fail to prepare for your incursion. This stratagem requires that you accept an inferior position today, as Wal-Mart does with its manufacturers, Doug did with his clients, and Xiang

Liang did with the governor of Wu, in exchange for a superior position in the future.

> "For such a prince cannot rely upon what he observes in quiet times, when citizens had need of the state, because then every one agrees with him; they all promise, and when death is far distant they all wish to die for him; but in troubled times, when the state has need of its citizens, then he finds but few. . . . Therefore, a wise prince ought to adopt such a course that his citizens will always in every sort and kind of circumstance have need of the state and of him, and then he will always find them faithful."[65]
>
> —Niccolò Machiavelli, The Prince

BORROW THE ROAD
TO CONQUER GAO

"When a small state, located between two big states, is being threatened by the enemy state, you should immediately send troops to rescue it, thereby expanding your sphere of influence. Mere talk cannot win the trust of a state in a difficult position."

—*From* The Thirty-Six Stratagems

Alliances are often viewed as roads of hope with uncertain ends. Partners take each other's hands and follow these roads, hoping they will last but uncertain where they will lead. Although the consequences of an unsuccessful alliance ending (agreements are filled with provisions that dictate rights and responsibilities if the alliance fails) can be contemplated at length, partnerships are generally viewed as marriages. Successful alliances are considered ones that never end.

But nearly 10 percent of the most competitive companies of the decade have expanded at least in part by taking an alternative view: that an alliance is a borrowed road. The road is borrowed because the actual goals lie beyond the alliance's lifespan.

Key Elements

You share a common objective or enemy with another.

You form an alliance to achieve this objective.

You then capture your ally.

Borrowing to Build an Advantage

In 1984, with $80,000 in seed funding, Liu Chuanzhi created a company with a vague mission: to commercialize technology developed by the Chinese Academy of Sciences. Over the next several years, the company, Legend, evolved into an average member of China's legion of domestic computer firms. Because the government would not grant Legend the authority to manufacture its own computers, Legend was relegated to distributing computers and related hardware for international manufacturers.

Legend, however, was learning. It would drain experience out of its partners and then build a formidable advantage. It was borrowing a road that would convert its inauspicious beginning into the third-largest computer manufacturer in the world.

Legend became the largest distributor of Hewlett-Packard (HP) computers and Toshiba notebooks in China. In this role, the company absorbed HP's practices. It simultaneously developed a unique understanding of how to serve Chinese consumers. For example, it created a breakthrough keyboard that facilitated writing Chinese characters; and, because Chinese consumers are less familiar with computers than are United States and European consumers, it ran computer education road shows countrywide. In addition, the company established an enviable distribution network comprising more than 2,000 distributors.

HP and Toshiba partnerships afforded Legend a valuable foundation of best management practices, customer understanding, and distribution infrastructure, which enabled the company to beat rivals decisively during the 1990s. However, this changed in 1992 when China lowered import restrictions. Foreign firms rushed in and quickly cut down local computer companies' collective market share from 70 percent to 30 percent.

Legend, which had begun manufacturing its own branded computers and still had a substantial distribution business, thrived under the pressure. Following U.S. practices, it took the radical move of offering shares in the company to the employees. This helped to attract top talent. It funneled its commercial and technological knowledge (borrowed from its alliances with HP and other foreign firms, including Intel) into the effort to become a highly competitive computer manufacturer. So while other Chinese computer firms retreated or closed down, Legend's share grew. From close to zero, it reached 5 percent in 1995 and continued to grow. In 1998, it captured 14 percent of the market, making it the top-selling computer brand in China and by the early 2000s commanded 30 percent, outselling international leaders such as IBM, HP, and Compaq.

But the company's ambitions remained unquenched. To assert its global aspirations, the company changed its brand name to Lenovo, a word composed of *Le* from "Legend" and *novo*, the Latin word for "new." Though it remained unknown outside China, the new Legend, Lenovo, proclaimed itself as innovative and not limited to a Chinese identity.

In December 2004, Lenovo announced it intended to buy IBM's PC business. Five months later Lenovo completed its IBM deal, paying $1.25 billion in cash and stock and solidifying its position as the third-largest computer company in the world.

Lenovo owes a debt of gratitude to its partners for helping it build a strong foundation. Liu Chuanzhi said, "Our earliest and best teacher was Hewlett-Packard."[66] HP concurs. HP executive Ken Koo says, "Legend grew with us. They learned vendor channel management from HP. We helped develop Legend into a strong PC company in China."[67]

Piercing Through Your Partners

Daniel Borel and Pierluigi Zappacosta never wanted to sell computer mice. They wanted to build software. Both were Stanford University engineering students who dreamed of bringing to their home continent of Europe the entrepreneurial energy they found so invigorating in Silicon Valley.

But European venture capitalists showed little interest in software companies, so Borel and Zappacosta had to adjust their plans. They followed a growth path surprisingly similar to Lenovo's and, indeed, many other technology firms: Align with larger players, build skills and capacity, and then expand beyond your former partners. This trajectory led them to create Logitech, one of the world's largest producers of computer mice and other input peripherals.

When venture capitalists turned down the pair's software ideas, Borel and Zappacosta switched to hardware. They bought the U.S. distribution rights for a computer mouse designed in Switzerland. Their timing was ideal. One year later, Steve Jobs revolutionized the computer industry by choosing to use a computer mouse on the Apple computer, which led to a broad adoption of the computer mouse throughout the industry. Borel and Zappacosta's sails filled and their small hardware business began to move.

Over the next six years, their company, eventually named Logitech, signed deals to produce computer mice for the world's leading computer manufacturers. By 1998, IBM, HP, AT&T, Olivetti, Convergent Technologies, and DEC were all buying their mice from Logitech. Logitech built plants in California, Ireland, and Taiwan. No competitor could convincingly claim more experience or capacity than Logitech.[68]

Though the company had won the world's leading computer companies as clients, it remained relatively small, with revenues of $40 million in 1988. To unlock further growth, the company decided to bypass the intermediaries and begin marketing directly to end-users.

Logitech hired a new CEO and began expanding its retail business. It invested in its brand, expanded its retail marketing skills, and widened its offering to include Webcams. Its revenues jumped 31 percent in 2000, hitting $615 million, and continued to grow at 20 percent per year for the next five years, reaching $1.8 billion in 2006. Its retail sales now comprise 80 percent of its total, and since the retail channel delivers far higher margins than selling to computer manufacturers does, Logitech's profitability has grown even faster than its size.

By following the road to consumers pioneered by HP and IBM, Logitech built a defensible foothold of skill and capacity. It then reached beyond its original channels to unlock extraordinary growth.

A Deposit of Jade

In 658 BC, the duke of Jin was contemplating how to continue expanding his state. He had, over the years, overtaken many other states and now enjoyed great power. He was particularly concentrating on two smaller states that bordered his own: Yu and Gao, which anticipated the duke's ambitions and so fortified their borders with his kingdom. They made an informal pact to support each other in case of an attack. As a result of this coordination, a successful incursion would cost the duke considerable resources.

One of the duke's generals suggested that if the duke could attack one of the small states through the other, his chances of success would be greatly improved, because their common borders were not heavily guarded. He proposed that the duke bribe Yu's leader, who was known to be greedy, with lavish gifts in exchange for passage through Yu to attack Gao. The duke countered that the cost might not be worth the gain. The general responded that the duke should think of the bribes as deposits, not gifts. Once successful, the duke could withdraw his bribes from Yu's stores again.

The duke agreed to the plan. He offered Yu's leader fine horses and jade in exchange for passage. An advisor to Yu's leader counseled him not to accept the gifts. "You have heard the saying, 'Without lips, the teeth would get cold,'" he said. "Gao and Yu are close neighbors and depend on each other for protection. Without Gao, Yu might not survive. Why should we let Jin pass?" But Yu's leader ignored the warning. He accepted the gifts and let the Jin army pass through his territory to attack Gao.

Gao fell easily to Jin's superior forces. The Jin army, on its way home, attacked and conquered Yu. The Jin general took back his duke's jade and horses from Yu's stores and returned them to the duke.

Through a temporary alliance, the duke of Jin upset his opponents' balance and overwhelmed them in succession, conquering both at minimal cost.

Summary

Social rules suggest entering an alliance as you would enter a marriage, without intending that it end. Yet highly competitive companies view alliances as borrowed roads. Just as the duke of Jin did 2,700 years ago, companies such as Legend and Logitec have pulled themselves toward dominance with the hand of partners to whom they later evolved into at least indirect competitors.

> *"And here it is to be noted that a prince ought to take care never to make an alliance with one more powerful than himself for the purpose of attacking others, unless necessity compels him . . . because if he conquers you, you are at his discretion, and princes ought to avoid as much as possible being at the discretion of any one."*
>
> —*Niccolò Machiavelli*, The Prince[69]

SHED YOUR SKIN LIKE THE GOLDEN CICADA

"Make your front array appear as if you are still holding your posi-
tion so that the allied force will not suspect your intention and the
enemy troops will not dare to attack rashly. Then withdraw your
main forces secretly."

—*From* The Thirty-Six Stratagems

A cyclical view of time makes it easier to accept loss today in exchange for gain tomorrow. This is playing with gain and loss across the dimension of time. Gain and loss can also be played with across other dimensions, such as markets and businesses. By linking businesses and shifting earnings, a company can manipulate competition and protect profitability.

This is like playing with the good and bad, the hard and the soft ground, in warfare. The key is to look at the whole, not the parts, and to let your adversary focus on a part and not on the whole.

Key Elements

You establish a façade.

Your adversary focuses on your façade, confusing it for the real action.

You move the real action somewhere else.

"Attain both hard and soft. This is the pattern of Earth."[70]

—*Sun Tzu*, The Art of War

Hollow Profits

The charter airline business is ruthless. It punishes with losses any airline that fails to achieve 70 percent utilization (an airline that achieves 70 percent utilization keeps its planes, on average, 70 percent full on flights). Keeping planes full, however, is a challenge. Charter airlines have few means, other than price, by which to differentiate their services and maintain high utilization rates. Passengers rarely can choose which particular charter airline to fly. Rather, institutions, such as tour operators and corporations, make buying decisions. They do not care about the airline's name or the details of its frequent flyer program, but they *do* care about safety. Regulations ensure airlines' records for safety remain similar, making it almost impossible for airlines to differentiate along this dimension. As a result, airlines are relegated to competing on price alone. Performance, to a great extent, depends on factors outside their control, such as macroeconomic trends.

The payoff for filling planes, however, is attractive. Revenue from each passenger above minimum utilization represents pure profit because carrying that additional passenger requires no meaningful additional cost. While growing profits in most industries usually involves increasing price, the way to expand the profit of an airline is to increase utilization.

The Thomson Travel Group of the United Kingdom has pieced together a system to improve the odds of its charter airline gamble. It beats the system by applying a clever stratagem to practically ensure full planes.

Thomson operates three related businesses. Its retail business, Lunn Poly, sells consumers travel services, such as hotel rooms, flights, and tour packages. Its tour operator, Thomson Holidays, packages and manages tours. Thomson's third business is a charter airline, Britannia.

While the three businesses are independent, they can coordinate their efforts to achieve an advantage that competitors cannot. For

example, Lunn Poly does not exclusively sell Thomson Holidays'
tour packages, but it sends a lot of business to this sister company.
Thomson Holidays, in turn, sends much of its business to Britannia,
which, in turn, benefits from well-utilized planes.

The impact of this structure is compelling. Thomson's retail and
tour businesses make little profit. Indeed, few companies in these
markets do. In forgoing retail and tour profits, Thomson benefits
in two ways. First, it wards off travel retail and tour competitors
with low prices and low profitability that diminish would-be competitors' appetites. Second, by ushering customers into Britannia planes, ensuring high utilization, the company can generate
abnormally high charter airline profits. Thomson's retail and tour
businesses not only serve as a conduit for the air charter business
but also act as a façade that discourages the competition while the
real action takes place elsewhere: Britannia earns unusually high
profits.

The False King

Xiang Yu, who collaborated with his uncle, Xiang Liang, to apply
the stratagem *Exchange the role of guest for that of host* and take control of Wu (see Stratagem Twenty-Three), continued his quest to
take down the Han empire. He and his uncle successfully took
control of their home state of Chu. Xiang Liang died later during a
mission to expand the revolution, and Xiang Yu became warlord of
Wu. In this position, Xiang Yu led many successful battles against
the king of Han, Gaozu.

After one such battle in the early second century BC, Gaozu
retreated with a diminished army to regroup in a fortified city.
However, Xiang Yu followed, surrounded the city, and prepared to
finally defeat his archrival.

Gaozu's situation looked dire. But one of his generals proposed
a maneuver to allow Gaozu to escape. The general proposed that
he pose as the king, focus their adversary's attention on him by
feigning a surrender, while the real king, Gaozu, escaped through
a side exit of the city. The general was offering his life to save his
king. The king accepted.

The general had 2,000 women dress as soldiers. Just before dawn, these women exited the main gate and took up battle formation. Xiang Yu's army reacted quickly. They assembled in formation and prepared for what they hoped would be the final confrontation. But just before daybreak, when the fighting would commence, the general appeared from within the city walls disguised as the king and signaled surrender. His people had run out of food, he explained.

Xiang Yu's soldiers celebrated their long-awaited victory in a joyous uproar. They did not yet realize that the man they thought was the king was actually a general, and the figures they thought were solders were actually women in disguise. Under the cover of this façade, with thirty horsemen, Gaozu quietly exited the city through the West gate.

The general's carriage slowly moved toward Xiang Yu. The king was to surrender in person. When Xiang Yu recognized the general and realized he had been tricked, he grew furious. When he learned that a group of horsemen had snuck out of the city and escaped, he had the general burned to death. Gaozu, the king of Han, was saved.

Summary

For millennia, to overcome adversaries, leaders have leveraged the tactic of creating a façade to hide the real action occurring somewhere else. Companies do this as well by, for example, linking businesses and pooling profits where they incite less competition.

THE STRATAGEM OF INJURING YOURSELF

"People rarely inflict injuries on themselves, so when they get injured, it is usually genuine. Exploit this naivety to make the enemy believe your words; then sowing discord within the enemy will work. In this case, one takes advantage of the enemy's weakness, and makes the enemy look as if he were a naive child easily taken."

—*From* The Thirty-Six Stratagems

M any of today's most powerful companies grew from positions of self-imposed weakness. They injured themselves to appear less threatening and thereby pacified the opposition. They then built their power within this protective sphere.

Key Elements

Your adversary's suspicion hinders your success.

You injure yourself to either win your adversary's trust or avoid appearing to be a threat.

Your adversary accepts you or lets down his guard.

You take advantage of this opening by attacking your adversary.

"The yielding can triumph over the inflexible;
The weak can triumph over the strong.
Fish should not be taken from deep waters;
Nor should organizations make obvious their advantages."[71]

—*Lao Tzu*, Tao Te Ching

Whole Foods Injures Itself

Injuring yourself can soften competitive resistance in at least two ways. A common approach is to injure yourself so that your competition, perceiving you as weak, discounts you as a threat and lets you advance. A more sophisticated approach entails wounding yourself in a way that entangles your competition in a dilemma, because defending themselves requires that they similarly injure themselves. Preferring your attack to a self-imposed one, your competition is likely to ignore you.

This stratagem has enabled Whole Foods to deliver unprecedented performance while facing minimal competitive resistance. In an industry growing at just 6 percent per year, Whole Foods is growing at 25 percent. While competitors squeeze out 4.5 percent profit margins, Whole Foods, operating on a far smaller scale, manages 8 percent.[72]

Since going public in 1992, Whole Foods has transformed from a lightweight, generating just a few hundred million dollars in revenue, into a serious contender. With $5 billion in annual sales, it now approaches the league defined by Supervalue, Safeway, and Kroger (which annually earn $60 billion, $40 billion, and $20 billion, respectively). Why did these incumbents allow a small natural-food store to take such a large share of their market? Whole Foods' rise shows the *Stratagem of injuring yourself* at work in two phases: first, in the founding of the chain, and second, in its organization on an ongoing basis.

In 1978 John Mackey, a University of Texas dropout, convinced a group of friends and relatives to lend him $78,000 to purchase a natural-food store called Safer Way Natural Foods. Two years later he partnered with a pair of entrepreneurs to open a new store in Austin called Whole Foods Market.

The Whole Foods concept was unique. Until that time natural-food stores had been small and had offered limited selections. At 12,500 square feet, the first Whole Foods Market approached traditional supermarkets in size and offered a broad selection of foods including meats, breads, wines, and cheeses.

The Whole Foods concept seemed to be working. By 1985 Mackey and his partners had opened two more stores. They then began acquiring existing natural-food stores, first in Texas, then in Louisiana, California, and Wisconsin. By January 1992, when the company issued its initial public offering (IPO) of stock, the company had grown to ten stores and $92.5 million in revenue.

Whole Foods' strategy of focusing on the natural-foods niche pre-empted competitive responses from the large incumbents. The natural-food segment was too small to be attractive to them. Whole Foods therefore appeared too specialized to be a threat. Larger supermarket chains, feeling no urgency to defend themselves against Whole Foods, allowed this small upstart to grow.

This competitive dynamic, in which an attacker commits itself to a niche deemed unattractive to incumbents, thereby pre-empting competitive resistance, has been termed the Judo Strategy. Numerous small companies have used this approach to carve out small businesses among giants.

But Whole Foods' strategy seems to be something bigger; for the company has achieved the scale few Judo Strategy companies enjoy, because Whole Foods "injures" itself in ways the competition chooses not to copy.

For example, Whole Foods gives each store broad control, allowing each to operate as a separate business unit. Its stores are run by teams of managers who make decisions that larger supermarket chains typically reserve for corporate headquarters. By granting such autonomy, Whole Foods spurs healthy interstore competition. Employees know how well their store is doing relative to other stores. They want to be the best so they strive to get better.

Unleashing such competitive energy would benefit any company, even traditional supermarkets, so why don't incumbents copy Whole Foods' approach? Because doing so would require inflicting a self-injury few large supermarkets can bring themselves to endure. For staff to play this interstore competition game, they must know their store's revenue, inventory turns, and profit-margin figures, and they must know how these compare with other stores. Indeed, to operate as it does, Whole Foods shares such detailed financial performance data with employees that the SEC considers each of Whole Foods' 6,500 employees an "insider," an outcome with far-reaching consequence no traditional supermarket chain would quickly embrace.

Whole Foods has also adopted a rule that its CEO cannot earn more than eight times the company's average wage. Hierarchical supermarket companies, which depend on large numbers of low-wage store clerks to support regional and headquarter managers, would strongly resist such a rule.

Matching Whole Foods' strategy would require an incumbent to self-injure in at least three ways: It would need to decentralize into autonomous stores, share detailed performance data with employees, and flatten its compensation structure. A copycat strategy is simply too painful to accept. As the incumbents ponder their alternatives, they pacify themselves with the view that Whole Foods, having injured itself, poses a minor threat. Meanwhile Whole Foods advances uncontested.

> *"There's this notion that you can't be touchy-feely and serious, we don't fit the stereotypes. There's plenty of managerial edge in this company—the culture creates it."[73]*
>
> —John Mackey, Founder and CEO, Whole Foods Market

Injuring an Assassin

During the Spring and Autumn period (770–476 BC), the emperor of Wu was preoccupied with the prince of Wei. The emperor had taken power by killing the prince's father and assuming the throne. The prince, seeking revenge, was assembling capable men to mount an attack. So the emperor decided to hire an assassin, Yao Li, to get rid of the prince's threat quickly and permanently.

To kill the prince, Yao Li would need to get close. But this would be difficult, because the prince was a careful and suspicious man. He would be wary of anyone who came from within the emperor's domain. So Yao Li proposed a plan to injure himself.

He publicly offended the emperor. In response, the emperor, playing along with the secret plan, ordered Yao Li arrested and his right hand severed in punishment. The one-handed Yao Li fled the emperor. He sought refuge with the prince and swore to hate the emperor and yearn for revenge.

The prince accepted Yao Li into his territory but remained suspicious. He sent spies to investigate the authenticity of Yao Li's falling-out with the emperor. The spies returned with shocking news. Not only had the emperor cut off Yao Li's hand, but he also had Yao Li's wife and children executed and their bodies burned in public. This news softened the prince's suspicions. Yao Li had reason to despise the emperor.

Yao Li eventually became one of the prince's advisors. When the prince was finally ready to take action, he launched a waterborne attack on the emperor. Yao Li was on the prince's boat. When their boat reached the middle of the sea, Yao Li turned to the prince and thrust a spear into him. While the prince bled to death, his men subdued Yao Li. But before they reached the shore, Yao Li committed suicide.

By injuring himself, Yao Li earned the prince's trust and made the prince pay dearly for this mistake.

Summary

People pity the weak and resist causing themselves pain. Play on both natural reactions by injuring yourself. You will gain their acceptance when they discount your threat and later benefit from their hesitation when your advance stirs concern.

BORROW A CORPSE FOR THE SOUL'S RETURN

"The powerful is beyond exploitation, but the weak needs help. Exploit and manipulate the weak for they need you more than you need them."

—*From* The Thirty-Six Stratagems

The practice of this stratagem differs somewhat from its original definition. *The powerful* has come to mean the living. *The weak* has come to mean the dead or the forgotten. So this stratagem advises picking up the dead or forgotten to battle the living. The tactic of reviving something old, dead, or discarded is called *Borrow a corpse for the soul's return*.

Webster's Dictionary defines *innovation* as "something new or different introduced." Companies often collapse "new" into "different," thinking that for something to be different it must be new. But companies achieve advantage through differentiation, not just newness. Of course, newness has benefits. It can, for example, complicate competitors' efforts to copy another's innovation. But it is neither sufficient nor necessary to creating an advantage.

Advantage requires being different. If your adversaries have shed old models, ideas, or technology to become "new," you can become different and gain advantage by adopting those discarded models, ideas, or technology. This is particularly powerful, as you shall see, when your adversary can no longer return to its old ways.

Key Elements

You adopt something forgotten or abandoned (a model, idea, or technology).

Because your adversaries have abandoned it, only you use this thing.

You convert this uniqueness into power.

Leapfrogging the Competition with Abandoned Technology

By the mid-1990s, pagers were dying. Once the mobile communications tool of choice among doctors and business executives and later embraced by the general public, pagers were losing their place on the hips of movie stars and drug dealers. As the cost and reach of voice networks improved, mobile phones and personal digital assistants (PDAs) with mobile phone capabilities were taking over. Why would anyone want a text message when they could have a two-way conversation?

The industry's shift toward adding more—combining Internet connectivity with voice and video and music—created an ideal opportunity for the innovative thinker willing to choose another path. It set the stage for a small, unknown Canadian company to steal the show once dominated by consumer electronic giants.

The steady decline of pagers forced BellSouth, at the time one of the leading pager service providers, to face up to a challenge. The company had invested millions in building a network of antennas, Mobitex, which passed text messages between pagers. BellSouth wanted to use its network investment. But to remain competitive, the company needed to expand its newer voice network and thereby push the older Mobitex infrastructure into obsolescence. BellSouth faced the classic "innovator's dilemma." It needed to destroy its old business to evolve.

Or did it?

A small wireless modem company convinced BellSouth it had a way out. The company, Research in Motion (RIM), had been founded about ten years previously by a twenty-three-year-old university dropout. He and two friends had built a business designing technology that enabled users to sell wireless data through a data network. Ericsson and a few other large companies were using RIM technology.

When BellSouth was looking for ideas for reviving their Mobitex infrastructure, RIM proposed developing a two-way pager. This idea cut across the mobile industry's dominant momentum. Mobile phone companies and hardware producers were abandoning old text networks and replacing them with more powerful voice networks. Their vision was to build devices that could deliver everything a user would need—voice, e-mail, Web pages, and videos—over one network.

RIM proposed moving in precisely the opposite direction. It convinced BellSouth to expand its Mobitex data network and launch a RIM-designed two-way pager.

The RIM device, eventually called the BlackBerry, was simple. It offered no voice service (it was not a phone) and no graphics (it only displayed text e-mails). Even the device's design ignored the aesthetics, which Motorola, Nokia, Palm Computing's Palm Pilot, and Compaq's iPac deemed essential to succeed in the market place.

The BlackBerry's utilitarian square black box with a screen and a small keyboard inspired no envy among the design-conscious. But it worked. Because RIM used an abandoned data network with excess capacity, e-mails sent from a RIM device transferred unhindered by the congestion common to newer voice networks. BlackBerry e-mails were fast and reliable.

The company introduced two other key technological innovations. It "pushed" e-mail onto its devices, while competing products required users to prompt e-mails to be downloaded. It also solved the "two e-mail" problem. At the time, people with mobile e-mail devices needed to maintain two e-mail accounts, one for the office and the other for the mobile device. RIM developed technology that enabled users to maintain one account linked to both their computer and their BlackBerry.

These innovations differentiated RIM's two-way pager, but they did not provide a sustainable advantage. With some technical investment, competitors could, and would eventually, duplicate push-e-mail and the one-e-mail-account ability. But RIM's strategic decision to build its business around out-of-date data networks was one that its competitors, all heavily invested in building devices that leveraged more modern voice networks, would resist copying. RIM, deemed out of place and pace, suffered the dismissive treatment most great companies experience in their early days.

Palm Computing had revolutionized the PDA with its Palm Pilot, at the time the most popular PDA in the world. Compaq was investing heavily in catching up with its iPac PDA. Mobile phone manufacturers were packing their phones with new features. Collectively the mobile phone giants were investing billions in creating a consumer's all-in-one digital device.

RIM's unorthodox, simplified offering quickly won over corporate executives. Its name became synonymous with fast, reliable e-mail. *Crackberry*, a word that acknowledges the addictive nature of the BlackBerry, entered the English lexicon. RIM leveraged its strength among corporate users to expand into adjacent segments. It later added voice capabilities and Internet capabilities as it steadily ate away at the market share of well-funded competitors. In 2005, ten years after introducing its first two-way pager, RIM's Black-Berry displaced the Palm Pilot as the most popular hand-held computer.[74]

The Shepherd Corpse

After the uncle-nephew team of Xiang Liang and Xiang Yu took control of the state of Wu (see Stratagem Twenty-Three, *Exchange the role of guest for that of host*), they continued their rebellion against the Qin Empire. Their first goal was to reclaim their home state, Chu, whose king had been humiliated and murdered by the Qin.

After they reconquered Chu, and before Xiang Liang was killed during a mission to expand the revolution, Xiang Liang vied for the Chu throne. The former king and his family were dead, so no clear heir existed. Xiang Liang, who came from a long line of respected

Chu generals, had as much right to the throne as anyone. Unfortunately for Xiang Liang, a rival warlord claimed he had found a descendant of a noble clan who could be linked, albeit through distant relationships, to the former king. The warlord argued that this person should take the throne.

Xiang Liang consulted a wise man to devise a strategy to maintain control of Chu. This wise man told Xiang Liang to find a direct descendent of the former Chu king. Although he would not directly rule Chu, he could exert influence over the new king. This would also invoke the spirit of the dead Chu king, ignite patriotism, and win Xian Liang broad support from the Chu people for having discovered a true heir of their beloved former king.

So Xiang Liang launched an exhaustive search. Time and persistence uncovered a direct grandson of the former Chu king—a poor shepherd. The shepherd agreed to become king and adopted his grandfather's name.

The shepherd's coronation marked a pivotal moment for Xiang Liang and the Chu state. It set a fire under the Chu rebellion against the Qin Empire and helped Xiang Liang and his nephew, Xiang Yu, become leading figures of that rebellion. Had Xiang Liang not found a true descendant to the Chu throne, it is not clear that Chu's patriotic drive would have exploded with sufficient force to put Chu and thus Xiang Liang at the forefront of rebellion that ended the empire.

Reviving the history of the Chu king was like borrowing a corpse and using it to awaken Chu's citizens. RIM and Xiang Liang each revived the past to chart a new future.

Summary

As corporations migrate from one model to another, from old technologies to new, they leave behind a valuable trail of sources of innovation—a junkyard of discarded models, ideas, and technology. These come pretested and, if truly abandoned, can provide a sustainable means of differentiation, of creating advantage. Often, competitors who have abandoned models, ideas, and technologies have invested so much in their evolution that they can return only with great effort. In such cases, the junkyard contains true jewels.

PART IV

SHANG BING WU BING: INDIRECT ACTION

The Eastern equivalent of chess is a strategic board game from China called go, or sometimes, I-go. The two games have similar objectives: to remove an opponent's pieces from the board until only the winner's pieces dominate. But the two approaches to winning are fundamentally different: Chess demands direct attack; go works by indirect attack.

In chess, a person captures an opponent's pieces by placing his or her piece directly into the target. This is like establishing a line of fire and pulling the trigger.

Go, on the other hand, takes the opposite approach. The go board markings resemble those of graph paper—a grid of nineteen horizontal lines and nineteen vertical ones. A total of 361 spaces are thus created. Each player begins with a pile of identical stones: One player plays white stones, the other black. The stones are placed on the intersections of lines, not in the squares as in chess. Stones are placed on the intersections by turn. However, go is unlike chess in that a player cannot place a piece on an occupied space. Instead, to remove an opponent's pieces from the board, a player must *surround* the opponent's pieces. Once a player has cut off the adversary's freedom of movement, the surrounded piece can be removed.

Chess and go are more than just games. For hundreds of years, they have symbolized different approaches to conflict. What they reveal and reinforce is that Western cultures tend toward direct attack while Eastern cultures move indirectly.

Indirect Warfare

The preference for indirect action exhibited in go is also evident in Eastern military philosophy. Sun Tzu and the Taoists advocated avoiding direct conflict at almost all costs. They counseled using indirect methods until and unless a situation became too desperate. Sun Tzu wrote, "One skilled at employing the military subdues the other's military but does not do battle,"[75] and "when ten to one, surround them. When five to one, attack them. When two to one, be able to do battle with them."[76]

In the West, the general rule is if victory is assured, attack; if victory is uncertain, contain; if victory is unlikely, avoid conflict. Both Eastern and Western military approaches contemplate indirect action. In the West, indirect actions are associated with weakness; whereas in the East, they are embraced as essential.

Sun Tzu wrote:

In all fighting, the direct method may be used for joining battle, but indirect methods will be needed in order to secure victory. Indirect tactics, efficiently applied, are inexhaustible as Heaven and Earth, unending as the flow of rivers and streams; like the sun and moon, they end but to begin anew; like the four seasons, they pass away to return once more. In battle, there are not more than two methods of attack—the direct and the indirect; yet these two in combination give rise to an endless series of maneuvers. The direct and the indirect lead on to each other in turn. It is like moving in a circle—you never come to an end. Who can exhaust the possibilities of their combination?[77]

In the gap between thought and decision lie invisible rules that in the West guide toward the direct path. Deeply routed Western metaphors for conflict encourage the direct path and hide circuitous, indirect options. However, by pausing in this gap and fighting your tendencies, you may reveal winning moves you would otherwise overlook.

Indeed, indirect competitive moves can deliver significant force using limited energy. They can be undertaken by powerful corporations, not just weak attackers. Thirty-eight of the 100 most competitive companies of the decade credit their success at least in part to one of the indirect approaches embodied in this section's stratagems. These stratagems can be used to break out of conditioned preference for direct approaches; they can trigger imagination and reveal new options that might not have been thought of before.

Point at the Mulberry but Curse the Locust

"When the powerful wants to rule over the weak, he will sound a warning. One's uncompromising stand will often win loyalty, and one's resolute action, respect."

—From The Thirty-Six Stratagems

Just as pulling on one strand of a spider web causes other strands to move, so too do actions have innumerable unintended consequences. Perhaps because these unintended consequences are so vast, people focus on just a few consequences, usually those intended. Within these unintended, unnoticed consequences lies an opportunity to act invisibly. For example, you can choose actions that send out hidden messages and cause other players in your game to adjust their behavior. As you shall see, corporations use this tactic to bring competitors into alignment and to lure customers. Similarly, political leaders have used this stratagem to influence new allies and induce them into compliance.

Key Elements

You want to influence your adversary's behavior.

Rather than attack your adversary directly, you focus your attention on a different target.

This action sends a covert message to your adversary, one that displays your power and communicates your intention.

Your adversary, appreciating your power and intention, alters her behavior.

Novell, Microsoft's Secret Messenger

In 2006 Microsoft surprised the software world by forming an alliance with a longtime nemesis. While the move was officially touted as a shift by Microsoft toward becoming more collaborative, many industry experts saw it as a tactic to deliver a secret threat to Microsoft's adversaries.

Novell and Microsoft are natural competitors. In the late 1980s Novell launched a revolution that threatened Microsoft's PC dominance. The company's vision was that, instead of using traditional PCs, employees would work through "dumb" terminals linked to a large central computer. Such an architecture would make Microsoft's desktop operating system unnecessary, thereby threatening the central hub around which Microsoft's advantages turned.

As Novell grew, it aligned itself with nearly every major Microsoft competitor. In 1991 it formed an alliance with IBM in which IBM agreed to market Novell's core software, NetWare. The next year it entered a product development agreement with Lotus, the company competing with Microsoft's Outlook and other collaboration products, through which Novell would connect Lotus more closely with NetWare. It then aligned with Sun Microsystems, another Microsoft rival. In 1994 Novell went head-to-head with Microsoft by purchasing WordPerfect and Quatro Pro, the leading competitors with Microsoft's Word and Excel programs, for $1.4 billion. Though Novell sold these businesses two years later, their purchase highlights Novell's long, proactive offense against Microsoft.

Between 2003 and 2005 Novell struggled against IBM and other competitors, losing market share and profits. But Novell still stands at the center of a movement in direct opposition to Microsoft's roots. Novell and its fellow open-source competitors believe a new open environment will emerge, which no company can own. They are part of a growing community of programmers who develop software anonymously, share it with others, and believe that this software should be part of the public domain, available for anyone to use at no cost.

The industry was therefore surprised in 2006 when Microsoft announced a $250 million deal with Novell. Through the agreement, Microsoft and Novell agreed to collaborate to jointly support customers who used both open source and Microsoft's proprietary software. They also agreed to work more closely to ensure that their software integrated easily.

Was Microsoft finally giving up its struggle against "open source"? Was it shifting its competitive position from confrontation toward collaboration? Microsoft claims its decision was a good-faith effort to serve the many Novell business customers running both Windows and open-source applications, but Microsoft's choice of partner seems to point to an entirely different motive.

Microsoft had many partners to choose from. By far the largest open-source vendor is a company called Red Hat. If Microsoft's primary goal was to service business customers using both open and closed software, it could have reached far more such customers by aligning with Red Hat. Why did Microsoft instead choose to partner with a weaker player?

We cannot know for sure. But if we consider this deal an attack rather than a capitulation, Microsoft's choice makes sense. As part of the Microsoft-Novell deal, Microsoft agreed not to sue Novell's customers. A string of lawsuits had been filed between open-source and closed-source software firms, with the latter claiming that open-source programs were stealing and embedding proprietary program codes into the software that was released into the public domain. Companies that use Red Hat or Novell to customize open-source solutions run the risk that, in the future, a company such as Microsoft might claim that some of that software was actually proprietary intellectual property.

By sending the message to Novell's customers that they will not be sued, Microsoft is implying that non-Novell customers may be sued. The secret message, then, is that if you are going to use open-source software and you do not use Novell, you expose yourself to a potential lawsuit.

This message has the potential to lead customers away from Red Hat, the leading open-source vendor, toward its weaker competitor, Novell. This, in turn, could disrupt the power balance emerging in the open-source community and potentially slow the movement's growth. This is not unlike, say, the U.S. government supporting a weaker opponent to remove an anti-Western leader from power.

The tactic of sending secret messages to scare potential clients away from the competition is so common in the high-technology space that it has earned a name: Fear, Uncertainty, and Doubt (or FUD). IBM was arguably the first to wield it successfully. Its famous marketing message that "nobody ever got fired for buying IBM" implied that not choosing IBM put your job at risk.

Though we cannot know Microsoft's true intentions, the impact of Microsoft's decision is clear. By aligning with a weaker player, it sent a message to any company looking at using open-source software: You may be sued.

What makes this tactic possible is the often-overlooked interdependency that links industries, companies, and actions. Actions propagate through these connections. This is similar to chaos theory: A butterfly flapping its wings in China may cause rain in Los Angeles; a decision to attack a small competitor has indirect effects, such as influencing the behavior of larger competitors.

By exploring these indirect effects, you may uncover levers of influence, means of achieving goals that you did not know you had.

Sending Secret Signals to Customers

You can apply the very same tactic to influence your customers. Movie marketers have found that young viewers dislike being marketed to, so they must appear to be targeting adults in order to sell films targeting youth. Movie posters, therefore, might display images of the adult leads but place a key teenage character not centrally but prominently. The ostensible message is, "This is a movie for adults," and the hidden message is, "But there is also something for younger viewers."

Take your children to Pixar's *Monsters Inc.* or a similarly successful children's movie, and you may catch yourself laughing out loud. You and the other chaperones will fill the theater with laughter but at different times than your children. This is because you and your children are laughing at entirely different things. The film is carefully designed to interweave plot lines that appeal to adults with those that appeal to children. Children miss most of the adult themes entirely. What is openly a children's movie is also one targeted at adults. This dual-message strategy is critical because adults are less likely to take their children to a movie they themselves will not enjoy.

Huan Unites Eight States

In 685 BC, a new duke, Huan, was installed as ruler of the Qi state. He claimed this position after years of military struggle, and he now wanted to secure peace and build prosperity.

An advisor suggested that the best way to achieve this goal would be to establish an alliance with the eight states in the region, with Duke Huan serving as the leader. The duke thought this would be an excellent plan for peacefully securing power. He invited representatives of the other states to jointly discuss his plan. He built a large platform for the conference; he assured his guests that they would enjoy lavish accommodations; and, as a sign of his peaceful intentions, he did not bring a single war chariot to the meeting.

To the duke's surprise and disappointment, only four of the eight warlords attended his conference. An alliance among just five states would be useless, even counterproductive, because such an alliance could threaten the four states outside the alliance and trigger further conflict. Nevertheless, the five states held the ceremony and appointed Duke Huan leader of their alliance.

At the meeting, Duke Huan proposed that the five new allies attack the four states that did not join the alliance. He requested their support. Three of the four states obliged. However, the duke of Song, did not.

The duke of Song was dissatisfied with the results of this meeting. While Song was the largest state, Duke Huan led the alliance. Further, Song saw little value in an alliance that excluded four of the eight states. The duke of Song believed that if he dropped out, others would as well and the alliance would collapse. So during the night, the duke of Song secretly left the meeting.

Song's exit from the alliance infuriated Duke Huan, who ordered a general to hunt down the duke of Song and kill him. But before his orders could be executed, one of his advisors made an interesting argument. He suggested that Duke Huan let Song alone for the moment. Instead, Duke Huan should focus his attention on a nearby state, one of the four that did not attend the meeting. Such an attack would be safer and cheaper and yet would be an effective warning to Song.

So instead of attacking his primary adversary, the state of Song, Duke Huan attacked a weaker, closer one. He led an army toward the capital city. When he reached the city walls, the head of this small state, fearing a painful defeat, sent an urgent message to Duke Huan explaining that he did not attend the alliance meeting only because he was sick and that he intended to join the alliance. In response, Duke Huan called off his attack, and this smaller state joined the alliance.

The veiled message in Duke Huan's tactic was powerful. Fearing attack and encouraged by the duke's willingness to forgive old enemies, each state that had missed the first meeting apologized and joined the alliance.

This left just Song outside the alliance. Duke Huan assembled a joint army and marched to Song's capital. But before this army engaged Song, the duke of Song himself, realizing the futility of waging war against seven other states, joined the alliance as well.

Duke Huan unified the eight states, ensuring peace and gaining supreme power without bloodshed. He did this by attacking a weak enemy—pointing at the mulberry while cursing the locust.

Summary

The colors of autumn call us to take walks through the woods. But their true message is intended for far smaller recipients: aphids and other tree-eating insects that dislike the color red.

In a similar vein, your actions send different signals to different players. Appreciating this, you can choose your actions for the broader messages they send. This gives you a powerful tool with which to influence your environment.

CLAMOR IN THE EAST; ATTACK TO THE WEST

"When the enemy command is in confusion, it will be unprepared for contingencies. The situation is like flood waters rising higher and higher; likely to burst the dam at any moment. When the enemy loses internal control, take the chance and destroy him."

—*From* The Thirty-Six Stratagems

Defense is commitment: It requires stationing armies, erecting barriers, and consigning assets. Forcing adversaries into defensive postures forces them into rigidity. Preparedness against one attack makes them vulnerable to another. So feigning one attack can increase the effectiveness of another genuine attack.

Key Elements

You feign an attack.

Your adversary responds to this false attack.

In responding to this attack, your enemy is exposed to your true attack.

You launch your true attack and defeat your adversary.

This pattern—feint east, attack west—is seen across all realms of competition. On the soccer field, a player pretends to shoot to the left; after the goalie has committed an airborne lunge in that direction, the attacker taps the ball into the right side of the net. In war, an army builds offensive force on one side and, after the opponent commits troops in defense, attacks an entirely different area. According to retired U.S. Marine Corps Brigadier General Samuel B. Griffith II, this tactic can be viewed as the central feature of guerrilla warfare.

Guerrilla tactics may be summarized by a four-character Chinese saying pronounced *Sheng Tung, Chi Hsi*, which mean "Uproar [in the East]; Strike [in the] West." Here we find expressed the all-important principles of distraction on the one hand and concentration on the other; to fix the enemy's attention and to strike where and when he least anticipates the blow.

This pattern appears less often in business, perhaps because it demands a level of secrecy difficult to maintain. But when executed correctly, it can be devastating.

Forcing the Competition to Expose Weakness
In the mid-1990s, John (who asked that his name and other key elements of this case be changed to avoid recognition) invested his savings and purchased a heating-fuel company. Soon thereafter he realized that the company faced a formidable competitive challenge. It had enjoyed a stable existence as the leading heating-fuel distributor in its small hometown (we will call this town Westville). Revenues were stable and sufficient to generate an attractive profit for its owners.

But history had moved on, and John's stable company was facing a new competitive threat that was eroding the company's revenue for the first time in years. Westville's neighbor was a far larger town called Middleville. The leading heating-fuel distributor in Middleville had squeezed out its local competition and was now seeking growth by crossing its former boundaries to try to win market share in Westville.

Had John been aware of this new competitive threat, he would have paid far less for his new company. But the transaction was complete. John needed to save his investment. John's obvious choices were (1) to defend by mounting a strong defense by bolstering his sales effort in Westville or (2) to launch a counterattack on his competitor's home turf of Middleville. But John chose neither option. Instead he focused his attention on Eastville, Middleville's other neighbor.

John had heard that a heating-fuel storage facility in Eastville was available for rent. Though he had barely enough cash to keep his business afloat in Westville and certainly insufficient capital to expand into a new, noncontiguous territory like Eastville, John leased this Eastville storage facility. He gambled that by leasing a facility he could not afford to use, he would save his company.

Heating-fuel distributors form a close-knit community, so it took little time for John's competitor to learn who had leased the East-ville storage facility. The implication of this news was obvious: John's company, the small heating-fuel distributor from Westville, was pre-paring to skip over Middleville and begin selling fuel in Eastville.

John's competitor had to respond. He needed to keep John out of Eastville for two reasons: he had to protect his business in East-ville where he had already started to expand, and he feared being hemmed in by John on two fronts. So to repel John's attack, this competitor strengthened his position in Eastville by redeploying his sales force across town.

But John's attack never came. His Eastville warehouse lay bare while John focused instead on his hometown, Westville. In the vacuum left by his competitor's redeployed sales force (salesmen had been moved from Westville to Eastville), John was able to grow. He recaptured his original market share and more. By the end of five years, John had nearly doubled his revenue and more than doubled its profitability. He later sold the company for far more than its original value.

By feigning a move into Eastville, John duped his competition into exposing itself to an attack in Westville. In this way he led a once-stable but then struggling company into a growth trajectory. John is not alone in misdirecting the competition with this strata-gem. Apple CEO Steve Jobs is known to throw off the market before a product launch by publicly scoffing at what he is secretly planning. Just one year before Apple launched an iPod that played video content, Steve Jobs told the press:

They love listening to music as a background activity . . . when they're exercising, when they are commuting and when they are just hanging out, and music is a wonderful thing because: A, it's music; and B, because it can be listened to as a background activity. And a lot of these other things that people are talking about building in such as video and things like that are foreground activities. You can't drive a car when you're watching a movie. You know? It's really hard doing that.[78]

"Attack him where he is unprepared. Appear where not expected."
—*Sun Tzu,* The Art of War[79]

Crossing a River, Luring a Leader, Ending a Siege

Two rival warlords, Yuan Shao and the great strategist Cao Cao, had been at war for many years. In AD 200, they prepared for what would be their decisive battle. Yuan Shao enjoyed two advantages in this battle. He occupied a superior position, and his forces outnumbered Cao Cao's.

Emboldened by his strength, Yuan Shao decided to cut off Cao Cao's supply lines, support, and escape route by attacking a small city called Baima at the rear of Cao Cao's forces (see Stratagem Ten, *Remove the firewood from under the pot*). He ordered enough soldiers to move against Baima so that Cao Cao's forces would be overwhelmed.

When Cao Cao heard of Yuan Shao's troop movement, he quickly assembled his advisors. They pondered his options but found few to choose from. If they moved to defend Baima, they would be far outnumbered and probably lose that battle. If they did not defend Baima, they would become crippled without supplies and support. They would have no chance against Yuan Shao.

Then one advisor suggested that Cao Cao pretend to attack Yuan Shao's old stronghold, Ye. Cao Cao understood how this move would play out and agreed.

Cao Cao led troops across the river toward Ye. When Yuan Shao heard of this incursion, he ordered half of his forces to turn back from their march toward Baima to return and defend against the imminent attack of Ye. After night set in, however, Cao Cao ordered his troops to change direction. They marched all night toward Baima.

The next morning, Yuan Shao arrived at Ye confused. He was prepared for battle but found no enemy. No one at Ye even knew an attack was coming.

That same morning, Cao Cao arrived at Baima with the troops he had redirected. His army now outnumbered the half that Yuan Shao had left to besiege Baima. He defeated Yuan Shao's forces, cut off their general's head, and saved the city.

Summary

Although they were strategists of different eras and scale, John and Cao Cao each used the same tactic to guide his adversary into an impossible situation. Each feigned an attack, the defense against which forced their adversaries to expose themselves to a second attack. By then launching this second attack, John removed a far larger competitor and Cao Cao saved a strategically important city from attack. Signal a false attack before you launch your true one.

"Appearance and intention inevitably ensnare people when artfully used, even if people sense that there is an ulterior intention behind the overt appearance. When you set up your ploys and opponents fall for them, then you win by letting them act on your ruse.

As for those who do not fall for a ploy, when you see they will not fall into one trap, you have another one set. Then, even if opponents have not fallen for your original ploy, in effect they actually have."

—*Yagyu Munenori*, The Book of Five Rings[80]

OPENLY REPAIR THE WALKWAY; SECRETLY MARCH TO CHEN CANG

"To pin down the enemy, expose part of your action deliberately, so that you can make a surprise attack somewhere else."

—*From* The Thirty-Six Stratagems

While their adversaries stare steadily at the orthodox path, the more creative companies and armies travel along the unorthodox path. Hannibal used this tactic when he crossed the Alps with elephants to steal the advantage and catch his Roman adversaries off-guard, Genghis Khan followed this practice regularly to surprise his opponents, and eight of the 100 most competitive companies of the decade used the same maneuver to ensure their success.

Key Elements

Your adversary is focused on a direct orthodox attack.

You launch an indirect unorthodox attack, crossing over a different border to your goal.

This unorthodox action, over an unexpected border, surprises your adversary.

You take the advantage.

Salesforce.com Secretly Marches onto Your Computer Screen

Marc Benioff, chair and CEO of Salesforce.com, showed from childhood a tendency toward the unorthodox path. In his teenage years in San Francisco, while his friends occupied their free time with sports, Benioff started a business producing and selling programs and games for the Commodore 64 computer. Long before his college peers at the University of Southern California had chosen the subjects they wished to major in, Benioff says, he had already decided he wanted to leave his mark on the computer industry. After graduating from university in 1986, he chose Oracle Corporation as the platform from which he could innovate.

Though Oracle was still considered a rebel by its peers, the company had grown into the world's second-largest software company. Benioff soon felt constrained. He spent his early career working on small PC and Internet-based businesses, none of which came to fruition. However, in 1996, a decade after joining Oracle, Benioff had an epiphany. While sitting at his desk surfing through Amazon.com, he found himself wondering why customers weren't able to access business software, such as that produced by Oracle, in the same way that customers of Amazon.com could access the shopping site via a Web browser. In the 1990s, it was quite common for software to be installed on company servers and computer desktops, yet Amazon.com users could access powerful technology without having to install anything. Why couldn't someone do the same thing for larger programs?

For the next three years Benioff persisted at Oracle, eventually becoming a senior vice president reporting directly to the company's chair, Larry Ellison. Despite his importance at Oracle during that time, Benioff's idea—that software could be delivered through a browser—was not embraced.

When a company restrains good ideas, the ideas usually win out in the end. In 1993, for example, an Oracle employee named Tom Siebel conceived the concept that came to be known as customer relationship management (CRM). He had recognized the potential of software to help companies automate and integrate their customer-facing processes. With one CRM solution, a company could efficiently find, win, and retain customers across diverse channels such as phone, fax, e-mail, and face-to-face interaction. By linking software used by the sales force with software used by the call center and the company's Internet engine, which tracks customer log-ins, for example, a company could get a full picture of one customer, regardless of when and how that customer interacted with the company. It is because of CRM software that the customer service representative helping on the phone knows that you requested technical help online last week and so may be following up on the same problem.

Rather than pursue his CRM idea through Oracle, Siebel left the company and cofounded his own, Siebel Systems, with Patricia House in 1993. Together they created the CRM market, which grew to $10 to $12 billion by 2005.

Benioff decided to follow Siebel's lead. Although he was not yet sure how he would capitalize on his vision, Benioff was nonetheless committed to it, and he left Oracle in 1999, embarking on a sabbatical to contemplate his options and form a plan. The year he returned he launched Salesforce.com, a service he created to help companies manage their sales forces more effectively, and that would, according to Benioff, put an "end to software" for good. Ironically, his decision to focus on sales force automation positioned him as a direct challenger to his fellow Oracle rebel, Siebel.

Benioff's approach to business was different from that of his competitors. For a start, he set up shop above a trendy restaurant in San Francisco, he often wears a Hawaiian shirt to work, and one of the company's most famous employees is its "Chief Love Officer," Benioff's golden retriever.

However, beneath these superficial differences lies a larger and more fundamental one. Microsoft, Oracle, SAP, Siebel, and other leading software companies all follow an orthodox path to the user, packaging software and loading customer databases on company-owned computers. Benioff did not fixate on this orthodox approach. As is often the case with highly competitive entrepreneurs, he recognized his competition was stuck, preoccupied with the expected, orthodox path. He used this insight to take his competition off-guard. He chose the unorthodox approach, crossing over to the customer in an entirely different way by putting the software and databases on Salesforce.com servers and allowing customers to access information through a Web browser.

As a result, Salesforce.com can adopt an entirely different fee model. For while Benioff's larger competitors sell multimillion-dollar software packages that take months to install, users of Salesforce.com need install nothing. Similarly, while Siebel and its peers charge companies large licensing fees, Salesforce.com charges a simple fee per user (currently about $65). This means that companies can decrease or increase their sales force automation cost in response to changes to their employee base. This is an attractive proposition when you consider that companies that are tied to a traditional software model must continue to pay heavy licensing fees to software companies, even if their business is suffering and they are being forced to lay off staff. With Salesforce.com those companies can simply pay for fewer users, providing instant cost savings.

This fee model also allows Salesforce.com to derive profits from those customers its competitors ignore. For while leading software companies focus their efforts on the "enterprise market" (generally companies with more that $1 billion in sales), Salesforce.com's flexible pricing model of $65 per user makes it an ideal package for smaller companies. Salesforce.com is able to serve such customers profitably because its servers and software are already paid for (and thus constitute sunk costs), so adding a new user costs close to nothing.

Salesforce.com's competitors have been slow to respond, perhaps because by copying Salesforce.com's Web-based model, Siebel and other large players would risk damaging the lucrative core of their business: selling and installing large software solutions. Even those companies that have developed lower-cost Web-based solutions have struggled to manage the awkward task of promoting such offerings while reassuring existing customers, who pay large licensing fees, that the Web-based offering is inferior to their chosen software.

By finding an unorthodox path to the customer, Salesforce.com has revolutionized the software business. Siebel, Salesforce.com's most direct competitor, hit financial difficulties and agreed to be sold to Oracle in 2005. Meanwhile Salesforce.com went public in 2003 and then grew 600 percent in the following three years, from $50 million in 2003 to $310 million in annual revenue in 2006. Its net income grew from a loss of $10 million to a gain of $30 million over the same period. While the scale of its competitor's figures may dwarf Salesforce.com's, the company is currently growing much faster than any major software company in its market. In the words of Marc Benioff, founder and CEO of Salesforce.com, "We will destroy Oracle and SAP because they won't be able to respond to the innovation we are about to unleash."[81]

The Circuitous March Eastward

In 207 BC, the Qin dynasty was in rebellion. Two rival rebel leaders struggled for control of Guanzhong, a strategically important kingdom of the Qin dynasty. One rebel leader, Liu Bang, had originally conquered the kingdom. But another stronger rebel leader, Xiang Yu, wanted the territory as well. Because Xiang Yu's forces outnumbered Liu Bang's, Liu Bang was forced to concede the kingdom.

Despite his capitulation, Xiang Yu remained wary of Liu Bang's ambitions. So he devised a plan to keep Liu Bang as far away from Guanzhong as possible. He divided the kingdom into eighteen parts and appointed Liu Bang as the leader of a remote area at the west end of the kingdom. To further insulate himself against Liu Bang's potential threat, he divided the area between the capital and Liu Bang's fiefdom into three parts and appointed three generals as leaders of each part. One of the fiefdoms was called Cheng Cang.

Liu Bang was already upset at having to give up the kingdom he initially conquered. He was now even angrier for being banished to a far corner of the region. As he and his soldiers marched out of Guangzhong's capital, one of his advisors suggested that they destroy the wooden road that connected their new home in the west with the capital. This would put Xiang Yu at rest by assuring him that Liu Bang had no intention of returning eastward to seek revenge. Liu Bang agreed, and so his soldiers destroyed roads and bridges as they traveled.

Once he established his new base, Liu Bang ordered his general to rebuild the army. When the army was so strong that Liu Bang felt it could defeat Xiang Yu's, he summoned his general. They discussed how best to march eastward and retake the kingdom. Two barriers stood in their way. First, three generals ruled the territory surrounding their new fiefdom that lay between them and the capital. Second, the wooden road that led to Xiang Yu was in ruins. However, Liu Bang and his general were wise men. They crafted a clever strategy to overcome, even draw strength from, these barriers.

Liu Bang ordered a contingent of men to set about rebuilding the wooden walkway. This impacted Liu Bang's adversaries in two ways. First, it put them off-guard. Liu Bang's work force was so small that it would take years for them to complete job—or so his adversaries thought. Second, his plan focused his enemies on the "obvious" path. Both Xiang Yu and the general of neighboring Cheng Cang saw that if Liu Bang ever did rebuild the walkway, they could easily block his attack by concentrating their forces at the mouth of the narrow passage.

But Liu Bang had no intention of using his walkway. His construction project was merely a diversion. He planned to attack Xiang Yu by a different, unorthodox route.

While his opposition watched the walkway, Liu Bang ordered his troops to attack Cheng Cang, his neighboring state. He surprised Cheng Cang's general and took the fiefdom. This move caught Liu Bang's adversaries off-guard and broadened Liu Bang's base of power. It laid the foundation for a campaign in which Liu Bang sequentially expanded his growing power base, defeating the states standing between him and Guangzhong's capital, until he reached Xiang Yu. Liu Bang ultimately won back control of Guangzhong, took command of the rebel movement, unified China, and became the founding emperor of the Han Empire.

Summary

Salesforce.com and Liu Bang found their adversaries focused on the orthodox path. They each capitalized on the opportunity their adversaries thereby presented, each crossing over an unexpected border, taking their adversaries by surprise, and seizing victory. This strategy has led numerous maverick companies to dominance. Dell's decision to bypass retailers and "go direct" to customers took computer firms by surprise and rocketed Dell from a one-man company operated out of a dorm room into a global computer leader seventeen years later. ING Direct has become the fastest-growing bank in the United States by similarly circumventing the traditional path to consumers. The bank operates no branches and instead serves customers exclusively over the Internet and by phone. By crossing an unorthodox border, you can often take your competition by surprise.

FOOL THE EMPEROR AND CROSS THE SEA

"The perception of perfect preparation leads to relaxed vigilance. Familiar sights lead to slackened suspicion. Therefore, secret machinations are better concealed in the open than in the dark, and extreme public exposure often contains extreme secrecy."

—*From* The Thirty-Six Stratagems

Every environment (e.g., market, sector, and industry) has background noise composed of everyday actions that attract no particular attention. Each day, for instance, realtors buy real estate, producers build factories, investors buy shares. In time, these familiar occurrences become background noise.

This background noise offers an opportunity, however, because in it, a company can hide its actions. It can weave a façade of normalcy around its adversaries and within, not behind the façade, execute its strategy. The tactic Disney used to acquire its land— hiding its actions in the open among everyday actions—is what the Thirty-Six Stratagems calls *Fool the emperor and cross the sea.*

Key Elements

Your adversary is vigilant.

You take actions that appear normal (i.e., that appear to be every-day actions).

Your adversary fixes his attention on this façade of normalcy. He does not see your true attack or intention.

You take your adversary.

This stratagem originates from the story of an emperor who refused to cross the sea despite his general's urging. The general ordered his soldiers to build large barges on the water and decorate them with dirt, trees, and military tents so that they appeared to be a normal encampment on solid ground. He then invited the emperor to enter the camp. As the emperor sat comfortably entertained inside a windowless tent, the barges were launched and navigated to another shore. The general fooled the emperor and crossed the sea. The core lesson here is that by making actions appear normal, you can hide your attack in the open and still not provoke a response from your adversary.

Hiding Action among "Normal Practices"

Industries tend to focus on a common set of variables to monitor competition. The television industry focuses on ratings; the pharmaceutical industry on new patents; and investors on transactions. If you are particularly careful not to disturb these variables, you can hide your actions in them. This is moving under the cover of stillness.

As an example, consider Krupp AG's 1991 acquisition of Hoesch AG in Germany. Throughout the 1980s, Krupp courted Hoesch with proposals of friendly mergers, all of which were rejected. Krupp nevertheless believed that a merger would be beneficial, perhaps even necessary, so it chose to pursue a more aggressive tactic. It decided to attempt to take over Hoesch by buying a controlling interest in the company.

Krupp knew, however, that Hoesch could easily mount an effective defense if it became aware of the plan. Krupp also knew that industry players would look for evidence of such takeover intentions in financial transactions, such as unusually concentrated purchases of Hoesch's stock. Therefore, the company had to find a way to hide its stock purchases and fend off a defensive response by Hoesch.

Both Krupp and Hoesch are German firms and, as such, practiced the "house bank" tradition, whereby a company maintains close ties with its primary bank. Typically, a German company's house bank is a significant shareholder in the company, sits on the company board, and is involved in upper-level management. In order to hide its actions, Krupp would have to deviate from this tradition. It did not inform its house bank or any of its major banks of the actions it was about take.

Over the course of six months, Krupp slowly and anonymously purchased Hoesch shares through a Swiss bank. Because the stock purchases appeared to be normal, everyday transactions, Krupp was able to collect 24.9 percent of Hoesch without triggering suspicion. By the time Krupp announced its holdings in October 1991, it was too late for Hoesch to defend itself effectively or for competitors to provoke a bidding war. Krupp successfully gained control of Hoesch by hiding its unusual actions behind a veil of normalcy.

The Walt Disney Company employed the same tactic when it purchased land for Disney World in the 1960s. Had landowners discovered that Disney was purchasing 30,000 acres of land in Florida, land prices would have risen quickly. By assembling the land from pieces purchased anonymously, Disney hid its intentions and avoided paying premiums.

Lulling an Opponent with Repetition

In the late 500s, the founder of the Sui dynasty defeated the northern kingdoms and decided to expand his successful military campaign south of the Yangtze River. He assigned a general named He Nuobi to lead his first southern effort: a siege of the Chen kingdom just across the Yangtze.

He Nuobi assembled an army and set up camp on the river's edge just opposite Chen's northern border. The Chen king ordered his troops to set up positions on the other shore in preparation for the attack. Both armies were poised for battle.

Soon, He Nuobi ordered his army to prepare for battle. At the sounds of the activity, the Chen army took their positions and prepared for an attack. The Sui army marched, drums beat, and dust rose into the air, but no attack came.

The Sui army was conducting maneuvers. These continued for several days. Eventually the Chen army grew weary of maintaining their vigilance. They grew accustomed to the sounds of war and stopped associating them with an attack.

He Nuobi had purchased boats and hidden them for just this moment. One evening, once he was sure he could move his troops without triggering a reaction from the Chen army, he quietly crossed the river. He and his soldiers reached shore at dawn and surprised the Chen forces. They easily defeated the Chen and established a foothold south of the Yangtze.

Summary

He Nuobi, Disney, and Krupp each outmaneuvered their opponent by hiding their actions within a façade of everyday occurrences. These occurrences incited no concern. Indeed, in each instance, they lulled the adversaries into inaction. By the time the adversaries realized they were being attacked, sold out, or acquired, or otherwise were giving up power, it was too late.

> *"The general who is skilled in defense hides in the most secret recesses of the earth; he who is skilled in attack flashes forth from the topmost heights of heaven."*
>
> —*Sun Tzu*, The Art War[82]

CREATE SOMETHING OUT OF NOTHING

"Design a counterfeit front to put the enemy off-guard. When the trick works, the front is changed into something real so that the enemy will be thrown into a state of double confusion. In short, deceptive appearances often conceal forthcoming danger."

—*From* The Thirty-Six Stratagems

When we play most simple games, like chess or football, we are limited to a fixed number of pieces and players. We cannot add new pieces to the board. In go, the Chinese and Japanese strategy board game, pieces can be added to the board but not moved. In chess, pieces can be moved but not added (you cannot, for example, pull a queen out of your pocket and continue playing with two queens). But real-world games, such as business, war, and politics, offer more freedom because pieces and players can be added and moved.

Real-world games are not closed systems; however, companies often overlook this fact. Business is often played as if it were chess or football. Companies do not usually think about adding new players to the board. This is why companies that break this unspoken rule surprise their competitors. While their competitors are thinking about what to do with the players on the field, creative companies introduce a brand-new player and change the game.

The Thirty-Six Stratagems calls the tactic of adding a new player to the game *Create something out of nothing*. Twelve of the 100 most competitive companies of the decade have used this stratagem in some form to gain strength.

Key Elements

Your direct attack (i.e., one using existing players) is ineffective.

You create a new player or entity.

This player or entity catches your adversary off-guard.

You, or the new player or entity, take your adversary.

"Things in the world arise of Existence, and Existence arises from Nonexistence."[83]

—*Lao Tzu*, Tao Te Ching

Outmaneuvering Resistance, Unlocking Growth

Reliance Industries of India was a common textile dealer—one of a thousand similar small ventures—that transformed itself into the country's largest private-sector company. It did so by "creating something out of nothing" at two critical turning points in its history.

The company's founder, Dhirajlal Hirachand Ambani, was born to a lower-middle-class family in a poor town in rural India. His father was a schoolteacher, but because his family could not afford to send him to university, Ambani was forced to choose a different career. At the age of sixteen, he took a job pumping gas. He applied himself to the gas retailing business for ten years, working his way up to a position as marketing manager.

But Ambani had greater aspirations; he wanted to start his own business. He rented an office (more accurately, a desk) for two hours a day and began trading anything he could get a margin on. His search for profit soon led him to textiles. Ambani jumped into the fray, battling hundreds of other small textiles traders seeking to match producers with buyers.

Ambani could have remained one of the countless traders, but he was able to create something his competitors could not. This set him apart and put him on a grand trajectory. As with most Indian industries, the textile business was dominated by a few large families. With the tacit cooperation of the Indian government, they dominated textile distribution and could demand low margins from traders like Ambani. Their presence, Ambani recognized, was hindering his growth.

While most traders were stuck thinking about how to better deal with these large distributors (i.e., trying to play using the pieces on the board), Ambani added a whole new piece to the game. He formed his own distribution business to sell his trading company's raw textiles and, later, even sold fashions he designed. His innovation changed the game, freeing him from the restraints of the large family-dominated buyers and allowing his growth to accelerate.

Ambani has successfully used this tactic again and again throughout his career, each time transforming the game to overcome an obstacle and unlock new growth. A few years later, for example, Ambani expanded into textile manufacturing. Because large Indian families blocked him from the capital he needed to build factories, he did something that was considered a radical maneuver at the time: he tapped the public financial markets by selling 2.8 million shares of his new company for $1.8 million. By issuing a new IPO, he sidestepped financial and manufacturing barriers, and a new manufacturing company was born from nothing. Ambani's manufacturing company soon dwarfed his original trading business, becoming one of India's largest textile producers.

Then, Ambani, joined by his sons, did twice more what had successfully transformed their business before.

Reliance had become India's largest producer of polyester and other synthetic products. Rather than share margins with the chemical companies that supplied Reliance with considerable raw materials, Ambani and his sons decided to enter the petrochemical business. In the 1990s, they opened a series of plants to produce the key raw materials they needed. Soon, the size of their petrochemical business rivaled Reliance's core textile business.

In the early 2000s, they realized they could leverage the expertise they had gained from producing chemicals to expand even further. They entered the petroleum business and produced some of the raw materials their petrochemical businesses depended on.

Petroleum refinement had always been a state-run activity; but in the late 1990s, it became clear that the state's petroleum operations were in trouble. Their reserves were running low, and they were not making the necessary investment in prospecting for new sources of oil. Reliance took advantage of this situation and began positioning itself to create a new oil company.

Reliance Refineries Private Ltd. came into being and built a gas distribution business, assembling a network of 1,000 gas stations. Ironically, the company was returning to its roots. Ambani had started his career in the gas distribution business years earlier as a gas pump attendant. When the Indian government was finally forced to liberalize the oil industry and allow private companies to produce and import oil, Reliance was well placed to take over. It won a large share of the government's bids to explore new fields, many of which proved unexpectedly large. One, for example, was the largest natural gas field discovered in India in decades.

By creating something out of nothing four times (a textile distributor, a textile manufacturer, a petrochemical producer, and an oil company), Reliance outmaneuvered growth barriers that blocked its peers and transformed itself into India's largest private-sector company. The company now generates annual revenues of $20 billion, 70 percent of which comes from its oil business, amounting to more than 3 percent of India's total gross domestic product.

Guerrillas

In 1937, Mao Tse-tung put down on paper his principles of guerrilla warfare in an influential book titled *On Guerrilla Warfare*. The principles outlined in his book proved powerful. By following them, his movement systematically captured land and power from the Chinese Nationalist government led by Chiang Kai-shek. Over the course of twelve years, the Communists routed the government and took control of the country.

Mao Tse-tung's guerrilla tactics were successful in part because they added new players to the game while his more orthodox and structured opponent maneuvered players already in the game.

When Mao Tse-tung's rebels set their targets on a new town, before taking up arms they launched a recruitment effort. Rebel teams walked the countryside to recruit, convert, and train local residents. These residents, in turn, recruited other residents, until eventually the rebels could count on an organized group of supporters.

Later, when the rebel forces launched their actual attack, they did so with a key advantage: a base of support to provide information and supplies. The town's leadership found itself battling an enemy it never expected. Its own citizens undermined the city's defense. In effect, Mao Tse-tung's rebels added a new opponent to the game before they engaged in battle.

Mao Tse-tung flustered his opponents, appearing in unexpected places. Using this principle, he was able to circumvent enemy lines by creating rebels behind them while attacking them. He repeated this pattern—recruit, build support, attack from inside and out—consistently and methodically until he routed the Nationalist government and seized control of the nation.

Summary

Your adversaries expect you to play with the pieces already on the board. They rarely think that you will introduce new pieces; so when you do, you take your adversary off-guard. By creating four new companies out of nothing, Reliance outmaneuvered its competitors and became India's largest private-sector company. Mao Tse-tung introduced a new enemy inside his enemy's town. Both surprised and outmaneuvered their targets.

HIDE A DAGGER BEHIND A SMILE

"One way or another, make the enemies trust you and thereby slacken their vigilance. Meanwhile, plot secretly, making preparations for your future action to ensure its success."

—*From* The Thirty-Six Stratagems

This stratagem rests on the same principles as Stratagem Twenty-Six, *The stratagem of injuring yourself*: A threatened adversary will resist, while a trusting one will not. In this case, however, instead of injuring yourself to appear weak, you adopt a helpful stance. Your "friendly" appearance, whether authentic or not, will avoid triggering competitive resistance. The Thirty-Six Stratagems terms this tactic *Hide a dagger behind a smile.*

Key Elements

A direct attack would generate resistance in your adversary.
You choose an approach that is, or appears to be, friendly.
Your adversary lets down defenses and welcomes this approach.
You advance unhindered.

The key goal of this stratagem is to convince your adversaries to lower their guard. In business, for example, companies are increasingly finding that taking a "friendly" stance toward the environment and society pre-empts costly resistance and leads to greater profits. In war, this may mean wielding "soft power," whereby rather than inducing your enemy into submission, you plant in him a desire to be part of you. The stratagem, of course, has a less honest side more aligned to its original meaning. You may feign "friendliness" to placate your enemy while hiding unfriendly intentions.

Google Smiles and Then Takes Over

By holding its smile before drawing its dagger, a small company can defer competition as it builds the strength to compete. Timing the switch from smile to dagger can transform David into Goliath. For example, by smiling for half a decade while it gathered strength, Google veered from the inevitable tracks laid by most Web upstarts. Instead of selling out to the Internet's behemoths, Google grew to rival them.

Google's founders, Larry Page and Sergey Brin, met at Stanford University, where they were both computer science graduate students. Though they did not initially get along, and argued over nearly every topic they discussed, they built a bond. About a year into their studies, they embarked together on a new research study. Their goal was to improve the effectiveness of online search engines.

At that time all search engines essentially looked for key words that matched their users' query and presented the results in a list. But as the Web grew and Web crawlers—programs that scan large portions of the Web and build an index—improved, the search results lengthened to the point of uselessness. Searches for common key words, for example, required users to scroll through hundreds of entries because search engines were ineffective at prioritizing their results.

So Brin and Page devised a new way to rank results. They assumed that if a Web page was linked by many other Web pages, it was probably important, so they designed an algorithm that measured links as votes and counted the number of Web pages between pages so, with some mathematical manipulation, they could measure the importance of every page on the Internet.

Their method, called PageRank, proved far more effective than those of existing search engines. Brin and Page decided to launch a business around their creation.

Their initial idea was to sell their technology to an existing search engine company. But these companies were not interested in improving their capabilities. Common wisdom among Internet experts was that searches offered no competitive advantage and that to survive, search companies needed to evolve into portals. As one CEO apparently explained to Brin and Page, "As long as we're eighty percent as good as our competitors, that's good enough. Our users don't really care about searching."[84]

The young entrepreneurs turned this initial cold response to their advantage. They launched a company that would take the search function away from the portals, who no longer wanted it.

In 1998 Brin and Page raised $1 million and moved out of their college dorms, where they had been running their project, into a garage. They launched a simple search engine called Google.com. That year they processed 10,000 queries per day and won recognition by *USA Today, PC Magazine*, and other major media publications as one of the most popular young Web sites.[85]

Despite a strong opening, Google remained small. Yahoo! was by far the most popular search engine, followed by a parade of other search engines, including AskJeeves and AltaVista. Google was last in popularity. To accelerate its growth, Google positioned itself as the back-end search provider to Web portals.

This position offered one major advantage. If Google could win Yahoo! as a customer, displacing Inktomi, the search engine Yahoo! was currently using, Google could instantly jump to the head of the line as the most popular search engine in the world. But to do this, Google would need to "smile." It would need to convince Yahoo! it posed no threat, and that it would be a valuable and loyal supporter.

Google made several strategic decisions that assuaged competitive fears. At a time when all search engines were using a new marketing tactic, banner advertising, to boost revenues, Google refused to accept banners. It refused to post any graphic ads at all, choosing instead to exclusively display simple text ads as part of its search results. Its homepage was also starkly different from any others. It was clean, composed of little more than a search window and logo.

Experts deemed Google's strategy flawed. Search engines had been evolving in precisely the opposite direction. AltaVista, for example, was successfully transforming its search engine into a portal. In 2000 AltaVista was the eighth most popular Web site, while Google was forty-eighth. Marc Krellenstein, chief technology officer of another leading search engine at the time, Northern Light, said, when asked about Google's strategy, "There isn't really good evidence, frankly, that companies focused purely on search, as Google has been, can support themselves with that model."[86] A 2000 *BusinessWeek* article warned that "when the whip comes down and shareholders start to demand a return on their investment, Google may have to swallow its scruples—particularly if it hopes to keep banner ads off its pages."[87] But Google endured the criticism. By sticking to its seemingly illogical strategy and keeping banner ads off its pages, Google was able to position itself as a helper rather than a threat to Yahoo! and other portals.

Yahoo! began as a search site or, more precisely, a search index. But it had evolved into a media company and was no longer seriously interested in search. Over the three years leading up to 2000, it had signed numerous deals with media-content providers, including Hallmark, NBC, Comedy Central, and A&E Television. Its strategy was to expand its online advertising expenditures, 7 percent at the time, by focusing on three priorities: building brand equity, providing high quality content and services, and ensuring wide distribution for its media franchise. Searching was not a priority, which is why Yahoo! had begun outsourcing its search services in 1996. The Google search engine was designed to fit neatly into this new strategy.

June 26, 2000, was a pivotal day for Google. On that day Yahoo! announced it would replace its current online search provider, Inktomi, with Google. Practically overnight Google became the most popular search engine in the world.

Google's newfound strength was insufficient to rouse competitive resistance. Even Inktomi, the company Google had ousted from Yahoo!, saw its loss with some indifference. Dick Pierce,

Inktomi's chief operating officer, argued that the loss would have "little impact with respect to profitability."[88]

The search function was a low-margin business. As a CNET analyst wrote in 2000, "The search market in general, meanwhile, remains a low-margin, commodity business."[89] A friendly, if apparently naïve, Google circled the world to take this commodity activity off the plates of richer rivals. It became Latin America's premier search engine in 2001 through a partnership with Universo Online (UOL) and that same year signed an agreement with Lycos Korea to bring Google to Asian Internet users. In just two years, Google solidified its search dominance.

But behind its "smile," Google had developed a service that would soon threaten its media partners' core businesses. AdWords was a self-service program that allowed advertisers to place ads on Google's search results in a matter of minutes with just a credit card. Those who had initially questioned Google's business model had not yet understood AdWords' potential.

Google launched a simple version of AdWords the same year it signed its landmark deal with Yahoo! At the time it was handling more than 100 million search queries per day. Over the next several years it maintained its position as an unthreatening search partner while it simultaneously evolved AdWords. As Google signed deals with more portals, it converted AdWords into a cost-per-click model and introduced a bidding system for advertisers.

By 2003 it had become clear that AdWords was beginning to attract advertisers away from Yahoo! and other online media companies. As Google's share of the online advertising market grew, Yahoo! realized the threat Google posed. In 2003, a year after renewing its original deal with Google, Yahoo! pulled its search activities away from its former partner. It purchased two Internet search services—Inktomi for $235 million and Overture for $1.6 billion—and decided to run its search activities on its own.

But by then Google had already built a dominant position in search. As of 2006, Google manages over 50 percent of all Internet searches and sells advertising on each one. By being careful not to draw its dagger too early, Google convinced its future competitors to help the company build a leading search position. It displaced once larger adversaries to emerge as the dominant search and online advertising option.

The Japanese Become American

To stave off the unexpected success of Japanese cars in the United States, the big three U.S. car manufacturers appealed to consumers' national pride. They launched a "Buy American" campaign.

Japanese manufacturers needed to devise a strategy for countering this campaign, for deflating the resistance to Japanese cars that was building among U.S. consumers. The obvious responses—increasing marketing spending, launching a countercampaign—might further agitate consumers.

So instead of attacking the "Buy American" campaign directly, Japanese car manufacturers simply became more American. They opened manufacturing plants in the United States and increased the number of American jobs supported by their car sales. When GM advised a consumer to Buy American, that consumer would consider buying a Toyota Corolla. Japanese car manufacturers pacified their adversaries' resistance by becoming friendly. The strategy worked so successfully, Japanese car manufacturers continued it, never dropping their smile. They continued the slow shift toward becoming friendly Americans. They raised revenues and profits while they increased their employment of U.S. workers. In 2007, Toyota eclipsed GM as the largest car manufacturer in the world. Figuratively, this was the point at which Toyota drew its dagger.

An Old Friend's Smile

In 342 BC, the states of Qin and Wei were at war. The king of Wei was worried. His army had recently lost a battle. It was weak, and its morale was low. It was in no condition to engage the 50,000 Qin soldiers marching toward one of Wei's cities. The king wanted to avoid battle, so he assembled his advisors to study his options.

One of his ministers offered a bloodless plan. As a boy, he had known the Qin general who was now in charge of the approaching army. He believed he could appeal to this friendship and persuade the general to call off his siege. The king of Wei approved his plan and charged his minister with defending the threatened Wei city. The minister rushed off to take his position in the city waiting for the approach of the Qin army.

When the Qin general arrived with his troops, he learned that his old boyhood friend, the minister, was in charge of the city's defenses and that he wanted a meeting to negotiate peace. The general chose his response carefully. He was not interested in peace, but he did not want to reveal this. As long as the city believed that peace was an option, their defenses would remain loose. If they felt that an attack was imminent, they would stay behind well-fortified walls, making the siege more costly. So the Qin general warmly welcomed his old friend's proposal.

Three days later, the two friends met at a designated location. To prove his good intentions, the Wei minister brought only 300 soldiers with him. The Qin general, to display his warm intentions, invited the entire Wei party to a banquet.

At the banquet, the Qin general and the Wei minister drank and ate together as one would expect of boyhood friends. But before the banquet ended, Qin soldiers kidnapped the Wei minister and his soldiers. They stole their captives' uniforms and marched toward the city disguised as Wei soldiers. When they arrived, the city's guards opened the gates, believing them to be the Wei minister and his party returning from their negotiations. The Qin soldiers rushed in and took control of the unsuspecting city.

By appearing pleasant, the Qin general was able to keep his adversary off-guard. He moved into the opening that this tactic created to defeat his adversary quickly, efficiently, and nearly bloodlessly.

Summary

The Qin general and Google each benefited from appearing friendly to their adversaries. Because they seemed nonthreatening, their adversaries offered no resistance. Companies are increasingly embracing this tactic as a long-term strategy. Nearly 10 percent of the most competitive companies in the world cite a friendly stance as central to their success.

DECK THE TREE WITH BOGUS BLOSSOMS

"Use deceptive appearances to make your troop formation look more powerful than it is. When wild geese soar high above, the grandness of their formation is greatly enhanced by the display of their outstretched wings."

—*From* The Thirty-Six Stratagems

To succeed against a stronger competitor, creative companies coordinate with their environments to build power. They form networks of alliances that together are stronger than their parts. A bee is a bother, but a swarm can be dangerous. A buffalo is no match for a lion, but a herd is safe. The Thirty-Six Stratagems terms this tactic *Deck the tree with bogus blossoms.*

Key Elements

You are too weak to attack your adversary alone.

You coordinate individual elements within your organization or in your environment.

Coordinated, these parts become a much stronger whole.

You are now strong enough to defeat your adversary.

Fighting Goliath

Microsoft is battling competitors across multiple fronts, competitors that are creating a network of alliances to contain their powerful adversary. In 2001, for example, about ten years after Microsoft toppled Britannica using Stratagem Three, *Invite your enemy onto the roof, then remove the ladder*, an unusual player entered the encyclopedia market.

Jimmy Wales and Larry Sanger had been working for Nupedia, a Web-based encyclopedia that provided free content reviewed and edited by experts. Nupedia was innovative in that it delivered its content exclusively via the Web, not CD-ROM or print, and it gave its content away for free.

But organizationally it differed little from its competitors. It maintained a network of subject experts who applied a seven-step review process. The process was about as slow, and the resulting content as stale, as any other encyclopedia.

On January 10, 2001, however, Nupedia added a new feature: an open encyclopedia that users could edit without the burden of expert review. This had the potential to unlock an ocean of content, as almost any user could submit articles, and an encyclopedia that changed daily, since this service would require no review process.

Contributors spontaneously organized to build content. By the end of its first year, the new service, called Wikipedia, grew to approximately 20,000 articles in 18 language editions. By the end of 2002, it expanded into 26 language editions, 46 by the end of 2003, and 161 by the end of 2004. By the end of 2006, Wikipedia, now a standalone business that absorbed its former parent Nupedia, wielded an army of over 4,500 "active editors" (those who do the bulk of the editing) who offer over 5 million articles in 229 language editions.[90] Its English-language edition offers more than 1.4 million articles compared with about 100,000 for Britannica and 68,000 for Microsoft's Encarta.[91]

By efficiently coordinating millions of individuals, Wikipedia has been able to replicate and arguably exceed the power of better-funded rivals. This pattern of competition—coordinating individual elements—has exposed Microsoft to another threat: open-source software.

The advantages of open-source software parallel the advantages of Wikipedia closely. Open-source software allows open communities of programmers to access, edit, and use software for free. In return, users agree to make their work—from debugging to developing entirely new utilities—available to the community for free. This arrangement cuts down development time considerably and multiplies the library of software available to developers by giving them access to a vast community of contributors.

While experts believe open-source software is unlikely to oust Microsoft from its position atop the software industry because of the company's impressive installed base, open source has been steadily gaining market share.

Ironically, Microsoft pursues the same tactic of coordinating the parts into a stronger whole, but it uses company-owned assets rather than adversaries in a coalition. As described earlier, the company coordinates its products so that they support each other. By bundling its software products and ensuring that they are compatible with each other, Microsoft creates a more valuable network of products.

Similarly, in 1998, a group of handset makers that included Nokia, Ericsson, and Motorola teamed up to create a new company, Symbian. Over the years, they had seen what Microsoft did to IBM—take control of a key lucrative component (the operating system)—and did not want their handsets to suffer the same fate. If Microsoft were to dominate the cell-phone operating system market as it does the market for computer operating systems, handsets would become commodities with little more margin than personal computer clones. Individually, none of the companies in the Symbian alliance have the cash or software competency to compete with Microsoft. But by coordinating their efforts, they were able to capture a 75 percent market share of handset software, effectively containing Microsoft's inroads into that market.

Bull Warriors

During the Warring States period (475–221 BC), five states joined forces against Qi. Unable to resist such uneven odds, Qi lost more than seventy cities during the course of five years, until only two cities remained. Both cities were surrounded. One was under the command of the capable general, Tian Dan.

Tian Dan knew that he was outnumbered and could not defeat his attackers with orthodox methods. Without a brilliant plan, he would remain trapped until his people either surrendered or died of hunger. So he analyzed his nonmilitary assets and wondered how he could coordinate them until they were powerful enough to break his enemy's encirclement.

He identified two useful nonmilitary assets: He had people— women, children, and the elderly—who were not slated for military duty, and he possessed more than a thousand bulls.

Tian Dan made three decisions. First, he ordered the children and elderly to guard the city walls and ordered the women to enroll in the military. Second, he had the bulls outfitted for battle. He ordered them covered with silk sheets painted in colorful patterns with knives fastened to their horns and oil-soaked straw bundles tied to their tails. Third, he collected gold from the citizens. Then he asked a group of wealthy men to bring the money to his enemy's general. They delivered the message that the city was about to fall and the general was requested not to take their wives and children. This third order put his enemy off-guard. The enemy soldiers celebrated their pending return home, and then they slept soundly.

That night, however, after his enemy's soldiers had fallen asleep, Tian Dan executed his plan. He had the oil-soaked straw bundles that were tied to the bulls' tails lit and released the bulls outside the city walls, where they ran wild. The enemy soldiers woke up to find themselves under attack by strange ferocious beasts. Many fled for their lives. Tian Dan then ordered his soldiers to march on the enemy forces. They could do this in greater numbers because women fought with them while the elderly citizens and children guarded the city walls.

Tian Dan's bewildered enemy fell. His city was saved. This triumph marked the beginning of a series of victories for Qi that led to the state recovering the cities that had been lost, returning Qi to its former splendor.

Summary

Sun Tzu repeatedly reminds us that power (*Shih*) is a result of formation and relationship not resources. A rock seems stronger than human flesh because it holds its form more tightly. Human beings can easily walk through air because flesh seems stronger than air. But when coordinated properly (e.g., when rushing down a ravine), water can move rocks. Sun Tzu points to "the rush of water, to the point of tossing rocks about. This is *shih*."

By coordinating individual parts in their environments (e.g., alliance partners, contributors), innovative companies and strategists are able to approximate the power of much larger adversaries. They transform themselves from bees to a swarm, from one buffalo to a herd of buffalos.

TO CATCH THE BANDITS, CAPTURE THEIR LEADER

"Capture their chief, and the enemy will collapse. His situation will be as desperate as a sea dragon fighting on land."

—From The Thirty-Six Stratagems

Creative and competitive companies pull levers that other companies do not consider. For example, to influence a competitor, they often save energy by going directly to their competitors' leadership. This is like leading a horse by directing its head. In The Thirty-Six Stratagems, this tactic is known as *To catch the bandits, first capture their leader.*

Key Elements

You face a persistent adversary.

You identify your adversary's leader or leaders.

You understand how the leader(s) interests differ from those of the organization.

You directly influence this leader or these leaders.

Your adversary's leadership brings your adversary's organization into compliance.

Turning Murdoch's Head to Capture DirecTV

This tactic is used most often during acquisition battles. When company A wants to acquire company B, it can either offer the highest bid or it can offer an incentive tailored to the interests of company B's owners. When the owners' incentives differ from the company's, this second approach can be less costly.

Consider the battle between two media moguls for the satellite television company, DirecTV. Rupert Murdoch, chair of the $68 billion media conglomerate News Corp, and John Malone, chair of Liberty Media, fought for control of DirecTV. One out-thought the market to win the battle; the other found his adversary's Achilles' heel and won the war.

Murdoch and Malone met at an industry gathering in 1983 and immediately struck up a friendship as two conservative outsiders in an industry dominated by liberals. Their friendship flourished in a decade-long series of collaborations.

In 1991, when Murdoch was facing a crisis with creditors, Malone was one of the first to buy convertible bonds from News Corp. This sign of confidence by an industry leader encouraged others to buy News Corp debt and contributed to Murdoch's avoiding bankruptcy.

Malone again evidenced his allegiance twelve years later when both media moguls coveted DirecTV. They each approached DirecTV's owner, General Motors, but lost out to a $19 billion bid from EchoStar, a pay-TV company. The EchoStar deal, facing tough opposition from the Department of Justice and the Federal Communications Commission, eventually fell through, leaving DirecTV again up for sale. Malone and Murdoch jointly bid for the company.

The following year, however, it became clear that their joint bid would fail. Malone and Murdoch faced two choices for winning control: They could compete with each other or one would need to step aside.

Malone wanted DirecTV badly. It represented a critical piece in his media puzzle because it would enable him to distribute his content across the country. But Malone seemed to place friendship above profit. He backed out of the battle and conceded the

DirecTV prize to Murdoch. In December 2003, News Corp purchased DirecTV for $6.78 billion, adding 12 million subscribers to Murdoch's empire.

Malone, however, had not given up on the prize. He knew what Murdoch cared about most and believed that by using this leverage he could convince News Corp to sell him DirecTV at a discount.

Murdoch was seventy-three years old when he bought DirecTV and was concerned with his empire's succession. With 30 percent of News Corp's voting shares, Murdoch effectively controlled the company, and he wanted to make sure that when he passed on his ownership to his three children, the Murdoch family would maintain its control. Malone knew that continued family control would be a higher priority for Murdoch than DirecTV. So Malone forced Murdoch to choose between the two.

Over the years, Malone had acquired 9 percent of News Corp. He was the company's second-largest shareholder behind his friend. Murdoch might have felt threatened by such a large shareholder and acted to guard his control, but the two were allies. Murdoch felt he could rely on Malone's support.

In 2004, however, Murdoch began getting nervous about his friend's intentions. That year, Malone doubled his stake in News Corp to 17 percent. Murdoch adopted a poison pill to protect himself against Malone. News Corp created a provision that allowed the company to issue new shares, holding Malone's ownership share to 18 percent. News Corp essentially made it prohibitively expense for Malone to increase his level of control. But the defense was not a permanent solution and upset other shareholders.

In 2006, News Corp and Liberty Media began discussions to avert a clash. Murdoch wanted to secure his family's continued control. Malone wanted what he had always wanted: DirecTV. The two agreed that News Corp would retire Liberty's 19 percent voting stake in News Corp. In exchange, Malone would receive News Corp's 39 percent stake in DirecTV as well as $550 million in cash and three regional sports networks owned by News Corp. All in all, Malone received $11 billion in assets for his 19 percent of News Corp.[92]

Many News Corp investors were displeased with the deal. They felt that Malone would have paid a multi-billion-dollar premium if forced to buy News Corp's DirecTV stake under different circumstances. But Murdoch controlled News Corp and was able to direct the company to accept the swap, despite investor discontent. By swapping DirecTV for Malone's shares rather than selling it outright, Murdoch increased his family's share in the company to 40 percent.[93] By playing on the discrepancies between Murdoch's priorities and those of News Corp's shareholders, Malone won the DirecTV prize.

Extinguishing a Siege with One Arrow

In AD 756, a city in China's Zhenyuan district was under siege by rebels. The governor of this district was able to hold off the rebels' attacks but unable to turn away the persistent attackers. The governor needed to extinguish the siege permanently, so he decided to implement the stratagem *To catch the bandits, capture their leader.*

One night, while the rebel army was sleeping, the governor led a surprise attack. His soldiers poured out of the city gates, surprised the rebel soldiers, and killed many of them. In the chaos of battle, however, the governor could not identify the rebel leader. He did not want to claim victory until the leader was found, because if he did, the rebel siege would continue.

To identify the rebel leader, he ordered his archers to use tree branches instead of arrows. The rebels believed by this action that the governor's forces had run out of arrows. Encouraged, the rebels reorganized for a counterattack. They assembled around one particular warrior—their leader.

As the rebels prepared for a counterattack, their leader mounted his horse and moved toward the front lines. But before the new battle began, the governor ordered one of his best archers to take aim with a real arrow, not a branch. This arrow hit the rebel leader in his left eye. Immediately losing his will to fight, he ordered a retreat.

Summary

When your adversary's leader holds an agenda different from that of his or her organization, you can save energy by focusing your attack on the leader. By focusing exclusively on Murdoch's interests, Malone won DirecTV; by aiming one arrow at his adversary's leader, the governor of Zhenyuan forced an entire army to retreat. One arrow aimed directly at your adversary's leadership can achieve what a barrage of arrows cannot.

THE STRATAGEM OF LINKING STRATAGEMS

"When the enemy possesses a superior force, do not attack recklessly. Instead, weaken him by devising plots to bring him into a difficult position of his own doing. Good leadership plays a key role in winning a war. A wise commander gains Heaven's favor."

—From The Thirty-Six Stratagems

Each stratagem, when correctly chosen and executed, can cause dramatic shifts in power, giving its wielder temporary advantage over her adversaries. But ambitions—in politics, war, or business—are longer lasting. Moving from a temporary advantage to a longer-lasting or even permanent advantage involves implementing a stream of linked stratagems. The most competitive companies of the decade each implemented at least three stratagems to outperform their peers. Some launched as many as fifteen. When artfully constructed and incessantly executed, this stream of stratagems will keep your competition off balance and make you a player few can challenge.

Key Elements

Rather than execute one strategy, you execute many (simultaneously or in succession).

If one strategy is not effective, the next one is. If the next one is not effective, the following one is.

Your adversary is eventually overwhelmed or caught in an impossible situation, then falls.

"When able to attack, we must seem unable; when using our forces, we must seem inactive; when we are near, we must make the enemy believe we are far away; when far away, we must make him believe we are near.

"Hold out baits to entice the enemy. Feign disorder, and crush him.

"If he is secure at all points, be prepared for him. If he is in superior strength, evade him.

"If your opponent is of choleric temper, seek to irritate him. Pretend to be weak, that he may grow arrogant.

"If he is taking his ease, give him no rest. If his forces are united, separate them.

"Attack him where he is unprepared, appear where you are not expected."

—*Sun Tzu,* The Art of War[94]

This mode of competition, in which companies attack adversaries with multiple stratagems, each delivering a temporary advantage, is what Richard D'Aveni termed *hypercompetition.* The aim in hypercompetition is to "hit the competitor from several different directions at once. These approaches leave the competitor harassed or stunned."[95]

As the cases in this book show, the most competitive companies maintain their long-term advantage not by executing one superior strategy, not by holding onto a permanent advantage, but rather by unleashing a series of moves (or stratagems) that keep their competition off balance. The sheer number of stratagems they execute and the pace at which they do so ensures that while some moves fail, in aggregate these highly competitive companies stay ahead of their peers.

Selling Music?

Many credit the iPod's success to Apple's creative ethic. Unconventional design choices—a flywheel, no on/off switch—surely made for a radically aesthetic product. Inventive marketing practices such as highlighting the iPod's white earphones, instead of the device itself, surely contributed to the generation of early buzz about the product.

But a careful dissection of the iPod's rise reveals numerous stratagems at work. Steve Jobs' creativity extended beyond the technology and into the business. Apple built and launched a set of interlocking strategies that deflated competitive resistance. If you had wanted to compete with iPod when it was launched, consider what you would have had to contend with:

- If you were Sony, you'd have been stuck with a conflicting agenda. Your consumer electronics group would have wanted to introduce a hard drive–based MP3 player like the iPod, but your entertainment business would have resisted. This is Stratagem Seventeen, *Seize the opportunity to lead the sheep away*.
- If you had been open to introducing a hard drive–based player, you would have been unable to match the iPod's size, because Apple had secured exclusive rights to a new hard drive capable of storing more songs in less space than previously possible. There would also have been music content that you could not have made available in your online music store because Apple had secured exclusive rights to some music content. This is Stratagem Ten, *Remove the firewood from under the pot*.
- Even if you could have gotten your hands on a small hard drive, you would have been forced to battle Apple on two fronts. Apple initially marketed the iPod only to consumers who owned an Apple computer (the iPod was initially compatible only with the Mac). Unless you had had a similarly strong business to link to your device, you would have faced unfair odds. This is Stratagem Seven, *Besiege Wei to rescue Zhao*.
- You would have to struggle to secure a music library as large as that which Steve Jobs rapidly lined up by his effective use of

Stratagem Six, *Kill with a borrowed knife*: He convinced music labels to give his iTunes music store a robust music catalog by using the threat of illegal digital music–sharing sites.

- If you had been able to launch a successful competing product, Apple would have made sure you remained on shaky ground by repeatedly implementing Stratagem Twenty, *Let the plum tree whither in place of the peach*, because the company is comfortable cannibalizing its products to prevent competitors from doing so first. In January 2004 Apple launched the iPod Mini, a lower-cost alternative to the iPod. One year later, in January 2005, it launched the Shuffle, an even smaller and less-expensive alternative. In September 2005 Apple replaced the Mini with the Nano. This was followed one month later by the Video iPod. Keeping pace with Apple is tiring.

Apple sets up a long line of barriers for its competitors to surmount. It continues to erect them, ensuring that its competitors' success comes only after considerable persistence and creativity.

Selling Software?

Microsoft, long an Apple rival, has grown as a result of a competitive ethic not unlike Apple's. Microsoft, of course, has succeeded on a greater scale than Apple. It executes multiple creative strategies across value chains, markets, and levels (from corporate strategy to operating tactics).

The company's core strategy is Stratagem Seven, *Besiege Wei to rescue Zhao*, which takes the form of one business contributing to the success of another (e.g., Windows contributing to the success of Microsoft's ISP, MSN). But Microsoft executes multiple strategies around this core strategy to confuse, frustrate, and outmaneuver its opponents.

- If you are profitable, Microsoft may sacrifice its own profits to win consumer loyalty, forcing you to give up your profits as well (Stratagem Two, *Exchange a brick for a jade*).

- If you beat Microsoft to market with an innovation, Microsoft may reveal its intention to soon make a similar innovation, thus drying up your supply of customers and investors (Stratagem Twenty-One, *The stratagem of the open city gates*).
- If you do launch your innovation successfully, Microsoft may let you proceed, and then launch a competing product only after you have proven your innovation to be successful (Stratagem One, *To catch something, first let it go*).
- If you command an advantage in your market, Microsoft may force you to play a different game, one it knows it can win (Stratagem Three, *Invite your enemy onto the roof, then remove the ladder*).
- If you are competing for distribution, Microsoft may use its cash to build influence over distributors, as it did to influence retailers (Stratagem Thirteen, *The stratagem of the beautiful woman*).
- Even if you win a battle, Microsoft may persist, launching small incursions that build its knowledge of your market and that incrementally erode your lead, until it overtakes you (Stratagem Fourteen, *Beat the grass to startle the snake*).

Competing with Microsoft or Apple demands agility. Both are examples of opponents that will come at you from multiple directions and will keep rising from the mat until you are too overwhelmed to keep up.

Designer Stratagems
Linking stratagems also means combining stratagems to create entirely new ones. This will gives you the power to generate nearly endless streams of moves. As Sun Tzu wrote, combining tactics can give rise to "an endless series of maneuvers. . . . It is like moving in a circle—you never come to an end. Who can exhaust the possibilities of their combination?"[96]

As an example, consider the "disruption" strategy heavily promoted by business strategists today: pursuing an approach that competitors will not copy because copying it would expose them to attack from other players in the market. This is the explanation often given for the successes of strategically innovative companies such as Southwest Airlines and Ikea, the furniture-store chain.

The Thirty-Six Stratagems would explain this strategy as being a combination of two stratagems: Stratagem Twenty-Nine, *Clamor in the east; attack to the west*, and Stratagem Six, *Kill with a borrowed knife*. First, attack your competitor in such a way that, in defending himself, he exposes himself to another attack (*Clamor in the east; attack to the west*). Then, rather than attacking your exposed competitor, let other players attack him (*Kill with a borrowed knife*).

If your competitor defends himself, he will be attacked by other players in his industry, weakening him and potentially forcing him to call off his defense against you. If your competitor decides that this makes it not worth defending against your incursion, you can move in unhindered. Either way, you win. If your competitor defends himself, he exposes himself to attack from *other* competitors.

The Generals' Three Strategies

The prince of Chu was being held prisoner by the state of Qi when his father died. He naturally wanted to return home to claim his throne. But the king of Qi demanded a high price for his freedom: The prince of Chu, soon to be the king of Chu, would have to give up great stretches of Chu's eastern lands to the kingdom of Qi. The prince reluctantly agreed.

After returning to his home and taking the throne, the new king of Chu faced a dilemma. A regiment of Qi soldiers had approached the Chu border, demanding that the king make good on his promise and surrender the eastern lands. The king was unsure how to deal with his promise—whether or not to fulfill. So he summoned three of his generals to ask their advice.

The first general believed the king's only option was to give up the land and later attempt to recapture it. He argued that a king's ability to rule depends on his reputation. If the king proved his word to be of no value by refusing to give up the eastern lands, his authority would be jeopardized. This general offered to travel to the Qi regiment on the Chu border and surrender the land.

The second general argued that the king should defend the land at any cost because it was too large a parcel to give up. The state's strength depends on its size, so giving up so much would be a disservice to the king's people even if it cost him some face. The general offered to lead troops to defend Chu's eastern borders.

The third general argued that Chu should seek an ally to help defend the land. He agreed with the second general that the land was too large to give up but feared Chu was too weak to prevent Qi from taking it. He offered to lead a diplomatic mission to a large neighboring state, Qin, to request help defending Chu's eastern land.

The king thanked the generals for their advice and dismissed them. He thought about his three options and decided not to choose among them. Rather, he decided to pursue them all.

The next day, the king ordered the first general to do as he had suggested and travel to the Qi regiment waiting on the Chu border. He was to announce to them Chu's intention to give up the land as promised. The general was pleased and left with a contingent of soldiers.

The following day, the king told the second general that he agreed with that general's advice; the land was too high a price to pay for keeping a king's word. He ordered this general to follow his own suggestion and lead troops toward Chu's eastern border to prepare to defend against an attack from Qi.

On the third day after his initial consultation with the three generals, the king told the third general to do as that general had suggested, and to lead a diplomatic mission to neighboring Qin to request assistance. This general assembled a small mission and set off for Qin.

The Qi were confused by the mixed messages they were getting from Chu's actions. One Chu general had approached them to surrender the land. But a day later, a second general was preparing to defend it. They decided it was time to bring certainty to their situation, so they sent for reinforcements and planned to take Chu's eastern lands by force.

When Qi's reinforcements arrived, the king of Qi was with them. He had planned to lead his army into battle himself.

As Qi's and Chu's forces lined up opposite each other and prepared to converge, the third general appeared. He was escorting Qin troops, led by a Qin general, who was ready to join forces with Chu.

Outnumbered, the king of Qi called off his attack. The Chu's eastern lands were preserved.

Summary

Just as Microsoft and Apple keep their adversaries off balance and win more consistently by unleashing multiple initiatives, the king of Chu confused his adversary (the king of Qi) and put multiple chances of winning in place by simultaneously executing three strategies. By launching multiple initiatives, you become more difficult to handle. By combining different stratagems to create entirely new ones, you become almost impossible to predict.

THE THIRTY-SIX STRATAGEMS AS PROBLEM-SOLVING TOOLS

This book proposes that all competitive interactions consist of only a limited number of patterns. Identifying these patterns requires significant time for research and synthesis. Luckily the thirty-six stratagems already represents such an effort. The process that created the text is identical to the one academics would undertake to identify the fundamental patterns of competition: Study cases, find common patterns, narrow them until you can add or remove no more (i.e., the patterns explain every case you can find, and you cannot combine any two patterns). The Thirty-Six Stratagems, then, represent a thousand-year-long research study of competition. Its conclusion is that there are only thirty-six patterns of competition.

Through your experience, you have learned a set of patterns. To navigate competitive challenges you consistently return to them. But because your experience is small relative to the thousand years the thirty-six stratagems represents, you have a limited number of patterns. By applying the stratagems, you learn new moves, you stock your reservoir, and you evolve into a more creative strategist.

This section will walk you through a simple process for using the stratagems as tools to solve immediate everyday problems. The CEO of a technology company used the stratagems to prepare for a negotiation. By spending one hour plotting his strategy with a few stratagems, he saw negotiating maneuvers he would otherwise have overlooked. One of these maneuvers won him a multimillion-dollar account with one of the largest travel Web sites. The regional head of a leading technology firm was struggling to expand revenue. When he looked at his challenge through the stratagem *Exchange a brick for a jade*, he saw an opportunity to trade internal information with key distributors. His program tripled his revenues over three years and was then copied by divisions of his company throughout the world.

Here is a simple approach to applying stratagems as templates to structure brainstorming in order to systematically generate creative, out-of-the-box strategies or solutions to your problems.

Step One: Define the Problem

To ensure that your problem-solving process remains focused and efficient, you must clearly articulate the problem you want to solve. This requires defining five elements:

1. Current situation
2. Current trajectory
3. Long-term aspiration
4. Desired trajectory
5. Key players

Defining the current situation means briefly describing what brought you to the problem at hand. It should be complete but brief (one sentence). Here are some examples:

- We are meeting with a key potential client tomorrow
- A new player has entered our market and is eroding our market share.
- Growth is slowing in our market.
- My initiative is being blocked by the XYZ department.

Defining your current trajectory means to honestly assess what is likely to happen if you execute your current strategy or plan (e.g., "We will not win the account now but will be invited to join a competitive bid," or "Our market share will continue to decline by 5 percent per year"). Ideally your trajectory is uninspiring but not dramatically so.

Defining your long-term aspiration means to concisely describe what future state you desire. Forgetting your past and your issues, what do you wish to be in the long run? For example:

- We will be the leading provider of our service to the ABC segment.
- We will be number one in our market.
- We will grow at 30 percent per year.
- I will be known as someone who can successfully drive projects through my organization.

Defining your desired trajectory requires working backward from your long-term aspiration and asking, "What needs to be true in the near term for me to ensure I will achieve my goal?" For example:

- We will win the account without discounting our service.
- We will grow faster than our competitor over the next three years.
- More that 50 percent of our sales will come from outside of our current declining market.
- The XYZ department will approve my project.

Defining the key players means simply that: State who you are (e.g., "ABC Company" or "the head of sales"), who your adversary is (e.g., "Acme Company" or "the head of purchasing from ABC company"), and any other key player (e.g., "XYZ regulatory agency" or "the head of marketing from ABC company"). Your adversary is not necessarily your competitor or enemy. Your adversary is any player in your game whose actions you want to influence because these actions will hinder or advance you in achieving your desired trajectory. In working with a leading customer-focused retailer, for example, we found that the company's customer was the most critical "adversary." With the customer in focus, the stratagems revealed to the company nearly fifty new strategies for convincing more customers to enter their stores. You may find that you want to specify more than one adversary—your customers and your chief competitor, for example.

Step Two: Choose a Stratagem

You do not have time to brainstorm using all Thirty-Six Stratagems. Depending on your time, you would be best served by choosing between three and seven stratagems with which to work. There are three ways to do this:

1. Having familiarized yourself with the stratagems, look for the ones that you intuitively feel "fit."
2. Pick a few at random.
3. Access a "Stratagemselector" tool through *www.strategylearningcenter.com*.

Step Three: Generate Options

Here is where you turn to the questions in this appendix. For each stratagem you've picked, you will already know your situation, objective, and players. The questions associated with each stratagem will prompt additional questions that will trigger your creativity and generate new options. Write these options down on paper, a white board, or a flipchart. Capture them quickly and resist the temptation to critique them. Before you complete this section, make sure you number each idea.

Step Four: Prioritize Your Options

Go through the options you generated in Step Three, consider each one independently, and for each ask two questions:

1. How attractive is it: If I had a magic wand and could make this idea work, how close would it get me to realizing my goal?
2. How achievable is it: With how little effort or risk can I execute this idea? Is it easy? How much time will it take?

For each idea decide whether you consider it to be of high, medium, or low attractiveness. Then plot the corresponding numbers on the following matrix. This will give you a visual depiction of your option set. It will help you focus on what you should do, what you should discard, and what you should spend more time considering. Specifically, I have found the greatest breakthroughs come from "highly attractive, low achievable" ideas that initially seem crazy but, after some creative thinking, become doable. You will find these ideas in the top left quadrant of the matrix.

Option Prioritization Matrix

Attractiveness
Criteria

1._____

2._____

3._____

Hi

Med

Low

Low   Med   Hi

Achievability
Criteria

1._____

2._____

3._____

Step Five: Choose Your Top-Priority Options

Choose from your prioritization matrix a maneagable number of ideas (between three and seven) that you want to "keep on the table" for further consideration. You may have several highly attractive, highly achievable ideas you are ready to pursue immediately without extensive analysis. Make sure that you also have a few "crazy" ideas on this list: ideas that you cannot obviously make work but that would offer an extremely high payoff if they did.

Step Six: Analyze Your Options

Do not act immediately. The process has so far been fact-free. You should now put facts behind your high-priority options (as identified in Step Five). The analysis and facts you need depend on the option you are considering and the level of confidence you want to have before you make a decision.

Begin

The rest of this appendix assumes you have done Step One, defining the problem. Each page contains the description of a stratagem, its key elements, and a few questions to prod your thinking. Let your hair down and open your mind. Now is the time to set aside judgment and have fun!

STRATAGEM ONE

To Catch Something, First Let It Go

"Press the enemy force too hard and they will strike back fiercely. Let them go and their morale will sink. Follow them closely, but do not push them too hard. Tire them and sap their morale. Then you will be able to capture them without shedding blood. In short, a careful delay in attack will help bring victory."

—*From* The Thirty-Six Stratagems

Key Elements

You "capture" your enemy.

Though you are able, you do not kill your enemy.

Implementation Questions

- Who is your adversary?
- What innovations could he introduce (list the three to five most likely and significant)?
- Assuming he makes each innovation, what action would you need to take to quickly catch up?
- What steps can you take now to ensure your adversary does not run too far away?

STRATAGEM TWO
Exchange a Brick for a Jade

"Use a bait to lure the enemy and take him in."

—*From* The Thirty-Six Stratagems

Key Elements

You give your adversary something on which you place relatively little value.

In exchange, your adversary gives you something you value much more.

Implementation Questions

- Who is your adversary (e.g., customer, competitor, supplier)?
- What "bricks" do you have that cost you little but that your adversary would value highly?
- What "jade" does your adversary have (something that she values less than you do)?
- What would it mean to exchange your "brick" for her "jade?" How would you give her that which costs you little and ensure she gives you that which you value highly in exchange?

STRATAGEM THREE
Invite Your Enemy onto the Roof, Then Remove the Ladder

"Expose your weak points deliberately to entice the enemy to penetrate into your line, then surround him by cutting off his exit."

—*From* The Thirty-Six Stratagems

Key Elements

You entice your adversary to enter your area of control.

You cut off your adversary's escape routes.

Implementation Questions

- Who is your adversary?
- What does your "roof" in this stratagem represent (e.g., your product segment, your market)?
- How can you entice your opponent to climb onto your roof?
- What does it mean to "take away the ladder"?
- What would be the impact of executing this stratagem?

STRATAGEM FOUR

Lure the Tiger Down from the Mountain

"Use unfavorable natural conditions to trap the enemy in a difficult position. Use deception to lure him out. In an offensive that involves great risk, lure the enemy to come out against you."

—From The Thirty-Six Stratagems

Key Elements

Your adversary is in a stronghold.

You avoid her stronghold by sticking to your own.

This lures your adversary out or prevents her from attacking you.

You either attack on open ground or attack the stronghold.

Implementation Questions

- Who is your adversary?
- What is her stronghold (e.g., market niche, capability)?
- What is your stronghold (e.g., market niche, capability)?
- What would it mean to stick to your stronghold and avoid your adversary's?
- Putting yourself in your adversary's shoes, how would your adversary respond? Would she leave her stronghold?
- In each scenario above, how could you win an advantage from your adversary either by staying in her stronghold or leaving it?

STRATAGEM FIVE
Befriend the Distant Enemy to Attack One Nearby

"It is more advantageous to conquer nearby enemies, because of geographical reasons, than those far away. So ally yourself temporarily with your distant enemies in spite of political differences."

—*From* The Thirty-Six Stratagems

Key Elements

You ally with a distant enemy.

You attack a nearby enemy.

Implementation Questions

- List as many of your adversaries as you can.
- For each, identify at least one common objective you share.
- Classify each adversary according to the degree to which his interests align with yours (i.e., high, medium, or low alignment).
- How might you cooperate or ally yourself with each adversary?
- What competition would you jointly attack? What would you jointly achieve?

STRATAGEM SIX
Kill with a Borrowed Knife

"Your enemy's situation is clear but your ally's stand is uncertain. At this time, induce your ally to attack your enemy in order to preserve your strength. In dialectic terms, another man's loss is your gain."

—*From* The Thirty-Six Stratagems

Key Elements

You induce a third party to attack your enemy.

You take no direct action.

You influence your adversary with a third party.

Implementation Questions

- What "borrowed knives" could influence your adversary? Have you considered suppliers, distributors, substitutes, or competitors?

- What sources of influence do you have over each of these "borrowed knives?"
- How could you use these sources to influence "borrowed knives" to attack your adversary?

STRATAGEM SEVEN
Besiege Wei to Rescue Zhao

"It is wiser to launch an attack against the enemy force when they are dispersed than to fight them when they are concentrated. He who strikes first fails, and he who strikes late prevails."

—*From* The Thirty-Six Stratagems

Key Elements

You are in direct conflict with an adversary.

Your ally defends you by attacking your adversary.

Your adversary disengages from its conflict with you to defend itself.

Your adversary must now fight on two fronts, multiplying your chances of success.

Implementation Questions

- Other than you, who else is an adversary of your adversary? Who else can influence your adversary's success? (List as many as you can.)
- Have you considered competitors or your other divisions and businesses?
- How could these forces attack your adversary or complicate his efforts?
- How would your adversary respond?

STRATAGEM EIGHT
The Stratagem of Sowing Discord

"Use the enemy's spies to work for you and you will win without any loss inflicted on your side."

—*From* The Thirty-Six Stratagems

Key Elements

You induce your adversary's agent to work in your favor.

Use this agent to topple a critical relationship on which your adversary depends.

Implementation Questions

- What critical relationships does your adversary depend on?
- How could you influence or remove each of these relationships?
- What would be the implications of removing each of these relationships?

STRATAGEM NINE

Trouble the Water to Catch the Fish

"When the enemy falls into internal chaos, exploit his weakened position and lack of direction and win him over to your side. This is as natural as people going to bed at the end of the day."

—*From* The Thirty-Six Stratagems

Key Elements

You create confusion around your adversary.

This blinds your adversary and hinders his ability to understand your intentions or see your approach.

Implementation Questions

- What action would you take if your adversary were too confused to react?
- What elements of your adversary's environment—or how he perceives his environment—can you combine?
- What elements can you disaggregate?
- How would you combine or disaggregate these elements?

STRATAGEM TEN
Remove the Firewood from under the Pot

"When confronted with a powerful enemy, do not fight them head-on but try to find their weakest spot to initiate their collapse. This is the weak overcoming the strong."

—*From* The Thirty-Six Stratagems

Key Elements

Rather than engage your adversary head-on, you attack her source of power.

This weakens your adversary or hinders her ability to attack.

You defeat your weakened adversary.

Implementation Questions

- What are your adversary's sources of power? What inputs does your adversary depend on?
- How could you limit your adversary's access to each source or input?
- Which of these methods of influence are most promising?
- What would be their impact?

STRATAGEM ELEVEN
Shut the Door to Capture the Thief

"When dealing with a small and weak enemy, surround and destroy him. If you let him retreat, you will be at a disadvantage in pursuing him."

—*From* The Thirty-Six Stratagems

Key Elements

You encounter a moment when your opponent is weak, divided, or dispersed.

You capitalize on this moment by surrounding your enemy, preventing escape, but avoiding direct attack.

Implementation Questions

- What actions do you want to prevent your adversary from taking? What threat does he pose?
- At what moments do you have influence over your adversary?
- How might you use these moments to contain your adversary (i.e., prevent him from taking action)?
- What would be the outcome of this approach?

STRATAGEM TWELVE
Replace the Beams with Rotten Timbers

"Make the allied forces change their battle formation frequently so that their main strength will be taken away. When they collapse by themselves, go and swallow them up. This is like pulling back the wheels of a chariot to control its direction."

—From The Thirty-Six Stratagems

Key Elements

Your adversary's advantage is built on key support structures.

You attack these structures.

By breaking her key support structures, your adversary's integrity falters; then you take her.

Implementation Questions

- What are your adversary's key support structures? If your adversary is a house, what are her beams?
- How could you attack these support structures or beams?
- What would be the outcome of each attack?
- Which attack seems most promising?

STRATAGEM THIRTEEN
The Stratagem of the Beautiful Woman

"When faced with a formidable enemy, try to subdue their leader. When dealing with an able and resourceful commander, exploit his indulgence of sensual pleasures in order to weaken his fighting spirit. When the commander becomes inept, his soldiers will demoralize, and their combat

power will be greatly weakened. *This stratagem takes advantage of the enemy's weakness for the sake of self-protection."*

—*From* The Thirty-Six Stratagems

Key Elements

Your adversary has a weakness or need.

You bait your adversary by feeding this weakness or need.

This encourages your adversary to act in a way counter to his benefit.

You take advantage of his misstep.

Implementation Questions

• What does your adversary have a need or weakness for? What could the "beautiful woman" represent?

• How could you provide what your adversary needs?

• How could you gain influence over him by providing it?

• What would be the likely outcome of each course of action?

STRATAGEM FOURTEEN
Beat the Grass to Startle the Snake

"Any suspicion about the enemy's circumstances must be investigated. Before any military action, be sure to ascertain the enemy's situation; repeated reconnaissance is an effective way to discover the hidden enemy."

—*From* The Thirty-Six Stratagems

Key Elements

You are unsure of your enemy's strength or strategy.

You launch a small-scale or indirect attack on your adversary.

Your adversary reveals his strength or strategy by his response to your "false" attack.

You plan your "real" attack with this new knowledge.

Implementation Questions

- What would a full-scale committed attack look like?
- What would a small-scale uncommitted attack look like?
- What new information could you acquire from a small-scale attack? What question might you be able to answer?
- Describe the possible outcome of a small-scale attack.
- Is this preferable to a full-scale attack?

STRATAGEM FIFTEEN
Loot a Burning House

"When the enemy falls into severe crisis, exploit his adversity and attack by direct confrontation. This is the strong defeating the weak."

—*From* The Thirty-Six Stratagems

Key Elements

Trouble strikes your adversary.

Your adversary freezes or retreats.

You capitalize on your adversary's inaction or retreat to build power.

Implementation Questions

- Whose house is burning?
- What opportunity does this create for you?
- What types of trouble create opportunities for you?
- Are you prepared to seize these opportunities? If not, what do you need to do to be prepared?

STRATAGEM SIXTEEN
Sometimes Running Away Is the Best Strategy

"To avoid combat with a powerful enemy, the whole army should retreat and wait for the right time to advance again. This is not inconsistent with normal military principles."

—*From* The Thirty-Six Stratagems

Key Elements

You face a powerful adversary.

You retreat.

You exert your preserved power somewhere else or at some other time.

Implementation Questions

- Describe what a retreat would mean for you.
- What resources (e.g., money, management time) would a retreat free up?
- How else could you use those resources?
- What would be the outcome of doing so?

STRATAGEM SEVENTEEN

Seize the Opportunity to Lead the Sheep Away

"Exploit any minor lapses on the enemy side, and seize every advantage to your side. Any negligence of the enemy must be turned into a benefit for you."

—*From* The Thirty-Six Stratagems

Key Elements

Your adversary fails to act (e.g., because he is distracted).

You take advantage of this moment to advance.

By the time your adversary realizes his mistake, you have already taken the advantage.

Implementation Questions

- What is a necessary task that your adversary performs in a routine, unimaginative way?
- If you were your adversary, what is something you do not want to do (e.g., because it would hurt you somewhere else)?
- What opportunity might your adversary's inaction offer you?

STRATAGEM EIGHTEEN
Feign Madness but Keep Your Balance

"At times, it is better to pretend to be foolish and do nothing than to brag about yourself and act recklessly. Be composed and plot secretly, like thunder clouds hiding themselves during winter only to bolt out when the time is right."

—*From* The Thirty-Six Stratagems

Key Elements

Your adversary is powerful and/or you are weak.

You appear mad or incapable in order to avoid being perceived as a threat.

When your adversary puts down her guard, you take her.

Implementation Questions

- What reaction by your adversary to your plans do you want to prevent?
- What would your adversary need to believe about you to choose not to react? What does appearing to be "mad" mean in your context?
- What actions might make your adversary believe you are mad?
- What would be the likely outcome of each approach identified?

STRATAGEM NINETEEN
Watch the Fire on the Other Shore

"When a serious conflict breaks out within the enemy alliance, wait quietly for the chaos to build. Because once its internal conflict intensifies, the alliance will bring destruction upon itself. As for you, observe closely and make preparations for any advantage that may come from it."

—*From* The Thirty-Six Stratagems

Key Elements

Your adversary is engaged in internal conflict or in conflict with his allies.

Your attack might unify your adversary and his allies.

You refrain from acting.

Allowed to continue, the conflict damages your adversary.

Implementation Questions

- What is your current battle?
- What might your next battle be?
- If you engaged in this battle, would your adversary become stronger or weaker? Would you be more or less prepared for the next battle?
- If you refrained from acting in this battle, would your adversary become stronger or weaker? Would you be more or less prepared for the next battle?
- How can you be better prepared for the next battle?

STRATAGEM TWENTY

Let the Plum Tree Wither in Place of the Peach

"When loss is inevitable, sacrifice the part for the benefit of the whole."

—From The Thirty-Six Stratagems

Key Elements

You cannot win on all fronts.

You allow your adversary a victory on one front.

You preserve, even strengthen, another front.

With this preserved front, you defeat your adversary.

Implementation Questions

- What are the "fronts" of your battle?
- For one of these fronts, what could your sacrifice be?
- What would be the positive and negative implications of such a sacrifice?
- What would be the net outcome of a sacrifice on each of your fronts?
- Does a sacrifice on one of these fronts put you in a better position than battling on all fronts?

STRATAGEM TWENTY-ONE
The Stratagem of the Open City Gates

"In spite of the inferiority of your force, deliberately make your defensive line defenseless in order to confuse the enemy. In situations when the enemies are many and you are few, this tactic seems all the more intriguing."

—From The Thirty-Six Stratagems

Key Elements

Your adversary is attacking or preparing to do so.

You reveal your strength or weakness.

Your adversary calls off his attack because he fears your strength or views you as weak and no longer considers you a threat.

Implementation Questions

- List as many adversaries as you can (e.g., direct competitors, suppliers, distributors).
- If you revealed your true strategy to your adversary, would he or she view you as a strong or weak threat? (Answer for each adversary identified.)
- How would he or she react to this knowledge?
- Given these answers, should you reveal your strategy or plans to anyone?

STRATAGEM TWENTY-TWO
Await the Exhausted Enemy at Your Ease

"It is an advantage to choose the time and place for battle. In this way you know when and where the battle will take place, while your enemy does not. Encourage your enemy to expend his energy in futile quests while you conserve your strength. When he is exhausted and confused, you attack with energy and purpose."

—From The Thirty-Six Stratagems

Key Elements

You predict the battleground will shift.

You set up a defendable position on the new battlground.

You wait for your adversary.

When your adversary arrives, you use your superior position to defeat him.

Implementation Questions

- Who is your adversary?
- How does he define the battlefield?
- Where might the battlefield shift? (List as many possibilities as you can.)
- Why might the battlefield shift (for each possibility given)?
- Which shift is most likely to happen?
- What actions could you take to prepare for this shift or to be there already when it does shift?
- What actions could you take to accelerate this shift?

STRATAGEM TWENTY-THREE

Exchange the Role of Guest for that of Host

"Whenever there is a chance, enter into the decision-making body of your ally and extend your influence skillfully step by step. Eventually, put it under your control.

—*From* The Thirty-Six Stratagems

Key Elements

Your adversary accepts you as nonthreatening.

You incrementally build power over your adversary.

You take control.

Implementation Questions

- Who is your adversary?
- What levers exert control over him (e.g., his capacity, access to funding, customer relationships)? List at least five.
- What weak position could you take now to gain his acceptance?
- How could you build on this weak position to begin controlling the levers you've identified?
- Of the strategies identified which is most attractive?

STRATAGEM TWENTY-FOUR
Borrow the Road to Conquer Gao

"When a small state, located between two big states, is being threatened by the enemy state, you should immediately send troops to rescue it, thereby expanding your sphere of influence. Mere talk cannot win the trust of a state in a difficult position."

—*From* The Thirty-Six Stratagems

Key Elements

You share a common objective or enemy with another.

You form an alliance to achieve this objective.

You then take your ally.

Implementation Questions

- What is your target?
- Who else has access to your target? List as many as you can.
- With which of these other companies or people could you partner to gain access?
- Which partner would yield the best outcome?

STRATAGEM TWENTY-FIVE
Shed Your Skin Like the Golden Cicada

"Make your front array appear as if you are still holding your position so that the allied force will not suspect your intention and the enemy troops will not dare to attack rashly. Then withdraw your main forces secretly."

—*From* The Thirty-Six Stratagems

Key Elements

You establish a façade.

Your adversary focuses on your façade, confusing it for the real action.

You move the real action somewhere else.

Implementation Questions

- Who are your adversaries, or what threats must you contend with? List as many as possible.
- What attracts these adversaries or threats?
- What façade could you create to hide from your adversaries?
- Where could you move the action to prevent your adversaries from noticing?

STRATAGEM TWENTY-SIX

The Stratagem of Injuring Yourself

"People rarely inflict injuries on themselves, so when they get injured, it is usually genuine. Exploit this naivety to make the enemy believe your words; then sowing discord within the enemy will work. In this case, one takes advantage of the enemy's weakness, and makes the enemy look as if he were a naive child easily taken."

—*From* The Thirty-Six Stratagems

Key Elements

Your adversary's suspicion hinders your success.

You injure yourself either to win your adversary's trust or to avoid appearing to be a threat.

Your adversary accepts you or lets down her guard.

You take advantage of this opening by attacking your adversary.

Implementation Questions

- Who is your adversary?
- How and why is your adversary hindering you?
- If you appeared less threatening, would she stop hindering you?
- How could you "injure" yourself to appear less threatening?
- What would be the outcome of such an action for both this game and the next?

STRATAGEM TWENTY-SEVEN
Borrow a Corpse for the Soul's Return

"The powerful is beyond exploitation, but the weak needs help. Exploit and manipulate the weak for they need you more than you need them."

—*From* The Thirty-Six Stratagems

The modern interpretation of this stratagem is to pick up the dead or forgotten.

Key Elements

You adopt something forgotten or abandoned (e.g., a model, idea, or technology).

Because your adversaries have abandoned it, only you use this thing.

You convert this uniqueness into power.

Implementation Questions

- What models, ideas, or technologies have your competitors abandoned? List at least five.
- For each, describe what would happen if you readopted it.
- Would you differentiate yourself?
- How would your competitors respond?
- Should you readopt any of these models, ideas, or technologies?

STRATAGEM TWENTY-EIGHT
Point at the Mulberry but Curse the Locust

"When the powerful wants to rule over the weak, he will sound a warning. One's uncompromising stand will often win loyalty, and one's resolute action, respect."

—*From* The Thirty-Six Stratagems

Key Elements

You want to influence your adversary's behavior.

Rather than attack your adversary directly, you focus your attention on a different target.

This action sends a covert message to your adversary that displays your power and communicates your intention.

Your adversary, appreciating your power and intention, alters his behavior.

Implementation Questions
- What do you want your adversary to do?
- What messages would induce him to do this? List as many as possible.
- What "false attack" might send him this message?
- Who might your apparent adversary be for this "false attack"?

STRATAGEM TWENTY-NINE
Clamor in the East; Attack to the West

"When the enemy command is in confusion, it will be unprepared for contingencies. The situation is like flood waters rising higher and higher; likely to burst the dam at any moment. When the enemy loses internal control, take the chance and destroy him."

—*From* The Thirty-Six Stratagems

Key Elements

You feign an attack.

Your adversary responds to this false attack.

In responding to this attack, your enemy is exposed to your true attack.

You launch your true attack and defeat your adversary.

Implementation Questions
- What attack does your adversary expect?
- What actions would your adversary take to defend against such an attack?
- In taking these actions, what real attack would your adversary expose himself to? List as many as possible.
- What would be the outcome of feigning the false attack and launching each real attack identified?
- How could you reinforce your adversary's expectation of the false attack?

STRATAGEM THIRTY
Openly Repair the Walkway; Secretly March to Chen Cang

"To pin down the enemy, expose part of your action deliberately, so that you can make a surprise attack somewhere else."

—*From* The Thirty-Six Stratagems

Key Elements

You focus your adversary, or let your adversary focus, on a direct orthodox attack.

You launch an indirect unorthodox attack, crossing over a different border to your goal.

This unorthodox action, over an unexpected border, surprises your adversary.

You take the advantage.

Implementation Questions

- What orthodox attack does your adversary expect?
- What actions will your adversary likely take to defend against this attack?
- What other borders exist around your goal (e.g., paths to the consumer)? List as many as possible.
- What would be the outcome of launching each of these unorthodox attacks? How would your adversary respond?
- How could you reinforce your adversary's expectation of the obvious attack?

STRATAGEM THIRTY-ONE
Fool the Emperor and Cross the Sea

"The perception of perfect preparation leads to relaxed vigilance. Familiar sights lead to slackened suspicion. Therefore, secret machinations are better concealed in the open than in the dark, and extreme public exposure often contains extreme secrecy."

—*From* The Thirty-Six Stratagems

Key Elements

Your adversary is vigilant.

You take actions that appear normal and everyday.

Your adversary fixes his attention on this façade of normalcy. He does not see your true attack or intention.

You take your adversary.

Implementation Questions

- What attack would you like to launch?
- What normal, everyday occurrences exist in your environment (e.g., stock purchases, real estate purchases)? List as many as you can.
- How could you hide your desired attack within these everyday occurrences?

STRATAGEM THIRTY-TWO
Create Something out of Nothing

"Design a counterfeit front to put the enemy off-guard. When the trick works, the front is changed into something real so that the enemy will be thrown into a state of double confusion. In short, deceptive appearances often conceal forthcoming danger."

—*From* The Thirty-Six Stratagems

Key Elements

Your direct attack is ineffective.

You create a new player or entity.

This player or entity catches your adversary off-guard.

You, or the new player or entity, take your adversary.

Implementation Questions

- What would a direct attack look like?
- What new player would improve your chances of success if introduced? List as many as possible.
- What would be the impact of each new player being introduced?
- What would it take to introduce each new player?

STRATAGEM THIRTY-THREE
Hide a Dagger Behind a Smile

"One way or another, make the enemies trust you and thereby slacken their vigilance. Meanwhile, plot secretly, making preparations for your future action to ensure its success."

—*From* The Thirty-Six Stratagems

Key Elements

A direct attack would generate resistance on the part of your adversary.

You choose an approach that is, or appears to be, friendly.

Your adversary lets down defenses and welcomes this approach.

You advance unhindered.

Implementation Questions

- How would your adversary likely respond to a direct attack?
- What would a "friendly" approach look like (whether genuinely friendly or not)?
- What could you do that your adversary would appreciate? What actions would your adversary welcome?
- How might you achieve your objective (i.e., of the direct attack) by taking the actions your adversary would welcome?
- What would be the outcome of this approach?

STRATAGEM THIRTY-FOUR
Deck the Tree with Bogus Blossoms

"Use deceptive appearances to make your troop formation look more powerful than it is. When wild geese soar high above, the grandness of their formation is greatly enhanced by the display of their outstretched wings."

—*From* The Thirty-Six Stratagems

Key Elements

You are too weak to attack your adversary alone.

You coordinate individual elements within your environment.

Coordinated, these parts become a much stronger whole.

You are now strong enough to defeat your adversary.

Implementation Questions

- What components are available for you to coordinate? List as many as possible.
- What potential allies exist?
- What internal elements compose your organization?
- What are the strengths and interests or objectives of each component listed?
- What combination of strengths, if coordinated, would compose a viable opponent for your adversary?
- How could you use each component's interest to induce it to cooperate?

STRATAGEM THIRTY-FIVE

To Catch the Bandits, Capture Their Leader

"Capture their chief, and the enemy will collapse. His situation will be as desperate as a sea dragon fighting on land."

—*From* The Thirty-Six Stratagems

Key Elements

You face a persistent adversary.

You identify your adversary's leader or leaders.

You understand how the interests of the leader(s) differ from the interests of the organizations.

You directly influence this leader or these leaders.

Your adversary's leadership brings your adversary's organization into compliance.

Implementation Questions

- What do you want your adversary to do?
- Who is your adversary's leader? Who commands significant influence?
- How could she influence your adversary to do what you want her to do?
- What does this person care most about?
- How could you use what she cares about to induce her into action?

STRATAGEM THIRTY-SIX
The Stratagem of Linking Stratagems

"When the enemy possesses a superior force, do not attack recklessly. Instead, weaken him by devising plots to bring him into a difficult position of his own doing. Good leadership plays a key role in winning a war. A wise commander gains Heaven's favor."

—*From* The Thirty-Six Stratagems

Key Elements

Rather than execute one strategy, you execute many (simultaneously or in succession).

If one strategy is not effective, the next one is. If the next one is not effective, the following one is.

Your adversary is eventually overwhelmed or caught in an impossible situation and falls.

Implementation Questions

- Which strategies are your favorites (e.g., which provide the greatest impact with the least effort)?
- Which might you combine? Which could you easily launch simultaneously?
- Which are completely unrelated but could nevertheless be launched simultaneously?
- What stratagems could you combine to create new stratagems?
- What new options do they offer you?

RAPID-CYCLE STRATEGY INNOVATION

"In battle, this ability to rapidly pass through the observation-orientation-decision-action loop (the Boyd cycle) gave American pilots a slight time advantage. If one views a dogfight as a series of Boyd cycles, one sees that the Americans would repeatedly gain a time advantage each cycle, until the enemy's actions became totally inappropriate for the changing situations."

—Robert Leonhard, The Art of Maneuver[97]

The OODA Loop

John Boyd was one of the U.S. military's most brilliant strategists. Today he is known to a small community of military tacticians and students of military methods. But his insights have come to define modern warfare.

During the Korean War, Boyd served as his squadron's commander and tactics instructor. The squadron's F86s had less firepower or thrust than their opponent's MIGs, yet Boyd's pilots averaged a 10:1 kill ratio against their enemies. Throughout much of Boyd's career as an instructor, advisor, military theorist, and fighter plane designer, he maintained a running bet that with forty seconds in the air he could beat any pilot in aerial combat. "Forty-second Boyd," as he came to be known, never lost this bet.

Asked to explain his methods, Boyd developed a theory of conflict that is now shaping military forces throughout the globe. Central to his theory is that the entity—the squadron, army, company, or government—that adapts fastest to changing events wins. He identified four interdependent phases an organization or organism must pass through to adapt to changing reality: observation, orientation, decision, and action (the OODA loop or the Boyd cycle). To beat your competition, you must cycle faster than them and/or hinder their ability to cycle through their OODA loop. Many of the Thirty-Six Stratagems achieve this dual objective by providing a creative response while concealing reality from your opponent.

Strategy Cycles

Boyd's principle has been at work for millennia, determining winners and losers on battlefields and in corporate conflicts. Cycle time was a determinant of competitiveness in business as early as the turn of the nineteenth century. In the early 1800s, Hudson's Bay, a trading company, faced collapse because a competing trading company, NorthWest Company, had adopted a new distribution strategy—with trading posts located more closely to customers—and a more flexible, decentralized management structure. Hudson's Bay's centralized bureaucracy hindered its reaction time, and by 1809 the company seemed destined to close. In that year, however, Hudson's Bay's ownership changed hands. The new leadership quickly copied its rival's approach, moving trading posts closer to customers and decentralizing operations.

By breaking through rigidity to react to a changing environment, the new owners saved their company. Hudson's Bay beat its rival, merging with it ten years later, and continuing as the Hudson's Bay Company, considered today to be the oldest surviving commercial enterprise in Canada.

The ability to cycle quickly proved definitive in the battle of Intel versus its early Asian competitors or Frontline versus rival oil tanker operators. The ability to react quickly and creatively to a changing environment is fundamental to competitive advantage.

Rapid, Creative Response

Few companies have proven able to consistently respond creatively and quickly to changes of environment. Companies stifle creativity, we have found, by relying too heavily on logical methods. When they face a strategic challenge, they inevitably turn to one of two approaches for solving it: option narrowing or rules. Option narrowing involves laying out a seemingly complete set of choices and then winnowing them out to arrive at the best one. The rules approach involves studying successful cases—companies, leaders, battles—and distilling from them a set of commonalities that, if followed, will lead to success. While both approaches are useful ways of problem-solving, they rarely lead to exciting, innovative solutions.

The Thirty-Six Stratagems are an effective complement to these methods. My colleagues have found the stratagems to be surprisingly effective tools for helping modern-day strategists see beyond the obvious, to conceive of the out-of-the-box strategic options that come naturally to history's most creative strategists.

The Seven Blocks to Strategic Innovation

To ensure that creative options, once conceived, transform rapidly into action, you must overcome one or more of seven barriers to strategic innovation. The vast majority of the most competitive companies of the decade achieved their strength by seeing and choosing a strategic option their competitors could not. They were able to surmount hurdles that their competitors tripped over. These seven barriers are as follows:

1. Failing to *observe* that your environment has changed and that new opportunities or risks have emerged.
2. Having observed the environment has changed, failing to *orient* yourself to the implication of this change. You may observe clouds are forming, for example, but fail to understand this means rain may soon come.
3. Having oriented yourself, you may lack a clear *aspiration* and so are not compelled to take action that might alter your current course.
4. Though you have a clear aspiration, you may fail to *conceive* of a good solution. You are then stuck with a few uninspiring options or, worse, are entranced with an option that is

merely good enough. As a result, you may adopt an uninspired, copycat strategy.

5. You have conceived of an exciting, out-of-the-box solution but will not *consider* it either because you find it unreasonable or because your teammates and your organization view the idea as "crazy."

6. You are willing to consider the solution but, after analysis, *choose* not to adopt it. This decision is usually based on sound logic that is shown to be flawed only after someone else—a successful competitor—proves that your idea was a good one

7. Though you choose a strategy, you may fail to *commit* to it. Because you are unable to convince others to support your strategy, you never align your real strategy (what you do) with your intended strategy (what you plan to do).

This framework is an expansion of John Boyd's OODA loop. My colleagues and I have used this framework to help companies across several sectors spur strategic creativity. By following how new ideas encounter these seven blocks in your company, you can diagnose what is hindering your company from responding rapidly and creatively to opportunities and threats. It is also a simple model for incorporating the Thirty-Six Stratagems into your strategy design process.

RESEARCH

The *Art of the Advantage*, which I completed in 2003, was based on research into 260 cases of corporate conflict. I was able to show that every case I could find fit one or more of the Thirty-Six Stratagems. Over the next three years I found myself working increasingly with the stratagems, helping companies incorporate them into their strategy development processes to become more fluid and creative organizations. I continued to collect cases, testing and classifying each, and found again that every case I could find fit the stratagems.

But these cases came to me arbitrarily. Occasionally my cases piqued the interest of a journalist, a businessperson, or an academic who liked my approach enough to remember it. I could not claim to have made a systematic approach to the problem.

So, I began to dissect competitiveness from the top down. I surveyed 9,000 publicly traded companies around the world, with stock traded on exchanges in Asia, Europe, and the Americas, looking for true evidence of competitive ability. I decided that to be able to call a company more competitive than its peers three things would have to be true:

1. **Revenue growth:** The company produced an extremely high rate of growth over an extended period and did this consistently. I judged this factor by calculating the average

revenue growth of each company over a ten-year period
ending in 2005.

2. **Profit margin:** The company consistently delivered high
profit margins over the same decade. This means that a
company did not achieve rapid revenue growth by under-
cutting the competition's price. Instead it convinced customers to pay a premium and/or configured a superior
cost structure. I measured this by calculating the average earnings before taxes, depreciation, and amortization
(EBITDA) margin over the same period.

3. **Value creation:** The company produced abnormally high
shareholder returns over the period. A company that
grows quickly and profitably but cannot produce value for
its owners is not, from an investor's perspective, competitive. I measured this by calculating the average total return
to the shareholder over the same period.

Of the 9,000 companies I studied, only 3,000 had been traded
long enough to have ten years' worth of financial data. For each
of these 3,000 companies, I calculated a "competitiveness" score
equally composed of the three metrics: revenue growth, profit
margin, and shareholder return.

The 100 companies with the highest competitiveness score are
the fastest-growing, most profitable, and most value-creating publicly traded companies in the world. I consider these the most competitive companies of the past decade.

The list contains some often-cited corporations including
Dell, Microsoft, Starbucks, and Nokia. It also contains relatively unknown star performers, many of which are mentioned
in this book, including Frontline Ltd, Reliance Industries, and
Wetherspoon plc. Notably absent from this list are several large
corporations that the press and business schools enjoy citing as
aspirational examples. General Electric, Southwest Airlines, and
Toyota are missing because we cannot mathematically say they are
highly competitive. They certainly offer valuable lessons, but this

is because they are "admired" not because they are competitive within the framework I established for this book.

The companies I included on my list have far outperformed their industries across all three dimensions of competitiveness. While commonly accepted strategic theory states that companies must choose between two generic strategies—differentiation or low price—these companies seem to contradict this accepted rule.

Measure	Most competitive	Industry average
Average annual total return to shareholder	41 percent	17 percent
Average annual revenue growth	23 percent	8 percent
Average annual profit (EBITDA) margin	17 percent	5 percent

I analyzed the histories of each company, looking specifically at how industry experts or the company itself explained the source of the company's competitiveness. I then analyzed the history of each company to assess whether its success can be linked to one or more of the Thirty-Six Stratagems.

My findings were that every case could be explained by the Thirty-Six Stratagems; therefore, the stratagems are a comprehensive framework for understanding competition. Ten stratagems stood out as those most commonly used by the 100 most competitive companies.

Ten Most Commonly Used Stratagems

Number (in book)	Stratagem Name	Frequency*
5	Befriend a Distant Enemy to Attack One Nearby	21%
22	Await the Exhausted Enemy at Your Ease	21%
10	Remove the Firewood from under the Pot	17%
7	Besiege Wei to Rescue Zhao	16%
32	Create Something out of Nothing	13%

Number (in book)	Stratagem Name	Frequency*
34	Deck the Tree with Bogus Blossoms	13%
24	Borrow the Road to Conquer Gao	12%
15	Loot a Burning House	10%
16	Sometimes Running Away Is the Best Stratagy	10%
33	Hide a Dagger Behind a Smile	10%

* Percentage of 100 most competitive companies of the decade whose rise can be traced at least in part to the use of this stratagem.

As I mentioned, I have been testing the Thirty-Six Stratagems against competitive strategy cases since 1995 and have collected hundreds of cases that are not derived from the earlier analysis. Here is a list of some of these cases categorized by the stratagem used to meet a challenge. I have listed each company name and either the company's principal corporate adversary or a description of the chief competitive challenge the company faced. In some cases, I have listed an industry or a group of companies rather than a specific company name. Not all the cases listed here are discussed in this book.

List of Cases and Stratagems

Stratagem	Company	Description
1	Barnes & Noble	Strategy against second-largest competitor, Borders
1	Barnes & Noble	Response to Amazon.com and online retailers in general
1	Bertelsmann	Acquisition of CD-Now
1	Coca-Cola	100-year competition with Pepsi
1	Dell	Strategy to attack traditional PCs
1	Estée Lauder	Acquisition of Gloss.com
1	FedEx	Launch of first overnight service
1	Gallo	Response to wine coolers
1	IBM	Overall innovation approach: follow closely
1	Kodak	Competitive strategy against Sony
1	Matsushita	Introduction of the VHS
1	Microsoft	Conversion of WordPerfect customers into MS Word users
1	Proctor-Silex	Launch of private-label products
1	Rohm & Haas	Strategy for attacking acetylene industry

Stratagem	Company	Description
1	Seiko	Overall strategy to closely follow competitors
1	Seven-Up	Response of Coca-Cola and Pepsi to Seven-Up
1	TiVo	Response of cable companies to TiVo innovation
1	Vonage	Response of cable companies to Vonage innovation
2	Adobe	Decision to offer free software
2	Amazon.com	Use of customer-generated book reviews
2	American Airlines	Launch of first frequent flier program
2	AOL	Customer acquisition strategy of giving away CDs with software
2	Camera manufacturers	Strategy to create common standard
2	Club Med	Ability to pay below-average wages
2	Coca-Cola	Use of grocery channel as loss leader
2	Coca-Cola	Designation of fountain accounts as loss leader
2	Consumer electronics firms	Profiting from financing business
2	Elevator industry	Profiting from servicing business
2	Gas stations	Offering leaded gasoline as loss leader
2	GE	Generating profits from financing business (and lower margins in other areas)
2	Gillette	Product pricing strategy: low-margin razors and high-margin replacements
2	GM	Decision to get into credit-card business
2	Hovnanian Enterprises	Low-price high volume strategy
2	Macromedia	Giving away of free software
2	Microsoft	Overall strategy to create standard OS
2	NVR Inc.	Customer acquisition and retention strategy
2	Pepsi	Designation of fountain accounts as loss leader
2	Ross Stores	Offer of deeply discounted merchandise
2	Skype	Decision to give away software for free
2	The Game Group PLC	Basing overall business model around customer loyalty program
2	Virgin	Trading brand value for equity in partnerships
2	Wireless service providers	Overall pricing strategy: deeply discounted phone for higher margin service contract
3	ABB	Decision to adopt corporate structure and expose managers to market
3	Mario Gabelli	Use of management compensation to expose management to market
3	Mercedes Benz	Rationale for listing on a U.S. stock exchange
3	Microsoft	Launch of Encarta vs. Encyclopedia Britannica
3	Morgan Sindall	Overall growth strategy vs. other construction firms
3	Pepsi	Use of Coca-Cola competition to motivate management
3	Procter & Gamble	Aligning management incentives to market performance
3	Thermo Electron	Adoption of corporate structure and culture that encourages entrepreneurship

Stratagem	Company	Description
4	Ben & Jerry's	Product strategy and Haagen-Daz' response
4	CarMax	New format strategy and AutoNation's response
4	Iowa Beef Packers	Strategy to transform the supply chain
4	Williams-Sonoma	Adoption of a multi-channel strategy (catalog)
5	3DO	Alignment of incentives with partners
5	Anheuser-Busch	Overestimation of synergies value in acquisition
5	Arctic Cat	Rationale for alliance with Suzuki
5	Autostrade SPA	Consolidation of independent infrastructure companies
5	Avned and Arrow	Joint purchase of #3 competitor
5	Century 21	Formation of first realtor coalitions
5	Corning	Overall joint venturing policy
5	Hero Honda	Partnership between Honda and bicycle company
5	Intel	Alignment of interests with Dell and Compaq
5	Kellogg	Product mix strategy vs. Post
5	Lincoln Highway	Formed by GM, Goodyear, and Prest-O-Lite
5	LogicACMG PLC	Growth through mergers of IT services firms
5	Lumberyards	Formation of buying groups
5	Man Group	Focus on growth through partnerships
5	Nokia	Overall collaborate approach to growth (e.g., pursuit of common standards)
5	OM Group	Growth strategy in specialty chemicals
5	Oshkosh Truck Corp	Use of partnerships to grow in truck and military vehicle manufacturing
5	Plexus Corp	Growth through agressively seeking alliances
5	Quaker Oats	Rationale for Snapple acquisition
5	Sears	Overestimation of synergy value
5	Skywest	Alliances with Delta and Continental airlines
5	The AES Corp	Strategy for engaging public utilities
5	Toyota	Strategic focus on developing supplier alliances
5	Vallourec SA	International expansion strategy
6	Carl Icahn	Serving as "white knight" during takeover pursuits
6	Coca-Cola	Use of Home Sweetener Company
6	European telecom cos.	Use of governmental protection to shield local players
6	Ford	Marketing strategy for Ford Focus
6	Latin American cocoa producers	U.S. and European strategy to build alternative African supply
6	Pharmaceutical industry	Use of FDA as competitive defense
7	Actividades Construction y Serv.	Overall growth strategy
7	Barbie	Launch of low-end products to protect high end
7	Canon	Leveraging optoelectronics capabilities to enter new sectors
7	Coca-Cola	Presence-building strategy
7	Fox	Launch of multiplatform strategy

Stratagem	Company	Description
7	Gillette	Bic launch
7	Honda	Leveraging motor capabilities to enter new businesses
7	Microsoft	Launch of Internet Explorer
7	Microsoft	Leveraging operating system platform to launch new products
7	Monsanto	Pricing strategy
7	Nong Shim Co. Ltd.	Growth strategy vs. rival Haetae
7	Seiko	Pulsar acquisition
7	Sharp	Leveraging optoelectronics capabilities to launch new products
7	Starbucks	Geographical expansion strategy
7	Swatch	Use of low-end products to protect high end
7	Teva Pharmaceuticals	Competitive strategy against Ikapharm and major U.S. pharma companies
7	Tietoenator OYJ	Growth strategy against global IT consulting companies
7	Toll Holdings LTD	Growth strategy against Asian and global logistics firms
7	U.S. auto manufacturers	Failure to protect low-end segments in 1960s
8	Amway	Use of distribution model in Japan
8	Avned	Marchall Industries acquisition
8	Avon	Use of distribution model in China
8	Coca-Cola	Conversion of Pepsi's Venezuelan bottler
8	Coca-Cola	Embracing Latin American shop owners during economic downturn
8	Enron	Use of lobbying activities
8	KFC	Success against McDonalds in China
9	Airlines	Use of bundling and disaggregation in pricing strategies
9	Blockbuster	Merchandising strategy
9	Coca-Cola	Product bundling
9	Financial trading firms	Product development strategy (bundling and disaggregation)
9	Genlyte Group Inc.	Focus on being close to customers
9	Hotels	Room bundling
9	Microsoft	Product bundling
9	Starbucks	Value proposition focused on experience rather than product
9	Telephone companies	Pricing strategies (bundling and disaggregation)
10	Alcoa	Attempted monopolization of power supply
10	AMR Technologies	Focus on strategic raw materials
10	Barr Pharmaceuticals	Attacking vulnerable pharmaceutical patents to launch generics
10	Coca-Cola	High-fructose corn syrup supply
10	Impala Platnum Holdings LTD	Growth vs. multinational mining companies
10	Kirch	Content supply strategy
10	Le Chateau CLA	Growth strategy against multinational retailers

Stratagem	Company	Description
10	McDonalds	Building hold on real estate supply
10	MCI	Local strategy against AT&T
10	Minnetonka	Launch of Softsoap by locking up pump supply
10	Postobon	Hipinto takeover
10	Procter & Gamble	Focus on supermarket display as competitive tool
10	Sony	Acquisition of Columbia pictures and CBS to own content
10	Tiffany & Co.	Overall turnaround in late 1990s
10	Xerox	Use of patents to pre-empt competing technologies
11	Borders	Upsell tactics
11	Capita Group	Overall growth strategy
11	Gallo	Building of control over growers and distributors
11	IBM	Early distribution strategy to upsell to existing clients
11	Matsushita	Sony/ licensing strategy
11	Microsoft	Growth strategy against Sun Microsystems
11	Movie studios	Strategic use of movie video business
11	Movie theaters	Strategic purpose of concession business
11	Nintendo	Attempt to lock up software developers
11	Peter Pan	Attempt to enter travel business
11	U-Haul	Launch of moving supplies business
12	Bloomberg	Overall marketing and sales strategy
12	Disney	Use of animated characters to reduce dependence on stars
12	Infosys Technologies	Use of outsourcing to attack higher-priced U.S. and European software companies
12	Kodak	Attack on Polaroid with one-hour processing
12	Salesforce.com	Distribution strategy against traditional software companies
12	Sony	Luring of Nintendo's game developers
12	Wetherspoon	Strategy focused on alternative locations
12	Wipro LTD	Use of outsourcing to attack higher priced U.S. and European software companies
13	Cisco	Suit against Apple for use of iPhone
13	Esprit Holdings	Launch of "what would you do to change the world" campaign
13	Hugo Boss AG	Appeal to "fashion" to sell at premium
13	McCaw	Attack on BellSouth
13	Microsoft	Investments in Best Buy and Radio Shack
13	QUALCOMM	Investments in mobile service providers
14	7-11	Rapid response to customer information
14	Audi AG	Growth strategy against Mercedes and other luxury brands
14	Bristol-Myers	Entry into acetominophen
14	H & M	Internation growth strategy focused on local (neighborhood) customer needs

Stratagem	Company	Description
14	Microsoft	Entry into server software
14	Microsoft	Entry into SQL server
14	Microsoft	Hosted-services entry strategy
14	Symantec Corp	Strategy against Microsoft and McAfee
14	Yamaha	Creation of listening lab in London
15	Bangladeshi textile industry	Growth during Malaysian textile industry crisis
15	Carlos Slim	Investment in MCI
15	Caterpillar	Strategy against Komatsu
15	Coca-Cola	Taking advantage of Mexican, Polish, and other economic downturns
15	Compac	Taking advantage of Alta Vista's trouble
15	Deloitte and Touche	Expansion during PriceWaterhouseCoopers consolidation
15	Forest Laboratories	Overall growth strategy
15	Michelin	Seizing advantage during International Rubber trouble
15	Nidec Corp	Overall growth strategy
15	Tata	Purchases AT&T fiber networks
15	Thor Industries	Acquisition of poorly performing companies to grow
15	Virgin	Timing of entry into Japan
16	Amorepacific Corp	Refocus on the global beauty industry
16	Apple	Steve Jobs cuts projects and products
16	Gallo	Exiting low-end jug wine
16	GE	#1, #2, or exit strategy
16	General Dynamics	Exiting F-16 program
16	Intel	Exiting memory chips
16	Sony	Exiting Betamax
16	TJX Companies	Exiting of non-core businesses during turnaround
16	Virgin	Selling of shares to fund expansion
17	Apple	Launch of iPod, seizing lead from Sony's MP3 players
17	AT&T	Entry into credit card business
17	Coca-Cola	Strategy to attack water consumption as competitor
17	Home Depot	Attacking building contractors
17	Intuit	Attacking pencil and paper (i.e., handwritten checks)
17	Microsoft	Multiple product launch strategies
17	Sage Group PLC	Strategy against Intuit and other accounting software firms
17	Sony	Development of transistor radio when RCA and GE would not act
17	Sony	Attacks Kodak with digital photos
18	Apollo Group	Attack on traditional universities using unorthodox tactics
18	Jones Soda	Adoption of unorthodox tactics to put traditional soda companies off-guard

Stratagem	Company	Description
18	Telecom Italia	Launch of hostile bid for Olivetti
18	Virgin	Decision to enter airline business
18	Virgin	Decision to enter U.S. mobile phone market
18	Whole Foods	Adoption of unorthodox tactics to put traditional grocery companies off-guard
19	Burger King	Selective expansion strategy
19	Chrysler	Avoiding Ford vs. GM competition
19	Daiwoo	U.K. market strategy
19	Dr. Pepper	Entry into cola market
19	Epson	Entry into laser printer business
19	Gallo	Distribution strategy
19	Ikea	Entry into funiture retailing
19	Intel	Adoption of non-compete policy
19	Jeffrey's and Company	Positioning relative to traditional banks
19	Mainstream airlines	Decision early on not to fight budget airlines
19	Porsche AG	Avoiding competition in luxury and superluxury segments
19	Puma	Decision to avoid direct competition with Nike and Reebok
19	Rolls Royce	U.S. entry strategy
19	Spil-Siliconware Precision	Targeting outsourcing clients
19	Swiss Post	Decision to enter office supply business
19	Tiffany's	Exit from mass retail after repurchase from Avon
19	Virgin	Overall Asia growth strategy
20	British Airways	Focus on long-haul travel
20	Dassault Aviation	Self-canibalization, innovation, and focus on military market
20	DeBeers	Strategy of limiting supply
20	Fugro NV	Strategy of serving two markets
20	IBM	RISC chip introduction
20	Intel	Multiple product introduction
20	IOI Corp	Diversified growth strategy
20	Morgan Stanley	Decision to focus on large deals
20	Nintendo	Focus on 16-bit game business
20	QUALCOMM	Abandoning of hardware business
20	Sony	Cannibalization strategy
20	TWA	Decision to remove seats
20	UK grocers	Early launch of online sales
21	Goodyear	Decision to reveal capacity and strategy
21	International Game Techs	Releasing of R&D plans to pre-empt competitive defense
21	Kiwi	Reveals limited aspirations to preempt competitive response
21	Lenovo	Transparent corporate reporting
21	Microsoft	Reveals digital home strategy
22	Amgen Inc.	Early research into leading biotech areas

Stratagem	Company	Description
22	Asahi	Focus on grocery store chains leading to toppling of Kirin
22	ATI Technologies	3-D card growth strategy
22	Beazer Homes	Focus on first time buyers in growth markets
22	Costa Coffee	Enters India and Middle East before Starbucks
22	Disney	Maintains non-core businesses
22	Forest City Enterprises	Regional growth strategy
22	Frontline LTD	Predicts demand for double-hull tankers will outstrip supply
22	GS Engineering and Constr.	Early focus on high-growth construction areas
22	H. Wayne Huizenga	Miami Dolphins acquisition
22	Hon Hai Precision Industries	Early investment in electronics manufacturing outsourcing
22	Honda	DaimlerChrysler
22	IOI Corp	Growth in palm oil
22	IPSCO Inc.	Positioned itself to piggy back on minimill revolution
22	MDC Holdings	Overall growth strategy
22	Meritage Homes	Focused growth in key markets
22	Microsoft	Software positioning
22	Persimmon PLC	Predicted in target markets
22	Shinsegae Co LTD	Competitive strategy vs. Wal-Mart and other large retailers
22	Unversal Health Services	Growth and acquisition strategy
22	Vornado Realty Trust	Predicted in target markets
22	Wal-Mart	Focus on early growth in rural areas
23	7-11 Japan	Acquires U.S. parent
23	Air Products and Chemicals	Strategic focus on industrial gas storage services
23	Ames	Acquisition of Zayre Corporation
23	Colombian coffee industry	Launch of international branding strategy
23	Douglas Knight & Assoc.	Launch of software to integrate with customers
23	Facset	Transformation from report delivery to database service
23	Intel	Early supplier agreement with IBM
23	LS Cable LTD	Mitsubishi and Samsung
23	Lumberyards	Creation of buying groups to build bargaining power
23	Microsoft	Early supplier agreement with IBM
23	Nintendo	Strategy of limiting product supply
23	Oral B	Introduction of a replacement indicator to move up customer decision process
23	Wal-Mart	Strategy to build buying power over manufacturers
23	Worldcom	MCI acquisition
24	Coca-Cola	Decision to follow U.S. troops during WWII
24	DHL	Sinotrans alliance to enter China

Stratagem	Company	Description
24	Hershey	Expansion strategy
24	Hindustan-Lever	Unilever alliance to expand in India
24	InterTrust	Alliance with AOL
24	Japanese government	Promotion of foreign alliances post WWII
24	Kingspan Group PLC	Strategy of growth through acquisition
24	Komatsu	Alliances with U.S. firms to gain knowledge
24	Lenovo	HP alliance to learn computer distribution and operating practices
24	Logitech International	Transformation from OEM supplier to retail
24	Michelin	Upward integration
24	Microsoft	Comcast alliance
24	Standard Pacific	Geographic expansion strategy
24	Virgin	Alliances with Asian firms
24	Wal-Mart	International expansion strategy
25	Disney	Entry into book publishing business
25	Kimberly-Clark	Expansion into consumer products
25	Thomson Travel Group	Linking of charter airline to travel businesses
25	Virgin	Decentralized corporate structure
26	American Airlines	Finding itself on defensive for being too strong
26	Apple	Focus on narrow market to avoid direct response
26	Express Scripts	Strategy against PBMs merged with pharma companies
26	Intel	Tactic to secure supply contract with IBM
26	Matsushita	Strategy to attract partners into VHS standard
26	Microsoft	On defensive for being too strong
26	Pilkington	Expansion into glass market
26	Sony	Entry into low-end radios
26	Virgin	Entry into U.S. cola market
26	Wal-Mart	On defensive for being too strong
27	Arm & Hammer	Creation of new usages to revive a commodity (baking soda)
27	China production	Use of labor instead of machinery to compete
27	Disney	Re-release of Snow White
27	Goodyear	New product development strategy
27	Google	Initial focus on pure search
27	Hexagod AB	Acquisition of historical brand to grow
27	Nucor	Focus on reusing old steel (minimills)
27	Perrier	Marketing strategy
27	RIM/ BlackBerry	Use of antiquated text data network
27	Southwest Airlines	Adoption of abandoned point-to-point model
27	Timberland	Return to nature look, feel, and values
27	U.S. consumer goods mfgs.	Introduction of made-to-order production to compete with low-price providers
28	Crazy Eddie	Offer of price guarantee
28	Dreamworks SKG	Marketing strategy for American Beauty
28	Kmart	Use of "Blue Light" brand
28	Microsoft	"Vaporware" announcements

Stratagem	Company	Description
28	Microsoft	Investment in Novell
28	New York Post	Deflection of competition by Daily News
28	Polaroid	Strategy of vigorous defense to ward off potential threats
28	Software developers	Early new product announcements
28	Sony	Columbia Records acquisition
28	Virgin	U.S. Congress lobbying efforts
29	Flick brothers	Unsolicited takeover campaign of Feldmühle Nobel
29	Hindustan-Lever	Branding and distribution strategies to target rural India
29	Home heating co.	False entry to remove competition from real target market
29	Microsoft	OS/2 and Windows introductions
29	Pepsi	12 oz. bottle introduction
30	Avon	Adoption of unique distribution model
30	Body Shop	Franchising strategy
30	Canon	Small- and medium-sized enterprise (SME) distribution strategy
30	Dell	Adoption of go-direct strategy
30	First Direct	Adoption of online bank model
30	Hanes	Overall distribution strategy
30	Harman International	Focus on growth through automobile channel
30	Japanese car manufacturers	Entry into lift-truck segment
30	Penn National Gaming	Launch of off-track betting
30	Polaroid	Alternative to (Kodak) picture development
30	Tata	Offer of car parts through mechanics
30	U.S. Airlines	Adoption of non-price competition
31	Alcoa	Capacity expansion policy
31	Krupp AG	Hoesch acquisition
32	Blockbuster	Creation of movie production company
32	Boeing	Creation of United Airlines
32	CJ CORP	Spin off from Samsung
32	Coca-Cola	Creation of independent bottling subsidiary
32	DeBeers	Creation of engagement ring tradition
32	Expeditors International	International expansion strategy of Washington
32	Ford	Ownership of Hertz car rental
32	Galencia AG	Backward integration
32	Miller	Lite beer segment creation
32	Pepsi	Entry into food-chain business
32	Reliance	Backward integration into chemicals and oil
32	Seaboard Corp	New business expansion
32	Virgin	Branded venture capital strategy
33	Chrysler	Offer of a price guarantee
33	GE	Using attractiveness as partner for bargaining power

Stratagem	Company	Description
33	IBM	Use of leasing policy to penetrate corporate market
33	Intel	Launch of branding strategy
33	Japanese car manufacturers	Response to "buy American" campaign
33	Retailers	Use of price protection plans
34	ABB	Decentralized corporate structure
34	ACER	Creation of network of alliances
34	Altran Technologies	Overall growth strategy
34	Bennetton	Creation of supplier and distributor network
34	Blogger.com	Use of community-created content
34	Coca-Cola	Creation of bottling network
34	CSL LTD	Growth through alliances followed by take-overs
34	Flickr	Use of community-created content
34	Ford and Chrysler	Creation of supplier networks
34	Liberty Alliance	Creation of alliance to battle Microsoft
34	MySpace	Use of community-created content
34	ODFJELL ASA	Configuration of small companies
34	Open-source software	Collaboration of independent programers to compete against large companies
34	Ryland Group	Multiple streams of revenue from different businesses of same industry
34	Saipem SPA	Strategic redirection in 2000
34	Symbian	Creation of alliance to battle Microsoft
34	USG People	Coordination of European staffing firms
34	Venture Corp	Unique organizational model
34	Virgin	Decentralized corporate structure
34	Wikipedia	Collaboration of independent experts to compete against large encyclopedias
35	Disney	Launch of Touchstone Pictures
35	Gucci	Takeover battle between LVMH and Pinault-Printemps-Redoute (PPR)
35	John Malone/ Liberty Media	Fight for DirectTV with Rupert Murdoch/ News Corp
35	Philips Electronics	B2B marketing strategy
35	U.S. aluminum industry	Conversion of steel cans into aluminum
36	Apple	Launch of multiple simultaneous strategies
36	Coca-Cola	Launch of multiple simultaneous strategies
36	Microsoft	Launch of multiple simultaneous strategies

NOTES

Part I: Yin Yang Polarity

1. Sun Tzu, *The Art of War*, trans. from *The Art of War, The Denma Translation* (Boston: Shambhala Classics, 2001), chap. 1, par. 7, 128–129.

2. "Can Microsoft Beat Sony and Nintendo at Their Own Game?" *Barron's*, May 14, 2001, 25.

3. Baltasar Gracian, *The Art of Worldly Wisdom*, trans. Christopher Maurer (New York: Doubleday, 1992), 47.

4. Niccolò Machiavelli, *The Prince and Other Political Writings*, trans. Stephen J. Milnder (London: Orion Publishing Group, 1995), chap. 17.

5. Sun Tzu, *The Art of War,* trans. Lionel Giles, *http://classics.mit.edu//Tzu/artwar.html*, chap. 10.

6. Janet Rae-Dupree, "Here's TV's Next 'Next Big Thing,'" *BusinessWeek*, August 9, 1999.

7. Warren St. John, "Friend or Foe? The Cult of TiVo Cometh," *New York Times*, April 20, 2003.

8. Roger Enrico, *The Other Guy Blinked and Other Dispatches from the Cola Wars* (New York: Bantam Books, 1988).

9. Sun Tzu, *Art of War*, trans. Giles, chap. 7.

10. Lao Tzu, *Tao te Ching*, trans. Stephen Mitchell, (New York: HarperCollins Publishers, Inc., 1988), chap. 78

11. "The World on a Disc," *The Guardian*, February 17, 1994.

12. Rajiv Lal and David Kiron, "CarMax," Harvard Business School Case Number 9-505-080, June 15, 2005.

13. Sun Tzu, *Art of War*, trans. Giles, chap. 6.

14. Richard Branson, *Losing My Virginity* (London: Virgin Publishing, 1998), 489.

15. Sun Tzu, *Art of War*, trans. Giles, chap. 13.

16. Mike Ricciuti, "Borland Sues Microsoft over Brain Drain," *CNET News*, January 2, 2002.

17. Saul Handell, "Giant Adjusting Slowly to Playing Google Game," *New York Times*, December 8, 2006.

18. "The Venezuelan Cola Wars," *Financial Times*, August 20, 1996.

19. Marguerite Reardon, "Cable Goes for the Quadruple Play," *CNET News.com*, November 7, 2005.

Part II: Wu Wei: Go with the Flow

20. Winston Churchill, speech to the Harrow School on October 29, 1941, *www.winstonchurchill.org*.

21. Sun Tzu, *Art of War*, trans. Giles, chap. 4.

22. "Patent Settlement Lifts Barr Laboratories Shares," *New York Times*, March 9, 1993.

23. Sun Tzu, *Art of War*, trans. Giles, chap. 9.

24. "Barnes & Noble, Inc.," *International Directory of Company Histories*, vol. 75 (Michigan: St. James Press, 2006.)

25. Sun Tzu, *Art of War*, trans. Giles, chap. 5.

26. Sun Tzu, *Art of War*, trans. Giles, chap. 10.

27. Alistair Osborne, "Wetherspoon Lashes Red Tape and Unveils Frothy Profits," *Daily Telegraph*, March 13, 1999.

28. Miyamoto Musashi, *The Book of Five Rings*, trans. Thomas Cleary (Boston & London: Shambhala, 1993), 41–42.

29. Microsoft press release, September 24, 2006.

30. Gracian, *Art of Worldly Wisdom*, 93.

31. Sun Tzu, *Art of War, Denma Translation*, chap. 1, par. 19, 132.

32. "Thor Industries," *Value Line* report, November 3, 2006.

33. "Thor Industries."

34. Sun Tzu, *Art of War*, trans. Giles, chap. 6.

35. Jeffrey S. Young and William L. Simon, *iCon: Steve Jobs, The Greatest Second Act in the History of Business* (Hoboken, NJ: John Wiley & Sons, 2005), 262.

36. Sun Tzu, *Art of War*, trans. Giles, chap. 4.

37. Nicole Harris, "Listen Up: Manufacturers of MP3 Players Say New Devices Are Smaller and Easier to Use," *Wall Street Journal*, March 5, 2002.

38. Frank Rose, "The Civil War Inside Sony," *Wired Magazine*, February 11, 2003.

39. Industry report from NPD Group for July 2005.

40. SoundScan, U.S. market share, July 2005.

41. Des Dearlove, *Business the Bill Gates Way* (New York: AMA-COM, 1999), 77.

42. Jennifer Drubner Eagan, "Method Ranks No. 7 in *Inc.* Magazine's 2006 Inc. 500 List," *Inc. Magazine*, August 23, 2006.

43. "Jones Soda Co.," *International Directory of Company Histories*, vol. 69 (Michigan: St. James Press, 2005).

44. Ryan Underwood, "Jonesing for Soda," *Fast Company*, March 2005.

45. Rick Aristotle Munarriz, "Keeping Up with Jones Soda," *MotleyFool.com*, January 19, 2006.

46. Underwood, "Jonesing for Soda."

47. Branson, *Losing My Virginity*, , 211.

48. "Business: Behind Branson," *Economist*, February 21, 1998, 63.

Part III: Wu Chang: Continuous Change

49. Gracian, *Art of Worldly Wisdom*, 135–136.

50. *Huai Nan Tzu*, adapted from Alan Watts, *Tao, The Watercourse Way* (New York: Pantheon Books, 1975), 31.

51. Danielle Sacks, "Masters of Design; The Catalyst," *Fast Company*, October 2006.

52. Lao Tzu, *Tao Te Ching*, trans. R. L. Wing, *The Tao of Power* (New York: Doubleday, 1986), chap. 43.

53. Dave Mock, *The QUALCOMM Equation* (New York: AMACOM 2005), 137–148.

54. Arensman, Russ, "Meet the New Qualcomm" *Electronic Business*, March 1, 2000

55. QUALCOMM 10-K (Annual Report) SEC filings for 1999 and 2003.

56. Mao Tse-tung, *On Guerrilla Warfare*, trans. Samuel B. Griffith II (Urbana and Chicago: University of Illinois Press, 1961), 52.

57. Jay Greene, Steve Hamm, Catherine Yang, and Irene M. Kunii, "On to the Living Room! Can Microsoft Control the Digital Home?" *BusinessWeek*, January 21, 2002.

58. Gracian, *Art of Worldly Wisdom*, chap. 99, p. 55.

59. Sun Tzu, *Art of War, Denma Translation*, chap. 6, par. 1, 158.

60. John Gorham, "Viking raider," *Forbes* magazine, April 30, 2001.

61. Sam Walton with John Huey, *Made in America* (New York: Bantam Books, 1993), 140.

62. Lao Tzu, *Tao te Ching*, trans. Stephen Mitchell, (New York: HarperCollins Publishers, Inc., 1988), chap. 69

63. *Why We Fight*, directed by Eugene Jarecki, 2005. BBC Storyville

64. Baltasar Gracian, *The Art of Worldly Wisdom*, trans. Christopher Maurer (New York: Doubleday, 1992), chap. 5.

65. Niccolò Machiavelli, *The Prince*, chap. 9

66. "Legend in the Making," *Economist*, September 15, 2001.

67. Andrew Tanzer, "A Legend in the Making," *Forbes* magazine, March 9, 1998.

68. Karlin Lillington, "Mouse That Roared Forms Basis for Logitech's Ongoing Success Story," *Irish Times*, October 18, 2002, 56.

69. Niccolò Machiavelli, *The Prince*, chap. 21

70. Sun Tzu, *Art of War, Denma Translation*, 249.

71. Lao Tzu, *Tao Te Ching*, trans. R. L. Wing, *The Tao of Power* (New York: Doubleday, 1986), chap. 36.

72. Ten-year average EBITDA margin for the period from 1994 to 2004.

73. Fishman, Charles, "Whole Foods is All Teams," *Fastcompany*, April 1996, p. 103.

74. Antone Gonsalves, "RIM's Blackberry Topples PalmOne in Handheld Market," *CDW*, May 4, 2005.

Part IV: Shang Bing Wu Bing: Indirect Action

75. Sun Tzu, *Art of War, Denma Translation*, 142.

76. Sun Tzu, *Art of War, Denma Translation*, 143.

77. Sun Tzu, *Art of War*, trans. Giles, chap. 5.

78. Transcript of Apple's iTunes conference call held April 29, 2004.

79. Sun Tzu, *Art of War*, trans. Giles, chap. 1.

80. Yagyu Munenori, "The Killing Sword," *The Book of Five Rings*, trans. Cleary (Boston & London: Shamhala, 1993), p. 70

81. Erick Schonfeld and Jeanette Borzo, "Former Oracle Exec: 'We Will Destroy Oracle,'" *Business 2.0*, September 20, 2006.

82. Sun Tzu, *Art of War*, trans. Giles, chap. 4.

83. Lao Tzu, *Tao Te Ching*, trans. James Legge, The Internet Classics Archive

84. "Google Milestones," taken from Google's corporate Web site, accessed February, 15, 2007.

85. Thomas R. Eisenmann and Kerry Herman, "Google Inc." Harvard Business Review case # 9-806-105, November 9, 2006.

86. Kalpana Mohan, "Will Google's Purity Pay Off?," *BusinessWeek*, December 7, 2006.

87. Mohan, "Will Google's Purity Pay Off?"

88. Jim Hu, "Yahoo Sheds Inktomi for New Search Technology," CNET News.com, June 26, 2000 (accessed June 11, 2007).

89. Jim Hu, "Yahoo Sheds Inktomi for New Search Technology," CNET News.com, June 26, 2000 (accessed June 11, 2007).

90. Wikipedia posting as of October 4, 2006.

91. Elsa Wenzel, "Digital Encyclopedias Put the World at Your Fingertips," *C-Net News*, September 13, 2006.

92. Anne Becker, "Murdoch and Malone Cut Deal for DirecTV," *Broadcasting & Cable*, December 7, 2006.

93. Joe Lauria, James Forsyth, and Rupert Steiner, "Murdoch Tightens the Family Grip on News Corp," *Knight Ridder Tribune Business News*, December 14, 2006, 1.

94. Sun Tzu, *Art of War*, trans. Giles, chap. 1.

95. Richard D'Aveni, *Hypercompetition* (New York: Free Press, 1994), 280.

96. Sun Tzu, *Art of War*, trans. Giles, chap. 5.

97. Quoted in Grant T. Hammond, *The Mind of War: John Boyd and American Security* Washington, DC: Smithsonian Institution, 2001), 35.

BIBLIOGRAPHY

Historical Sources

Note

There are many existing translations of the great Chinese classics, particularly of Sun Tzu's *The Art of War*, which in recent years has become widely known in the West. I have included in the bibliography and notes the Giles translation, originally made in 1910 but widely reprinted since then, and the Denma translation, made by a modern group of scholars, which is my personal favorite.

Ames, Roger T., comp. *The Art of Rulership*. Albany: State University of New York Press, 1994.

The Art of the Warrior: Leadership and Strategy from the Chinese Military Classics. Compiled and translated by Ralph D. Sawyer. Boston and London: Shambhala, 1996.

Bin, Sun. *Sun Bin Bing Fa*. Translated by Jinjun Xia. Boulder and Oxford: Westview Press, 1995.

Bin, Sun. *The Lost Art of War: Sun Bin's Art of War*. Translated by Thomas Cleary. New York: HarperCollins, 1996.

Bozan, Jian, Shao Xunzheng, and Hu Hua. *A Concise History of China*. Beijing: Foreign Language Press, 1981.

Brahm, Laurence J. *Negotiating in China: Thirty-Six Strategies*. Hong Kong: Haga Group Limited, 1996.

Champion de Crespigny, Richard Rafe. *The Last of the Han*. Canberra, Australia: The Australian National University, 1969.

Chan-Kuo Ts'e (Zhan Guo Ce). Translated by J.R. Crump Jr. Oxford: Clarendon Press, 1970.

Chu, Chin-Jing. *The Asian Mind Game*. New York: Scribner, 1991.

Cleary, Thomas. *The Japanese Art of War*. Boston and London: Shambhala, 1992.

Gracian, Baltasar, *The Art of Worldly Wisdom*. Translated by Christopher Maurer. New York: Currency Doubleday, 1992.

The Han Civilization. Translated by K. D. Chang and Zhongshu Wang. New Haven: Yale University Press, 1982.

Hookham, Hilda. *A Short History of China*. New York and Scarborough, Ontario: The New American Library of Canada Limited, 1972.

Lao Tzu. *The Tao of Power: Lao Tzu's Classic Guide to Leadership, Influence, and Excellence*. Translated by R. L. Wing. New York: Doubleday, 1986.

Lao Tzu, *Tao Te Ching*, Translated by Stephen Mitchell. New York: HarperCollins Publishers, Inc., 1988.

Legge, James, editor and translator. *The Ch'un Ts'ew with the Tso Chuen*. Vol. 5 of *The Chinese Classics*. Hong Kong: Hong Kong University Press, 1970.

Machiavelli, Niccolò. *The Prince and Other Political Writings*. Translated by Stephen J. Milnder. London: Orion Publishing Group, 1995.

Mote, F.W. *Imperial China 900–1800*. Cambridge, MA: Harvard University Press, 1999.

Munenori, Yagyu, *The Book of Five Rings*. Translated by Thomas Cleary. Boston and London: Shambhala, 1993.

Pan Ku. *History of the Former Han Dynasty*. Translated by Homer H. Dubs. Baltimore: Waverly Press, 1938.

Pin, Sun, *Sun Pin Military Methods*. Translated by Ralph D. Sawyer. Boulder, CO and Oxford, UK: Westview Press, 1995.

Sawyer, Ralph D. *The Six Secret Teachings on the Way of Strategy.* Edited and translated by Mei-Chun Lee. Boston and London: Shambhala, 1997.

Ssu-Ma Ch'ien. *Records of the Grand Historian of China.* Compiled by W. M. Theodore de Bary. New York: Columbia University Press, 1968.

Ssu-Mae Ch'ien. *The Grand Scribe's Records; The Basic Annals of Pre-Han China.* Translated by Tsai-fa Cheng, Zongli Lu, William H. Nienhauser Jr., and Robert Reynolds. Bloomington and Indianapolis: Indiana University Press, 1994.

Ssu-Ma Ch'ien. *Records of the Grand Historian.* Translated by Burton Watson. New York: Columbia University Press, 1995.

Sun Tzu. *Sun Tzu on the Art of War: The Oldest Military Treatise in the World.* Translated by Lionel Giles. Australia: Deodand Publishing, 2002.

Sun Tzu. *Sun Tzu, The Art of War: The Denma Translation.* Boston: Shambhala, 2002.

Three Kingdoms: Chinese Classics. Translated by Luo Guanzhong, Moss Roberts, and Lo Kuan-Chung. Beijing: Foreign Language Press, 2001.

The Tso Chuan: Selections of China's Oldest Narrative History (*Zuo Zhuan*). Translated by Burton Watson. New York: Columbia University Press, 1989.

Twitchett, Denis, ed. *The Cambridge History of China.* Cambridge: Cambridge University Press, 1979.

Tzu, Sun. *The Art of War. The Denma Translation,* (Boston: Shambhala Classics, 2001).

Unorthodox Strategies. Translated by Ralph D. Sawyer. New York: Barnes & Noble Books, 1996.

Verstappen, Stefan H. *The Thirty-Six Strategies of Ancient China.* San Francisco: China Books & Periodicals, 1999.

Von Senger, Harro. *Stratageme.* Bern, Munich, and Vienna: Scherz Verlag, 2000.

Wee Chow Hou and Lan Luh Luh. *The Thirty-Six Strategies of the Chinese.* Singapore: Addison-Wesley, 1998.

Wong, Eva. *The Shambhala Guide to Taoism*. Boston and London: Shambhala, 1997.

Wright, Arthur F. *The Sui Dynasty*. New York: Alfred A. Knopf, 1978.

Wright, David C. *The History of China*. Westport, CT: Greenwood Press, 2001.

Xuanming, Wang. *Thirty-Six Stratagems*. Singapore: Asiapac, 1992.

Zen Flesh, Zen Bones. Compiled by Paul Reps and Nyogen Senzaki. Boston and Rutland, VT: Tuttle Publishing, 1998.

Online Sources

http://kongming.net/novel/
www.bellum.nu/literature/36stratagems.html
www.chinastrategies.com
www.geocities.com/Area51/Shire/5882/36s.html
www.pipeline.com/~tkd-pix/36_strat.htm
www.strategeme.com
www.threekingdoms.com
www.sonshi.com

INDEX

About the Author

KAIHAN KRIPPENDORFF is a former consultant with McKinsey & Company and author of the forthcoming *The Way of Innovation*. He is president of the Strategy Learning Center, a firm that helps companies worldwide—including Microsoft, Ryder, Pfizer, and DHL—outthink their competition. He holds an MBA from Columbia Business School. He has been mentioned in or written for publications such as *Inc.* magazine, *Harvard Business Review*, and *Harvard Management Update* and has appeared on many radio programs, including NPR's *Marketplace*.

2336094R00153

Printed in Great Britain
by Amazon.co.uk, Ltd.,
Marston Gate.